American Foreign Aid and Global Power Projection

The Geopolitics of Resource Allocation

EARL CONTEH-MORGAN

International Studies Programme
University of South Florida

Dartmouth

Aldershot · Brookfield USA · Hong Kong · Singapore · Sydney

Published by

HC
60
· C6534
1990

Dartmouth Publishing Company
Gower House, Croft Road, Aldershot
Hants. GU11 1HR, England.

Gower Publishing Company
Old Post Road, Brookfield, Vermont 05036
U.S.A.

British Library Cataloguing in Publication Data
Conteh-Morgan, Earl, 1950–
    American foreign aid and global power projection: the
    geopolitics of resource allocation.
    1. Developing countries. Foreign assistance by United
    States. Policies of United States government
    I. Title
    338.917301724

    ISBN 1 85521 006 1

Printed in Great Britain by
Billing & Sons Ltd, Worcester

Contents

Dedicated to the memory of
Pa Morgan and Ya Thombo

List of Tables and Figures

FIGURES

Preface

This book is the result of research that focused on foreign aid's articulation into American foreign policy. It sets out to identify the various roles of resource transfers in the pursuit of specific US foreign policy objectives in regions and countries of the Third World. It is also an attempt to reconceptualize and reinterpret the donor-recipient relationship which I hope will open up new avenues of analysis and research. Accordingly this book's intended audience includes all those who must describe, explain, or analyse rationales underlying foreign assistance within the wider context of US-Third World relations. The most obvious consumers are those in academia--students in particular--who may be required to discuss various aspects of American foreign aid policies in their foreign policy courses. The reader will find a substantial dosage of foreign policy analysis, Third World politics, and geopolitical perspectives as they relate to the political economy of American foreign policy.

I of course owe a number of debts to those who helped me complete this book. The staff of the Word Processing Centre at the College of Social and Behavioural Sciences, University of South Florida, very willingly typed and retyped the manuscript, such that without their tolerance I doubt whether this book would ever have been completed. I am especially thankful to Marianne Bell, Nita Desai, Jerry Hren and Carole Rennick for having helped me in innumerable ways. My profound gratitude is expressed to the Faculty and Staff of the International Studies Programme, University of South Florida, for giving me a semester off from teaching and other responsibilities to complete the final chapters of the manuscript. Mark Amen, Ann Bell, Kofi Glover, Abdelwahab Hechiche, Marilyn Myerson, Harvey Nelson, Festus Ohaegbulam, Darryl Slider, David Stamps, Susan Stoudinger, and Linda Thompson, all in one way or the other gave me moral support as a junior faculty member in their midst.

It is the author's hope that this book will not only stimulate the interest of students, scholars and policymakers alike, but will also help to provide fresh insights into the role of foreign assistance in world politics. I alone am responsible for any problems in the book that may have eluded me. Hopefully, they will not seriously detract from the main thrust of the analysis.

Earl Conteh-Morgan
Tampa, Florida 1989

Introduction

As the United States nears the twenty first century, its foreign aid programme is increasingly being examined in relation to, the changing international strategic landscape, its flexibility and utility, its growing constraint in its use by the more recent presidents, and its weakened effect on future presidents as a vehicle of American foreign policy. In the January 1988 Report of the Commission on Integrated Long-Term Strategy, the Commission vigorously underscored the importance of foreign aid as the key instrument of the US to preserve Third World nations against activities that could endanger a struggling democracy (as in El Salvador), increase pressures for large-scale migration to the United States (as in Central American Wars), jeopardize important American bases (as in the Philippines), threaten vital sea lanes (as in the Persian Gulf), or provide strategic opportunities for the Soviet Union and its proxies, among other concerns. [1]

Identifying foreign aid as a key element of foreign policy, which for the past forty years has helped project US power in the countries of Asia, the Middle East, Africa, Latin America, and the East Caribbean, the Commission recommended an unrestrained use of foreign aid, and its increased provision by the 101st Congress to future presidents for protecting American interests in the Third World. In particular, the Commission, among other things, called for the following:

Appropriate more funds for foreign aid and reallocate funds among aid claimants to provide more for developing nations threatened by low intensity conflict. It should recategorize such nations so that they may be treated in budget actions separately from Israel, Egypt, and the base rights countries.

DOD training exercises should be used to help allies and friends in the Third World. [2]

The above recommendations focus on the provision of more foreign aid funds for zones of conflict and competition, an issue that often engages the attention of the United States as the Third World experiences its political and social upheavals.

Foreign aid became a cornerstone of US global power projection because towards the end of World War II a new geostrategic environment was emerging in which the traditional Great Powers of Europe occupied a secondary place in the configurations of power and influence created by the impact of the war. The US emerged from the ravages of war as the only power with an enormous economic and military advantage. By 1945 it possessed gold reserves of $20 billion, approximately two-thirds of the world's total of $33 billion. [3] By 1947, it owned roughly 50 per cent of the world's GNP, a reflection on its standard of living which was higher than that of any other country. Instead of being exhausted by the war, the American economy in fact grew at an unprecedented rate due to enormous increase in war expenditures. In constant dollars the country's GNP surged from $88.6 billion in 1939 to $135 billion in 1945, a result of the full utilization of resources and manpower and the extraordinary industrial expansion that took place during the height of the war.

This overwhelming economic superiority of the United States was reflected in its military strength; in sum in its land, air, and sea power. The US Navy was unquestionably the most powerful with a fleet of roughly 1,200 major warships hinged upon many aircraft carriers rather than battleships. The American air dominance was even more awe-inspiring with over 2,000 heavy bombers, in addition to the more powerful jet-propelled strategic bombers like the B-36. [4] To crown it all, the US was the only country with the atomic weapon. The American global power projection during the war was so overwhelming that by 1945 it had 7.5 million military personnel overseas out of a total of 12.5 million.

The new configuration of power and influence resulting from the changed geostrategic landscape characterized by political vacuums and Soviet competition compelled the US to use its enormous economic and military power to compete with the

Soviets by first revitalizing Europe and Japan, and second containing the Soviets in both Europe and other regions of the world. Achieving these two objectives meant maintaining in many areas formal security commitments in the form of alliances, arms transfer agreements, economic and military assistance, as well as embarking on a continuous search for influence in geostrategic locations of the world.

Other pressures spurring a US power projection came from two groups, the corporate and military sectors. [5] On the one hand, exported-oriented sectors of the American economy were concerned that a decline in US government spending would produce a postwar recession unless the triple economic objectives (investments, markets, raw materials) were pursued vigorously to absorb the American economic boom. On the other hand, the military called for and pressured the government to ensure unhindered American access to critical resources like oil, cobalt, among others. All these reasons, among many others, which are products of the war and the changed international context committed the US to a global foreign policy underpinned by political, military, ideological, and economic factors in which the distribution of US resources played a central role.

In the early 1950s, Paul Hoffman, a key executive who administered Marshall Plan aid in its early years, predicted the global mission of American foreign aid in later years when he said: 'We have learned in Europe what to do in Asia, for under the Marshall Plan, we have developed the essential instruments of a successful policy in the arena of world politics.' [6] More than $13 billion in US foreign economic assistance was transferred to Marshall Plan countries between 1948 and 1952. Success with the plan, particularly with the rapid reconstruction of capital assets damaged during the war, encouraged the US to expand the scope of its assistance to include the provision of economic development aid to Third World countries struggling to achieve economic self-sufficiency and develop stable democratic political institutions. With the passage in 1949 of the Act for International Development, which authorized the famous Point Four or technical assistance program, the US foreign aid effort in the developing world began in earnest.

The 1950s and 1960s were dominated by traditional East-West political rivalries and concern for the rapid economic growth of the newly independent nations. It was not until 1973 when a major switch in focus on aid objectives was made with the passage of the Foreign Assistance Act which stressed the redirection of economic assistance to the poor majorities of the recipient countries. The 'New Directions' approach as it was called was the result of a major evaluation of the foreign aid programme. However, even before the New Directions emphasis on foreign aid-giving both economic and military aid rationales had to adjust to changing regional and global configurations of power as well as the ongoing US-Soviet competition. The Draper Committee was appointed by President Eisenhower in 1958 to examine US military and economic assistance programmes. Then in December 1962, President Kennedy appointed the Clay Committee to conduct an examination of US foreign assistance policies in terms of their relevance to the changing times and conditions. [7] Furthermore, in 1969 the Peterson Commission was established as a Presidential Task Force on International Development and constitutes the most recent government-sponsored public examination of US foreign aid policies and programmes prior to the appointment of the Carlucci Commission (the Commission on Security and Economic Assistance) by Secretary of State George Schultz in February 1983. The Carlucci Commission was formed especially because of the concern over the lack of popular and legislative support for foreign aid, declining real resource levels and widespread skepticism regarding programme effectiveness. Noting that international political, economic and security concerns are increasing in number and complexity, the Commission was charged with examining all aspects of US foreign aid programmes and proposing ways these programmes can make a greater contribution to meeting foreign policy objectives in the 1980s.

In addition to these Commissions which are a reflection of the need to adapt to changing times, new geostrategic realities, and socio-economic imperatives, major foreign assistance acts were also passed by the US to respond to regional and international systemic changes. The Mutual Defense Assistance Act of 1949 established the Military Assistance Program and created the authority for foreign military cash sales of US military equipment and services. Activities authorized by the Act are also known as the Mutual Defense Assistance Program. The Mutual Security Act of 1951 established the Mutual Security Program which incorporated most of the then existing programmes of economic and military assistance into one programme for legislative purposes. In 1954 the Act was amended to establish the basis for Foreign Military Credit Sales. In that same year the Agricultural Trade Development and Assistance Act was passed and established the Public Law 480 food aid programme. Moreover, the Foreign Assistance Act of 1961 was the legislation that established the basis for the current framework of US economic and security assistance programmes. Beginning in 1968, however, a number of legislative steps were taken to consolidate legislation relating to US arms sales under a separate legislative authority. This process was completed with the passage of the Arms Export Control Act in 1976.

More recently, Admiral William Crowe, the Chairman of the

Joint Chiefs of Staff, underscored the continuing importance of foreign aid in the balance of power equation in the Third World when he testified before a Congressional Committee that:

> Security Assistance is a vital pillar of our national strategy...yet Fiscal Year 1987 was extremely disappointing in terms of Congressional action on the program and deep trade-offs required to stay within funding levels not fenced by Congress...in many developing parts of the world we are slipping dangerously behind the power curve...simply not enough for smaller, poorer countries to protect their sovereignty, deal effectively with state-supported terrorism and subversion, and curtail local trafficking in drugs...I caution you against repeating last year's legislation which skewed the program disproportionately toward the eastern Mediterranean. Too much is at stake and risk elsewhere in the world. [8]

In the above testimony the importance, geographic articulation, dwindling availability, and the overall role of American foreign aid in US global power projection are emphasized. To underscore the above concerns, President Reagan in a January 1988 speech on the National Security Strategy of the US identified American development aid and security assistance among the components of national power. But he lamented the fact that the US government currently spends less than two percent of the annual federal budget on foreign assistance. [9]

It is in terms of the above numerous but interrelated contexts that the issue of foreign aid in American foreign policy is analysed. Overall, and in relation to the above concerns about the future role of foreign aid and its decreasing availability to American presidents, there seemed a need for new conceptualizations and interpretations of the United States foreign aid relationship with Third World Nations. In the following analyses, integrating the past, present, and future developments in US foreign policy, we shall attempt to weave the evolving patterns of foreign aid distribution to the spatial, military-strategic, ideological and economic components of American global power projection in completion with the Soviet Union.

In conceptualizing and interpreting the various articulations of US foreign aid into the global objectives of American foreign policy since the immediate post World War II period the following focus of analysis will be pursued. Chapter 1 will identify the varied forms and dimension of foreign assistance in relation to the assumptions, objectives, patterns, and rationale that underlie them; they are then placed within the proper context of US foreign policy and the changing international system. In recent years, there has been a growing reference to a geopolitical dimension in US-Soviet Third World competition. Newspapers, periodicals, and reference works in international relations are full of such references. In Chapter 2, we will describe and interpret the corpus of nineteenth and twentieth century geopolitical theories and relate them to the current US-Soviet competition. In particular, the role of foreign aid in spatial location, regional conflicts, and the like will be emphasized in connection with current uses of the term 'geopolitics.' Chapters 3 and 4 will discuss and analyse how the regional problems of Africa, Asia, Latin America, and the Middle East spawn external interventions aimed at maintaining geopolitical and economic balance in relation to superpower competition. The different emphases given to economic and military aid in connection with shifting US regional objectives, the doctrinal proclivity of American foreign policy as reflected in the Truman, Nixon, and Carter Doctrines, among others will be the focus of Chapters 5 and 6. The argument will be made that doctrines are one element of US foreign policy that give structure and justification to the use of foreign aid in the pursuit of global objectives.

Since the mid 1970s the US and the Soviets seemed to have shifted the locus of their competition to the acquisition of military-strategic (military alliances, arms sales agreements, and basing access) advantages in the Third World. Chapter 7 will examine first, the renewed interest of the superpowers in the South Atlantic and the Indian Ocean. Second, the changing character of military basing in relation to foreign aid as a quid pro quo, and in terms of the post World War II proliferation of military and space technologies.

Ideology (the antagonism between Capitalism and Marxism-Leninism) has been a key element of the post World War II international system. The events, conflicts, crises, and issues of the Cold War and thereafter are replete with examples of ideological divisions. For example, is there a strong correlation between the ideological preferences of Third World regimes and the level of United States foreign aid they receive? This and related questions will be the focus of Chapter 8. Chapter 9 by way of conclusion, will offer an alternate interpretation of the foreign aid relationship that will provide a set of alternative clues and insights that it is hoped, will be useful in understanding specific evolving patterns of US foreign policy and future trends in foreign aid distribution.

[1]   See, for example, 'Commitment to Freedom: Security
      Assistance as a US policy Instrument,' a paper by the
      Regional Conflict Working Group submitted to the
      Commission on Integrated Long-Term Strategy
      (Washington, DC: Government Printing Office) May,
      1988.
[2]   These are only two out of the twelve basic reforms
      advocated by the Commission.   The entire strategy
      recommended to the 101st Congress is found in the above
      mentioned paper, 'Commitment to Freedom,' pp. 2-4.
[3]   For more details on the international political economy
      of the interwar and war years, see, for example, B.M.
      Rowland (ed.), Balance of Power or Hegemony: The
      Inter-War Monetary System (New York: New York
      University Press, 1976); and A.S. Milward, War,
      Economy and Society 1939-1945 (Berkeley: University of
      California Press, 1979).
[4]   A vivid description of the US military and economic
      dominance following the end of the Second World War is
      found in Paul Kennedy, The Rise and Fall of the Great
      Powers (New York: Random House, 1987) pp. 347-437.
[5]   Gabriel Kolko, The Politics of War: The World and US
      Foreign Policy, 1943-1945 (New York: Random House,
      1968).
[6]   Paul G. Hoffman, Peace Can Be Won (New York:
      Doubleday, 1951) p. 130.
[7]   See, for example, David Wallace, 'Commissions on
      Foreign Aid: An Evolution of Thought,' in John Wilhelm
      and Gerry Feinstein (eds.) US Foreign Assistance:
      Investment or Folly (New York: Praeger, 1984) pp.
      18-23.
[8]   Admiral William J. Crowe, USN, Chairman of the Joint
      Chiefs of Staff Statement before the House Foreign
      Affairs Committee on Security Assistance, 18 Feb.,
      1987.
[9]   Reagan, R.   National Security Strategy of the United
      States, Washington, DC.   Jan. 1988.

1 Forms and Dimensions of Foreign Aid

The developments that led to the institutionalization of foreign aid as a cornerstone of US foreign policy originated with the abandonment of America's isolationist stance between 1939-1941. The immediate reasons for the shift in policy orientation came from the threat posed by a potential Fascist victory over other European powers that shared American culture, democratic institutions, and values. The post World War II period presented a different situation for US security concerns. With the defeat of Fascism in Europe and Asia both the short and long term threats to US and Western European security originated from the Communist bloc and in particular Soviet Communism.

By the early 1950's the new security problem had become a reality and was summed up by Secretary of State Dean Acheson in these words:

> In the compact world of today, the security of the United States cannot be defined in terms of boundaries and frontiers. A serious threat to international peace and security anywhere in the world is of direct concern to this country. Therefore it is our policy to help free peoples to maintain their integrity and independence, not only in Western Europe or in the Americas, but wherever the aid we are able to provide can be effective. [1]

Efforts to handle the new security problem was done through

the distribution of economic and military assistance, collective defense planning, regional economic arrangements, and protection of sources of strategic materials. The policy of containment initially expressed in the Marshall Plan and the North Atlantic Alliance was adopted to signal the determination of the US to safeguard the geopolitical and security interests of Western Europe and by extension those of the entire Western hemisphere. Containment as a policy was first categorically expressed in the Truman Doctrine of 1947. Its emphasis on the preservation of the institutions of freedom in other parts of the world presupposed the containment of Soviet influence on a national and regional basis structured by US actions, and reactions to Soviet geopolitical conduct in the international system.

With the acceleration of the decolonization process in the late 1950's and early 1960's there was a shift in the locus of competition between the US and the Soviet Union from Europe to the Third World regions of Asia, Africa, Latin America and the Middle East. This shift made the security problem more complex because of the indirect Soviet challenges to US interests through surrogates like Cuba after the 1950's and Vietnam as from the mid 1960's. Regional conflicts which originally had no external factors are sooner or later super-imposed by the East-West competition. By the mid 1970's the regional conflicts in the Horn of Africa, Southern Africa, Central America, the Middle East, and South-East Asia had all been tainted by the ongoing Superpower competition.

In all commission reports on foreign aid since the time of President Eisenhower to now, the threat of communism has often been a key concern for both supporters and detractors of the programme. Discussions of foreign aid during the Cold War and thereafter have generally been framed in the narrow context of the East-West rivalries. The Draper Commission of 1958 and the Clay Report of 1963 specifically emphasized the challenge posed by the communist bloc in its efforts to dominate the world. The emergence of new issues complicating security goals was reflected in the Peterson Commission of 1970 which though it emphasized strategic concerns, did not specifically mention a communist threat. By 1970 a changed international environment had shifted the security focus by transcending narrow Cold War thinking. According to the Peterson Report, the challenge for the 1970's was the need to work out a programme 'designed to meet the new national priorities facing today's pluralistic world.' The findings and recommendations of the Draper and Clay Commissions were reflective of a prevailing environment and world view -- the Cold War, East-West rivalries, whereas the recommendations of the Peterson Commission were the products of a new order characterized by changes, increased pluralism, and stronger assertions of national sovereignty and independence by multiple actors.

The continuing diversity and complexity of national and regional issues as a consequence of the changed international context are emphasized in the 1980's and reflected in the State Department's Fiscal Year 1984 foreign aid request. The State Department's aid request was justified in terms of: (1) promoting peace in the Middle East, particularly the Middle East Peace Process involving Egypt, Israel, Lebanon, and Jordan; (2) strengthening the NATO members of Portugal, Spain, Greece, and Turkey; (3) ensuring access to the Southwest Asia region which is comprised of Morocco, Tunisia, Sudan, Oman, Yemen Arab Republic, and Pakistan; (4) promoting stability and development in the Caribbean Basin with particular emphasis on El Salvador, Honduras, Costa Rica, Jamaica, Guatemala, and the Dominican Republic; (5) protecting US pacific interests in South Korea, the Philippines, Thailand, Indonesia, and Malaysia; (6) enhancing a strategic balance in the Indian Ocean with particular reference to Djibouti, Kenya, and Somalia; (7) promoting peace in Zaire in particular and Southern Africa in general; (8) maintaining peace in West Africa, in particular Senegal, Niger, and Liberia; and (9) promoting regional stability generally and specifically preventing the spread of nuclear weapons. [2] Much more than in the 1950's, the objectives which the distribution of foreign aid in the 1980's are expected to achieve are varied and include military security, political stability, international security, and economic development among others. These objectives are basically located within the context of regions and subregions such as the Caribbean Basin, Western Africa, the Indian Ocean, and so on.

Before elaborating on the US foreign policy objectives that foreign aid programmes are believed to serve, it is essential to first of all clarify the concept of foreign aid and also make reference to particular aid programmes that are integral to the conduct of foreign policy. This initial discussion of major aid-giving programmes as well as the fundamental trends in the aggregate flow of foreign aid will help to lay the foundation for subsequent analyses of the aid phenomenon in later chapters of this book. We will now focus on some basic facts about the foreign aid issue.

SOME CLARIFICATIONS ON FOREIGN AID

To start with, this study of aid flows focuses on both economic and military aid. A broad disaggregation of the concept of foreign aid is useful at this stage in the analysis and will also be relevant for later references to

10

specific categories of aid distribution. Economic aid is itself a broad category of resource transfer that includes PL 480 Food Assistance, the Economic Support Fund (ESF), and Development Assistance (DA). [3] PL 480 involves commodity transfer in kind from the US to recipient countries. It was established in 1954 and is now a major component of the US bilateral economic aid programme. The PL 480 programme itself currently distributes approximately $1.2 billion of commodities annually to recipient countries. The ESF another major arm of the economic aid programme provides funds to promote economic or political stability in countries where the US has special interests. It is increasingly gaining in popularity; in 1975 it amounted to $1.2 billion, in 1982, $2.8 billion. It now constitutes over 50 per cent of US economic assistance. Most funds that are used in the Middle East peace process and stability in Southern Africa come under the ESF programme. In 1982 the Middle East was allocated 59 per cent ($1.6 billion) of the share of which 97 per cent went to Egypt and Israel. [4] The ESF used to be called the Security Support Assistance. Development Assistance is extended for the purpose of promoting development and includes Project Aid and Program Aid. The former is usually given for a specific function such as the provision and development of goods and services like factories, dams, oil refineries and the like; the latter has a broader focus and is geared towards promoting overall development such as reducing inflation, reforming the fiscal and monetary structure, or balancing the budget and fighting unemployment.

Three basic components make up the US military aid programme: the Foreign Military Sales Credits (FMSCR) Programme, the Military Assistance Programme (MAP), and the International Military Education and Training (IMET) Programme. The overall purpose of US military aid programmes is to lend or grant funds for military equipment and training primarily to Third World countries. FMSCR are credits for foreign military sales which can be converted to grants by forgiving repayment. For example in 1983 $1.2 billion of FMSCR were forgiven credits or grants, all allocated to Egypt and Israel. [5] The MAP provides grant financing for the purchase of defense articles, services, and training. The IMET aid is used primarily to reduce some of the costs incurred when foreign military personnel attend US military schools and war colleges. IMET has been declining in importance because of the fewer number of foreign military students trained or studying under this programme. Between 1972 and 1982 there was a drop in 19,000 students; in 1972 the number was 22,000 and in 1982, only 3000 students.

As I have already started citing a variety of foreign aid figures, it will be best to continue with a discussion of

11

major data sources on foreign aid flows. For the purposes of this examination of the aid phenomenon the most relevant sources of data are: Agency for International Development, US Overseas Loans and Grants, various issues; the Geographical Distribution of Financial Flows to Less Developed Countries (Paris, OECD), various issues; United States Foreign Policy: A Report of the Secretary of State, published annually by the Department of State; American Foreign Policy: Current Documents, also published annually by the Department of State; and Executive Office of the President, Budget of the United States Government, various issues published by the Office of Management and Budget.

In reference to foreign aid figures and tables a few distinctions must be made to ensure maximum understanding. First it is useful to distinguish between foreign aid commitments and foreign aid disbursements. The former refers to obligations to provide aid to recipient nations under specified terms; funds may be committed in one year but not disbursed until later years; the latter refers to the actual transfer of the resources. A second distinction that is essential to this study is that between figures in current dollars (i.e. figures based on actual price recorded at the time of the aid disbursement), and constant dollars (i.e. values reflecting prices that prevailed in a single base year). Most of the data sources listed above are based on current dollars only. A final word of caution is that even when foreign aid contains a loan element it is still concessional in character. This should be contrasted with grants which are usually outright gifts, in money or in kind, for which no repayment is required.

Distributional Trends

A significant development in the aid phenomenon that both proponents and opponents of aid flows are familiar with is that there has been a noticeable decline in the value of US aid distribution since the inception of the programme in the immediate post World War II era. Table 1.1 presents in current and constant 1982 dollars the relative levels of economic and military aid. Compared to earlier years the combined grant and loan levels of military aid for FY 1982 are lower in constant dollars, than during 1968 or 1977. A closer examination of the table further reveals that between 1968 and 1982 foreign aid funds have undergone profound changes in size and distribution. There was a 50 per cent increase in current dollars in foreign assistance from an average of about $7 billion in the 1968-72 period to a little over $11 billion in the 1978-82 period. However, after
• correcting for inflation, and expressed in constant 1982 dollars, the reality is that the level of aid flows has

Table 1.1
US Foreign Aid Programmes, 1968-1982
(in Current and Constant dollars, millions)

	Current dollars			Constant dollars		
	1968-72 Average	1973-77 Average	1978-82 Average	1968-72 Average	1973-77 Average	1978-82 Average
Economic Aid						
PL 480	1,220	1,182	1,362	2,817	2,403	1,601
Economic Support Fund	548	1,154	2,254	1,260	1,905	2,647
Development Assistance	1,387	1,477	1,940	3,201	2,515	2,292
Contribution to MDBs	341	735	1,292	806	1,271	1,534
Contribution to International Organizations and Programs	153	192	302	349	289	322
Other	83	126	207	189	190	220
Total	3,732	4,866	7,357	8,622	8,253	8,659
Military Aid Concessional	3,078	2,206	904	7,007	4,070	1,050
Non-Concessional	378	1,203	2,771	850	2,011	3,273
Total	3,456	3,409	3,675	7,857	6,081	4,323
Grand Total	7,188	8,275	11,032	16,479	14,334	12,982

Source: Derived from annual data in US Overseas Loans and Grants (Washington: AID, 1968-82).

13

steadily declined by nearly 18 per cent from an annual average of $16.5 billion during the 1968-72 period to $13.0 billion in 1978-82.

Figure 1.1 represents the general trend in the aggregate flow of economic and military aid from 1946 to 1984. Although the current dollar figures of most aid tables indicate an increase in aid flows in the 1980's, measured in constant dollars, US foreign aid in the five year period ending in 1959 was nearly double the amount distributed between 1980 and 1984. According to calculations by the Department of State, $40 billion of foreign aid between 1946 and 1952 would equal $150 billion today. [6] In 1982 the US share of total official development aid distributed by the world's key donors fell to 22 per cent from a high of 37 per cent in 1970. In conformity with the falling trend of US aid-giving share, in 1985 the official development assistance was only two-thirds of 1 per cent of its GNP making it the lowest ranking donor among seventeen Western foreign aid donors in terms of aid-giving as a percentage of GNP. [7]

Since the end of World War II, the US foreign aid programme has gone through four major stages: (1) the Postwar Relief Period (1946-1948); (2) the Marshall Plan Period (1949-1952); (3) the Mutual Security Act Period (1953-1961); and (4) the Foreign Assistance Act Period (1962-1984). The Marshall Plan officially known as the European Recovery Programme (ERP) was the first major peace time utilization of foreign aid as an instrument of foreign policy and was extended mostly to Western European nations. It disbursed over $13 billion between 1948-1952 to West European countries organized under the Organization for European Economic Cooperation (OEEC). The aid mostly in the form of grants emphasized the economic recovery of Europe. By the early 1950's there was a shift in aid emphasis from recovery to containment. In 1951 in particular the Mutual Security Act united military and economic programmes and technical assistance, establishing the Mutual Security Agency. Europe still received the bulk of the aid as shown in Figure 1.2. However, there was also a regional shift to include the Middle East and Asia. During this period military aid dominated the aid programme. Countries bordering the Communist bloc were the recipients of 63 per cent of US military assistance and 54 per cent of development aid during the Security Act period.

By 1960 the distributional emphasis on aid had shifted significantly to the Third World regions of Asia, Africa, Latin America, and the Middle East. In that year, Europe received only about 16 percent of overall US aid compared to about 78 per cent in 1950. The Foreign Assistance Act of 1961 further shifted the aid focus to issues of economic development instead of just military aid. The underlying rationale for the issue-oriented shift is two-fold: (1) the

Figure 1.1

Trends in the Aggregate Flow of Economic

and Military Aid, 1946 - 1984

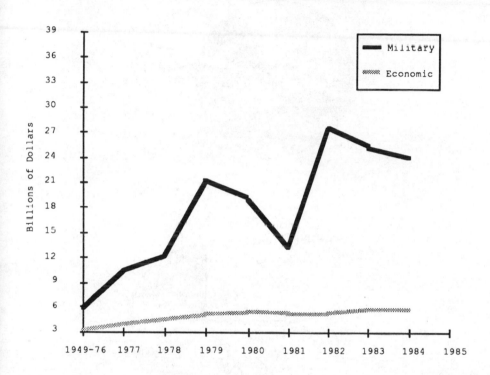

Source: Adapted from U.S. Overseas Loans and
          Grants and
          Assistance from International
          Organizations, 1945-1980, 1981-1984.

Figure 1.2

Regional Distribution of U.S. Overseas

Loans and Grants, 1950 and 1984

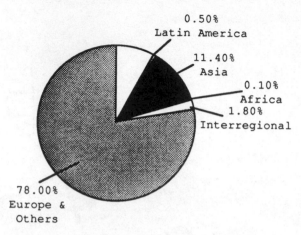

0.50%
Latin America

11.40%
Asia

0.10%
Africa

1.80%
Interregional

78.00%
Europe &
Others

1950

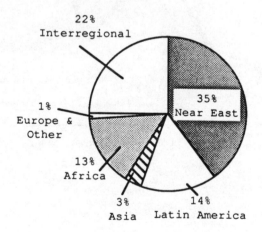

22%
Interregional

1%
Europe &
Other

13%
Africa

35%
Near East

3%
Asia

14%
Latin America

1984

Source: Adapted from U.S. Overseas Loans and
          Grants and
          Assistance from International
          Organizations, 1950 and 1984.

Note: Items in the interregional category
          include Food for Peace emergency relief
          and economic aid contributions to
          international financial institutions.

realization that security and socio-economic concerns are not necessarily mutually exclusive; and (2) the obvious concern of the newly emerging nations for rapid social and economic progress.

A continuing trend about foreign aid is that it has generally been extended in significant levels to countries that either border the communist bloc or are threatened by internal opposition with undertones of communist support. Figure 1.3 reveals the proposed concentration of country programmes for FY 1966. The 11 countries in which 72 per cent of the military programmes were concentrated are: Greece, Turkey, Iran, Pakistan, India, Laos, Vietnam, Thailand, the Philippines, South Korea and Taiwan. Since the Mutual Security Act Period military aid in particular has been highly concentrated with certain countries always among the top 20 recipients of aid. Between 1947 and 1973 Turkey, Thailand, the Philippines, and South Korea were among the top 20 recipients of military aid on a per capita basis. In FY 1983 the same four countries were also among that category. [8]

The shifting trends and patterns of US aid flows are better grasped when put in the context of aid-giving rationales and specific instances of US foreign policy behavior. The interlocking relationship between US political conduct, regional conflicts, and aid distribution are discussed later in this book to underscore the regional orientation of US foreign aid programmes. A dominant aspect of US foreign policy is that despite its bilateral emphasis the issues involved have profound subregional and regional implications.

The distribution of aid is predicated on certain beliefs or expectations that specific foreign policy goals will be realized either in the short or long run. Specifically aid-giving is motivated by expectations which lead us to ask questions such as: Does US aid distribution ensure political and economic stability in the Third World? Do aid programmes promote US military security? Or is US global or regional influence strengthened by aid-giving? These are some of the questions we will be attempting to answer indirectly through a discussion of rationales and objectives of American foreign aid.

BELIEFS AND EXPECTATIONS: THE POLITICAL AND ECONOMIC FACTORS

The political economy of US foreign aid distribution is predicated on four fundamental national interests: preventing the expansion of Soviet power and influence in Third World regions; upholding the commitment to the independence and security of friendly countries; developing and strengthening political and economic cooperation

Figure 1.3

Proposed Concentration of Country Programs, FY 1966

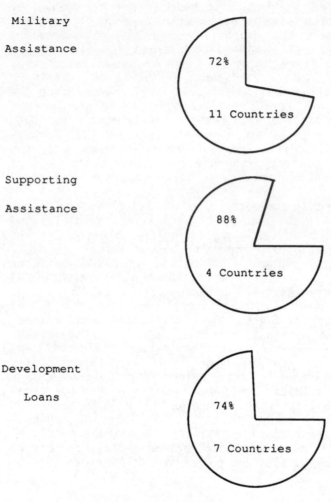

Military

Assistance

72%

11 Countries

Supporting

Assistance

88%

4 Countries

Development

Loans

74%

7 Countries

Source: AID, _Department of Defense, Summary_
             Presentation to the Congress, March
             1965:5.

Note: These are countries considered to be of
             geopolitical, economic and need
             priority and best performance.

internationally to enhance US security; and maintaining freedom of access to critical raw materials and sea passages. Emanating from these four broad US national interests are specific goals and objectives that have historically shaped, and are currently guiding, US foreign aid policies. Collectively they constitute a set of rationales and expectations about the utility of foreign aid flows in pursuit of regional goals and objectives. However, because of the uncertainty involved in international relations and the constantly changing array of complex issues these goals are not always achieved. Examples abound in which aid has proved counterproductive of US interests. But both the short term and long term perception regarding its utility has fixed in the Congressional consciousness that aid-giving should be considered a sine qua non of US foreign policy.

Political, strategic, economic, and developmental factors in combination define and structure the conduct of a superpower's regional foreign policy. A superpower donor transfers resources on concessional terms thereby incurring some sacrifice in the process. Since Superpowers usually have a number of foreign policy objectives they wish to achieve and protect, allocating aid is a valid manifestation of the need to conduct an effective foreign policy. In addition, because the amount of aid available is finite, we would expect most of the disbursed aid to be targeted to the most salient geostrategic and economic regional recipients. The more the number of salient recipients within a region, the more aid will be targeted to the region on a competitive basis.

Political and Strategic Rationales

A traditional and dominant rationale of US aid distribution is the overall enhancement of US national and international security. Regional imbalances, and threats to friendly nations can jeopardize US interests. From the early postwar period to the present, economic and military aid have focused on three objectives in the area of international security and regional balances. The first is to prevent establishment of new Soviet bases in strategic locations. Reinforcement and resupply in a time of crisis would be made easier if Soviet aid and naval bases are kept at a minimum in strategic passages like the Persian Gulf, the Indian and Pacific Oceans, and the Cape of Good Hope.

The second objective is to create a network of allies that will be useful as a source of resupply and local support facilities for US forces in crisis periods. The security of the US is clearly diminished when other countries succumb to Communism, as did China in 1949, North Vietnam and Laos in 1954, or Cuba in 1960. For example, Cuba is now practically

19

a Soviet base with a 2,600-man Soviet combat brigade operating a sophisticated electronic eavesdropping and communications station. In Ethiopia, the Soviets in a five year period ending in 1983, provided 1,380 artillery pieces and supersonic fighter aircraft, 1,250 tanks, including Armored Personnel Carriers (APCs) and Armored Reconnaissance Vehicles (ARVs) because it is in the Horn of Africa which has geostrategic importance since it borders upon the air and sea lines of communication and commerce to the Persian Gulf. [9]

The third objective is the enhancement of US security and that of friendly nations through the process and development of mutual defense. President Truman's message to the Congress of March 12, 1947, had declared that the policy of the US would be 'to support free peoples who are resisting attempted subjugation by armed minorities or by outside pressures.' It was against this background and in conformity with other security arrangements that the Mutual Defense Assistance Act was authorized by Congress in October, 1949. The programme underscored the essence of international security for all nations. The essential purpose of the programme was defined in the following terms:

> The Congress hereby finds that the efforts of the United States and other countries to promote peace and security in furtherance of the purposes of the Charter of the United Nations required additional measures of support based upon the principle of continuous and effective self-help and mutual aid. These measures include the furnishing of military assistance essential to enable the United States and other nations dedicated to the purposes and principles of the United Nations Charter to participate effectively in arrangements for individual and collective self-defense in support of those purposes and principles. [10]

As a result of this resolve by Congress, military aid to allies has developed into a bulwark of the foreign policy of the US in the past four decades.

Even before the enactment of the Mutual Defense Assistance Act, the MAP had already been created in 1947 as a vital and specific instrument for enhancing the collective defense and military strength of pro-American nations. It was designed to extend military assistance to friendly free nations. In 1950 $300 million was extended to Greece, Turkey, South Korea, the Philippines and Iran. In October 31, 1951, the Mutual Security Act expanded the role of both economic and military aid in the whole process of mutual security involving the US and friendly nations. For the first time nonmilitary aid was also used to guarantee the political stability and internal military strength of developing

countries. In his message to the Congress on the Mutual
Security Program for FY 1958, President Eisenhower expressed
the main objective of nonmilitary aid as follows:

This part of the [Mutual Security] programs helps less
developed countries make the social and political
progress needed to preserve their independence. Unless
these peoples can hope for reasonable economic advance,
the danger will be acute that their governments will be
subverted by Communism. [11]

Aid flows have been based on the underlying argument that
poor and new nations are susceptible to a gap between their
value expectations and the capabilities needed to satisfy
them, resulting in a condition of actual and potential
political vulnerability.

Enhancing the political and military security of friendly
nations became even more important from the 1970's with the
Nixon Doctrine's emphasis on the assumption of more defense
responsibilities by individual recipient countries. The
AWACS aircraft delivered to Saudi Arabia are there to warn
the Saudi military of any air attack across the Gulf. The
commitment of the US to Israel's security is reflected in
the level of US aid flows to Israel. Well over 33 per cent
of the entire US security assistance is extended to Israel.
In FY 1983 alone, Israel was the recipient of $750 million in
FMS grants, $950 million in FMS guaranteed credits, and $785
million in ESF cash grants. Other nations that are part of
this US commitment are Egypt, Pakistan, and Somalia among
others.

The Mutual defense and security objectives of the US find
motivation in the fact that the Soviet Union is also actively
engaged in strengthening the security posture of its allies
around the world. In 1982, Cuba was the recipient of $3.5
billion in economic aid and $500 million in military
equipment. In 1983 Syria received substantial amounts of
Soviet weapons including an advanced Soviet-run air defense
system and an improved Syrian Electronic Countermeasure (ECM)
capability. [12] The Soviets are also a part of the mutual
defense and security of India in South Asia, Vietnam in
Southeast Asia, Angola in Southern Africa, and Ethiopia in
the Horn of Africa.

Strengthening the political and military security of
recipient countries has underscored extending economic and
military aid to those nations whose security is vital to the
security of the US. In terms of foreign assistance it means
supplying finished items of military hardware, providing
technical assistance and training, and supplying the
technological materials and components that would enable such
nations to develop the technical know-how of weapons

21

production. The objective of mutual security between the US and salient regional nations is predicated on four arguments: (1) the US and its allies consider their collective and individual security to be threatened by Soviet expansionist moves; (2) it is only through the global enhancement of political, economic, and military strength that the Soviet threat can be contained; (3) the only strength sufficient to contain the Soviets is a collective one; and (4) it is only with US assistance that other nations can build the strength required for the common defense.

The expectations and beliefs that geopolitical and military objectives are enhanced through foreign aid are not always borne out. Since the 1970's in particular the US has suffered some foreign policy and security setbacks in regions of the world. In 1977 the Soviets gained a foothold in Ethiopia resulting in a security loss for the US at least in that part of Africa. In 1979 US aid to Afghanistan did not prevent instability in that country and an eventual invasion of it by the Soviet Union. In the same year the Sandanistas seized power in Nicaragua, and the Shah fell in Iran resulting in the establishment of an anti-American regime. In the Asian region Laos, South Vietnam, and Cambodia came under the aegis of North Vietnam.

A corollary objective to enhancing political security is the one of maintaining a regional balance to prevent war between two or more hostile nations. There are instances when this objective has not been realized through foreign aid. Aid flows to Israel and the Arab states in the mid 1960's by the US and USSR did not prevent the 1967 Arab-Israeli War or the 1973 Yom Kippur War. The idea of regional balance may cause another nation to react negatively. For example, the Shah of Iran's significant military build-up in the 1970's aroused some concern in Saudi Arabia and led the Saudis to also ask for US military assistance.

Finally, enhancing the political stability and internal security of friendly governments is at times achieved at the expense of political freedom and democracy in recipient countries. The repressive regime of the Shah which received support from US technical assistance eventually resulted in strong resentment of the Shah's rule and the ultimate loss of Iran in 1979. In Nicaragua, Samoza maintained his regime with the support of US economic and military aid, and his overthrow resulted in rule by a leftist regime. In the Middle East, the increasing anti-Americanism can be partly attributed to the perception Arabs have that it is American weapons that are used by Israel to bombard their territories.

The Influence Relationship

The belief and expectation that control over the distribution of foreign aid will enhance influence, leverage, and power is another traditional rationale of foreign aid programmes. The three concepts -- influence, leverage, and power--will be used interchangeably to refer to 'the capacity to achieve intended effects,' through aid programmes. [13] As relational concepts they signal the implicit and explicit communication of preferences from donor to recipient regarding specific political, military, economic, and developmental issues. Such issues revolve around a donor-recipient interaction process that can be based on either a permanent influence relationship or a temporary one. The multidimensional nature of influence, leverage and power are better understood within specific foreign policy contexts. Influence is strengthened by the credibility created through the steadfast maintenance of aid obligations from year to year. A good example of aid attempting to play the role of influence is the enormous amounts of aid extended to Egypt, Israel, and Lebanon to promote the Middle East Peace Process. In FY 1984 President Reagan requested $1.7 billion in military grants and $4.4 billion in military loans. [14] Over 50 per cent of the requested aid was eventually distributed to Egypt and Israel, the two major countries in the region involved in the Peace Process. Foreign aid in this case is enabling Egypt and Israel to support a policy that is among the foreign policy priorities of the US in that region. It is more likely that Egypt and Israel would have been unable to support the Peace Process had they not been the frequent recipients of significant levels of foreign aid from the US.

In terms of some recipients, like El Salvador, US aid-giving imputes legitimacy upon the government, which essentially translates into leverage over the actions of the regime. For example, military aid from the US to an unstable country is perceived as a mutual security relationship that confers prestige on the recipient country because it is viewed internally as capable of providing security. The recipient country is then expected to be open to US influence because it stands to gain by maintaining that relationship. The foreign aid relationship in this case necessitates the recipient country to maintain a particular policy in a manner advantageous to US foreign policy in the region because the aid relationship guarantees political benefits in the form of security and prestige.

In the game of influence buying it is usually a special relationship that the donor wants to establish vis-a-vis the recipient. In such a situation a recipient does not necessarily have to be an ally or overtly pro-American. The

US supplies foreign aid to a wide variety of nations: allies, neutrals, Communist, and socialist regimes. This behavior is predicated on the belief that resource transfer offers access to elites and builds friendships. In the Middle East, the US offers military assistance to both Israel and Saudi Arabia, and before the fall of the Shah to Iran as well. This is supposed to enhance US influence in the region even though the three nations are all suspicious of each others intentions. The special relationship between Poland, Romania, Yugoslavia, and the US is not based on ideological affinity but on the need to demonstrate American generosity which, hopefully, will translate into influence. The Soviet Union since the 1950's has been extending economic and military assistance to Arab states because it saw the need to establish a foundation from which to build its influence in the region. Other examples are the extension of military assistance to distant regional recipients like Peru, Indonesia, and India. The kind of aid relationship that is not predicated on ideological affinity but has the objective of establishing a foothold in the recipient country at times takes the form of a benefactor-before-beggar strategy. [15] Before the US or USSR pursues an objective in a recipient country aid is first granted thereby obligating the recipient to future repayment of favors. This type of influence buying is similar to the transfer of arms by the US to the People's Republic of China in 1981.

The assumption that foreign aid could guarantee friendship, cooperation, and political compliance should be regarded with caution. Power, influence, and leverage are again relational concepts, and since relationships are subject to the vicissitudes of international and regional politics, these justifications for resource transfers are not always supported. Concerning the general distribution of foreign aid, experience indicates that countries will acquire foreign aid even when the US decides not to extend it. In the area of military assistance, US arms to Latin America declined from about $900 million in 1973-76 to about $450 million in 1977-80. At the same time total Latin American purchases from alternative sources doubled from about $3.5 billion to $7 billion. [16] This indicates that even when certain resources are curtailed, recipients are generally capable of finding alternative donors. An influence relationship is easily shattered when rival donors are available.

There are at times when the 'misuse' of the donor's aid by the recipient consequently diminishes the donor's influence following a change of regime. The US was able to develop a close military relationship with Iran during the Shah's reign, such that the two countries maintained a sophisticated listening and electronic device for intelligence gathering about the Soviet Union. The 1970's saw Iran as perhaps

America's most strategic ally in the Middle East, and the relationship guaranteed Iran the most sophisticated US fighter planes. However, there developed a gradual association of the Shah's oppressive rule, through the Savak, with American presence in the country, such that when the Shah lost power in 1979, American influence was also lost. This example signifies that even though aid relationships can develop influence, they are also capable of creating the wrong perceptions that produce guilt by association after a regime change that results from unfavorable domestic conditions.

In a similar fashion, the apparent ineffectiveness of Soviet weapons and technical advice especially during the 1967 Arab-Israeli War cost the Soviet Union its close relationship with Egypt. The influence the Soviets had gained since 1955 which resulted in their use of the naval facilities in Alexandria and access to air bases was lost when in 1972 Sadat expelled Soviet military advisers and turned to the US for support. Another indication that resource transfer and technical assistance do not always guarantee influence and leverage is the fact that the Third World is full of many American-trained elites that do not promote Western democratic principles where critical issues like regime stability, elections, and the like are concerned. To put it in another way, US foreign aid programmes have not promoted or restored human rights, nor have they strengthened democracy in some recipient countries.

However, the belief and expectation still exist that foreign aid flows will reap such rewards as: overt manifestation of friendship and cooperation between the US and recipient nations at the expense of the Soviet Union. In the final analysis the continuity of the aid relationship is believed to eventually cement and prolong traditional friendship based on influence, leverage, and power.

Economic Imparatives

Another set of broad objectives that underlie the justification of aid flows are the commercial advantages that they can produce. Regionally, and in terms of the Third World, US aid distribution is believed to promote the triple goals of trade expansion, continued access to scarce resources, and new avenues of investment. These interrelated trade and investment goals stem directly from the rationale underlying the second national interest as stated by the Special Senate Committee on Foreign Aid, and runs as follows:

> A [second] national interest --- is the long range economic well-being of the United States. The future growth of this nation --- requires an expanding world

25

commerce as well as expanding sources of raw materials. This dual expansion depends to a considerable extent on the economic development of other countries --- especially the so-called less developed nations. [17]

The PL 480 aid programme is designed to fulfill several objectives in recipient countries, with the most persistent ones being trade expansion and economic development in the Third World. Since 1975 in particular PL 480 distribution has been designed:

> --- to expand international trade; to develop and expand markets for United States agricultural commodities; to combat hunger and malnutrition and to encourage economic development in the developing countries . . . ; and to promote in other ways the foreign policy of the United States. [18]

As a tool of trade expansion PL 480 is concerned with surplus disposal to reduce domestic stocks in periods of commodity surplus, lower producer prices, and depressed farm income. For example, between 1961 and 1970 agricultural exports increased in value by an average of 17 per cent per annum; during the same period the average annual growth in net farm income was over 12 per cent. In 1981 the trade balance for agricultural goods averaged $26.6 billion annually an increase from an average of $1.6 billion annually between 1961 and 1970. PL 480 also enhances market development for US foreign commerce. The recipient nations of South Korea, Taiwan, Spain, Portugal, and Brazil are an integral part of the programme. In FY 1981 alone, South Korea purchased $2.14 billion of agricultural products from the US on Commercial terms and was also among the top five importers of US agricultural commodities. [19]

Another aspect of US foreign economic policy underscores the rationale that foreign aid is used to promote US commercial policies. The Johnson-Bridges Amendment to the Mutual Security Act of 1959 mandated the suspension of foreign aid within six months to any host country that did not compensate US Corporations that were the victims of nationalization. In addition, the Hickenlooper Amendment of 1962 also authorized the immediate suspension of foreign aid flows unless US investors are compensated promptly for nationalized assets. In 1968, the Pelly Amendment particularly targeted military aid by authorizing the suspension of military sales and credit to any nation prohibiting, and seizing US fishing vessels beyond twelve miles off their coasts. [20] Finally, the Gonzalez Amendment of 1972 mandated the refusal of loans from international financial institutions to countries that disrupt US investment efforts.

By 1975 Peru had nationalized almost all extractive multinational companies: International Petroleum Company (IPC) in 1969; Cerro in 1974; and Marcona in 1975, among others; the US response was initially economic pressure in the form of freezing aid. For example, as far back as 1963 the US pressured Peru to arrive at a satisfactory solution with IPC, by authorizing a freeze on US foreign aid authorizations. In 1964 the freeze was made permanent and was not lifted until 1966. The economic pressure continued under the Nixon Administration and by February 1969 the US threatened to cut $2.5 million in aid and $65 million in sugar quotas. The IPC conflict was treated with such seriousness that Peru became the target of multilateral loan cuts. Loans from the Inter-American Development Bank and the World Bank were significantly reduced, such that by 1969 overall foreign aid to Peru had fallen to $9 million. [21] However, by 1975 all the investment disputes between Peru and the US had been settled through negotiations and Peru was again restored to a favored nation status regarding foreign aid flows.

Finally, the ESF plays the role of providing trade incentives and strengthening a recipient's economy and by extension its trade relationship with the US. ESF's are designed to meet the critical economic needs of recipient nations through the creation of stable environments conducive to foreign US investments. Because the ESF plays the dual role of promoting US economic interests and maintaining political stability, it has become the fastest growing US economic aid programme. It is primarily used in the effort to rejuvenate the economies of the Caribbean Basin. In 1982, 20 out of the 32 recipients of ESF were low income countries with incomes below $1,200 per capita.

The belief or expectation that foreign aid promotes trade and investment is not always supported considering the fluidity of Third World politics, the transitory nature of world politics, as well as the cyclical nature of the global economy. During the Cold War many countries especially in Latin America were far more stable and encouraged American investments through the enactment of very liberal investment codes. The conservative regime of General Manuel Odria enacted the Peruvian Mining Code of 1950 and the Petroleum Law of 1952 as a way of attracting foreign investment. [22] However, with the 1960's, and the changing international context as well as the emergence of new leaders and the new spirit of nationalism the situation began to change. In Cuba the change came as early as 1959 and 1960. By the late 1960's and 1970's American investments were being nationalized and at times expropriated despite the existence of foreign aid relationships between the US and recipient

27

nations. Between 1951 and 1965 there were three takeovers of
US companies in Latin America; between 1965 and 1974 there
were as many as 24 takeovers in the same region. In the same
period (1965-1974) there were 10 takeovers in Africa. [23]
   Besides, political considerations seem to outweigh economic
considerations in the US response to nations that nationalize
US   corporations.   Congressional   provisions   like   the
Hickenlooper Amendments   or   the   Gonzalez Amendment   are
reluctantly invoked when host countries nationalize US
companies.   In fact, in 1973 the Hickenlooper Amendment like
the other Amendments repealed the mandatory provisions of the
bill, giving the President discretion over whether or not to
curtail foreign aid flows.   In 1973 when Zambia nationalized
the Anglo-American Corporation the US did not apply any
sanctions.   Only in the cases of Guatemala in 1954, Cuba and
the Dominican Republic in the 1960's, and Chile in the early
1970's did the US use tough measures to protect trade and
investment because in all three cases the threat of communism
was an underlying factor.
   Foreign aid comprises of both loans and grants, with the
loans expected to be repaid after a number of years.
However, economic recessions such as that in 1973 and 1979
affect the ability of aid recipients to adequately service
their debts.   The sluggish economic growth of the 1970's
coupled with the global inflation and high interest rates
resulted in a large number of Third World nations being
unable to honor their debts.   The lack of foreign exchange
and debt-service burden affects trade leading to the
conclusion that instead of always promoting trade, foreign
aid and its accompanying debt burden can in fact reduce
imports thereby affecting the US ability to sell its finished
goods to trading partners.   The cutback in imports by the
developing countries then affects the recovery of industrial
economies like that of the US According to the Treasury
Department the Mexican debt crisis of 1983 cost the US $10
billion in export sales because of Mexico's lack of foreign
exchange.   A continuing or recurring debt crisis could hurt
the US in the future because currently the Third World is the
recipient of 40 per cent of all US exports.

The 'Interdependency' Factor

   The three broad discussions of politics, influence, and
economic enhancement are three basic utilitarian rationales
that are often used as justification for US foreign aid
flows.   The three categories could be divided into more
specific motivations like the promotion of democracy, access
to markets and raw materials, and promotion of higher living
standards in the Third World.   The specific motivations
contained in the above discussions are presented in Table

1.2. In addition to the foreign aid dimensions usually articulated, the interdependency of economic and military aid has often been emphasized.

First, the extension of military aid is primarily done to ensure security and at the same time attain economic stability. The ability of a recipient nation to contain both domestic and external threats is as important from the point of view of economic stability as the right set of economic policies promoted by aid flows. For example, during the era of European reconstruction, the Mutual Defense Assistance Program was designed to safeguard the politico-military security of Western Europe without undermining the goal of economic stability which the ERP was designed to promote. This interchangeable use of foreign economic and military aid results in aid flows being predicated on mutually supportive and complementary rationales. This seems to have been the case regarding US foreign aid to South Vietnam in the late 1960's. The US was already spending $30 billion per year on the war in Vietnam, at the same time, total gross economic aid was $700-800 million. Even the amount of nonmilitary aid most of which was labelled supporting assistance, placed a major emphasis on defense and economic stabilization not only in South Vietnam, but in Cambodia, Laos, and Jordan. In these cases economic aid was being used as a supplement to political and military goals. Economic and military aid were simultaneously being used to: (1) defend Vietnamese and US national security in the region; (2) contain Communist expansionism in the region; (3) provide budgetary support to the governments of the three countries; (4) supply resources to the peoples of those countries thereby improving their standard of living; and (5) ensure regional peace and stability by defending the national self-determination of those countries from external threats.

A usual pattern is the use of military aid programmes to buttress countries receiving little economic aid. US military aid to South Korea consistently plays a substantial role in protecting US economic interests. South Korea is a key military ally of the US and also happens to be a major market for US goods and a supplier of goods to the US.

The mutually supportive role existing between economic and military aid results in interrelated rationales underlying their distribution. The 'interdependency' factor which produces interrelated motivations for aid can be seen in the context of US aid to a particular region or nation. Southeast Asia received billions of dollars in US aid in the late 1960's up to the mid 1970's because interrelated motivations were more or less operating at the same time. In other words, aid flows to a recipient country will tend to be significant when there is a constellation of politico-military, economic and development factors justifying its

Table 1.2
US Aid Objectives

Category	Objective
Geopolitical	1. A Cold War weapon against communism. 2. Enhancement of local military preparedness of recipients 3. Promotion of democracy and maintenance of the status quo 4. A rewarding/punishing instrument 5. Territorial security and external military security 6. Selective targeting of priority regions 7. A back-up to the interests of allies 8. A favorable international image
Economic	1. Access to markets and raw materials 2. Removal of barriers to foreign investment and free trade 3. Promotion of exports in the form of procurement-tying
Humanitarian	1. Higher living standards in the Third World 2. A conscience-satisfying instrument towards poorer countries.

flows. For example, the ESF is based on the argument that no threatened country can provide for its security or adequately share the burden of security with the US without an economic base strong enough to withstand the resource demands placed on its economy by security requirements. The ESF is therefore given to countries like Pakistan, Turkey, and El Salvador to help promote economic and political stability through balance-of-payments support and short term project assistance, in addition to real military aid.

A major US concern in countries like El Salvador, Pakistan, and Turkey is that a severe inflation would result in great economic deprivation, make it very difficult for the survival of any regime. Lack of political stability caused by adverse economic conditions would reduce the ability of the governments to resist communism. In the final analysis, the enhancement of US security in Third World regions depends on effective containment of Communism by militarily strong regional allies. Achievement of that goal is enhanced by supplementing military strength through economic support in the form of reducing inflation to acceptable limits and increasing the recipient nation's standard of living.

In terms of the evolution of foreign aid programmes, two interrleated propositions are worth considering. First, the interdependence among broad politico-military interests, economic interests, and other national interests has become a dominant factor in the aid relationship between the US and recipient nations. This signifies that a change in economic circumstances or in national economic policies in a recipient country will have significant implications for US national security in the region. Similarly, a change in political and military circumstances in a Third World Country is bound to affect US economic interests and the role of foreign aid in articulating regional objectives. For example, political changes in Libya and Chile in the 1970's resulted in the nationalization of American companies and the subsequent strained relations between the US and those countries.

The second proposition is that the multiple motivations underlying the distribution of US foreign aid underscores the significant role played by the US in the maintenance of the international political-economic system characterized by free trade, competition, and capital flows. The system which is based on Western economic principles is the foundation on which the aid relationship between the US and recipient countries rests.

While the 'interdependency' factor emphasizes the multiple functions of aid within a recipient Country, the extension of aid also creates a balancing problem between economic and military aid. Between how much or whether or not to give military aid to authoritarian regimes. In other words, should the US extend military aid to dictatorial regimes in the Third World? Or should it emphasize the promotion of human rights over the containment of Communism? The question whether a recipient nation merits US military assistance, and how much, is a question that involves debate about the domestic policies of the recipient state regarding its citizens. Favouring the distribution of more economic aid over military aid raises the issue of fungibility or the interdependence and complementarity factor in the aid process. In 1976, during the Carter Administration, the International Security Assistance and Arms Export Control Act was passed making it an offense to extend military assistance to any country 'which engages in a consistent pattern of gross violations of internationally recognized human rights.' [24] At the same time military aid to Argentina, Uruguay, and Ethiopia was reduced because of human rights violations. The very politically salient countries like South Korea and the Philippines were hardly affected by the Act, partly due to the fact that they were beset by both domestic and external Communist threats. The first country based report on human rights completed by the Carter Administration in 1977 found that human rights were being violated in most of the 82 countries that received some form of security assistance. These were mostly countries from the Third World. Although the Reagan Administration operated under the same Act, the emphasis has shifted to security and the containment of Communism.

The dilemma -- whether or not to extend military assistance to dictatorships -- in the politics of foreign aid distribution presents the US with difficult and conflicting choices particularly with regard to the Latin American region where the human rights violations of the Chilean regime and a few others are now topics of controversy. The dilemma discussed above has a direct bearing on two US national interests: (1) the promotion of democracy in the Third World, and (2) the containment of Soviet influence. These two national interests are brought into mutual conflict in the conduct of US foreign policy. As long as Third World countries continue to be threatened by revolutionary politics inspired by Soviet support, this dilemma will continue to confront US officials in their conduct of foreign policy.

RECIPIENTS' ATTITUDES TOWARD AID

Analyses of foreign aid flows tend to focus almost exclusively on donor rationales, objectives, and preferences in the entire aid relationship. Such partial analysis is permissible if the time frame is the 1950's and 1960's when most aid, was in the form of grants and targeted at Cold War objectives. Since the 1970's when the debt burden became an issue and the grant element in aid was drastically reduced, it has become worthwhile to consider the recipients' reaction to aid flows. Attitudes, aspirations, feelings, and perceptions regarding aid programmes significantly affect the volume and types of aid a Country is willing to receive or demand from a donor. At the same time as aid flows have been declining since 1967, the attitude of recipient Countries towards foreign aid has also been increasingly critical particularly of the types of aid given and the conditions accompanying such aid. The former President of Tanzania, Julius Nyerere expressed the attitude in this way:

> Loans which carry no interest or have very low interest rates, contain a large amount of aid -- particularly at times of world inflation. But the aid element can be nullified or reduced if such a 'soft loan' is tied to purchases from a high cost lending nation. Indeed, our experience, has shown us that a tied 'soft loan' from some countries can be almost as expensive as free commercial money would be. [25]

A Common attitude is thus the negative reaction on the part of recipients regarding the real benefits generated by aid after it is disbursed. The common concerns of recipients are the conditions of procurement-tying, duration of the payment period, the rate of interest on the loan, and the rate of return for them. Closely related to the issue of the benefits of the aid distributed is the fact that the history of aid-giving has been plagued by failure and general developmental stagnation. Such an outcome has been partly a consequence of domestic and international systemic interactions that lead to a distortion of aid objectives with regard to proper orientation and implementation. This situation has also resulted in disillusionment with aid programmes over the years because of their failure to accelerate the development process in recipient countries. The reaction of recipient nations signifies that they like donors also have objectives they would like to achieve through the aid relationship. Negative reactions tend to have a strong bearing on economic concerns like rapid development and access to industrial goods without suffering a heavy debt-service burden.

The debt burden has become one of the major issues within the aid relationship that has affected the attitudes of both donor and recipient. To start with, the oil crisis of 1973-74 and the oil squeeze of 1979 coupled with global recessions and high interest rates drastically weakened the economies of Third World countries. These developments culminated in the debt crisis. In 1978 the OECD estimated the long term debt of all Less Developed Countries (LDC's) at only $340 billion, but by 1982 their long term debt was estimated at $626 billion, a significant increase in only four years. The rate of increase of developing country debt was about 20 per cent a year during the 1970's. After 1980, the significant decrease in LDC export earnings caused the ratio of total debt to exports to rise from 83 percent to 114 per cent between 1980 and 1982. [26]

There seems to be an inevitable relationship between aid distribution and debt accumulation. If the aid relationship is to be viable, gross aid disbursements must increase faster than debt services on past aid. In the case of US aid flows, military aid has risen sharply while economic aid has declined. As a result, the military aid debt has complicated the debt problem. In 1984, the interest payments on US. foreign military sales credits alone were estimated at $2 billion; this despite the fact that most US military aid is provided on either a grant or very concessional basis.

US aid flows perform a dual role with regard to the debt problem. They are at the same time a part of the problem as well as a part of the solution. The various US foreign aid programmes are characterized by different financial terms ranging from very concessional rates to rates at the cost of money to the US Treasury. On the one hand, PL 480 and ESF loans are traditionally very concessional whereas FMS military credits extended by the Federal Financing Bank with near-commercial interest rates contribute to the debt-servicing difficulties of some Third World Countries. However, with the emergence of a debt crisis, nonproject ESF is willingly given to recipient states experiencing critical balance-of-payments problems as one way of alleviating their debt problems. The recipients are primarily states that are central to, or are of some special importance to US national security.

Two other provisions exist for the alleviation of debt problems of LDCs. The first is the debt forgiveness option of the PL 480 food aid program and the other is the 'Retroactive Terms Adjustment' (RTA) option. One component of the PL 480 food aid programme known as Title III provision permits the forgiveness of PL 480 Title I loans if the recipient is willing to implement agreed upon economic development programmes. This option is part of the food aid relationship with Senegal, Sudan, Honduras, Egypt, Bolivia, Bangladesh, among others. The RTA option converts outstanding concessional loans into grants. It was adopted in March 1978 by the Trade and Development Board (TDB) of the United Nations Conference on Trade and Development (UNCTAD). [27] It called for measures by developed donor nations to adjust the terms of past bilateral aid to more concessional terms as a means of increasing net Official Development Assistance (ODA) aid to LDC's. The US Congress amended the

Foreign Assistance Act in 1978 to accommodate the measures of the RTA option. However, RTA is limited only to the 30 poorest countries and therefore does not solve most of the current debt problems facing middle-income countries.

The burden of debt services or repayment has had a formidable influence on the recipient's attitude to aid flows. The general lack of any visible signs of substantial economic growth has added to the disillusionment and frustration experienced by recipient countries with regard to the aid they receive. Suspicion and negative reactions surface when the recipient countries consider themselves perennially vulnerable to the conditions accompanying the aid such that they perceive a threat to their sovereignty. President Nyerere succinctly voiced this sentiment:

> But we poor nations insist that aid should be given as an expression of partnership, and therefore without political strings being attached to it. Poverty has no ideology. We are poor whether we are socialist, capitalist, or communist. We feel very strongly on this issue: our independence is not for sale. [28]

The expression of the above concern is an indication that the aid distribution process has a strong element of action-reaction-over reaction pattern between donor and recipient. The aid-giving (action) directed by the donor towards the recipients may be perceived (reaction, overreaction, or attitude) either positively or negatively by the recipient nation.

In the final analysis the viability of the aid relationship is bound to be shaped by the debt issue for the rest of the 1980's and on to the 1990's. If recipient countries increasingly experience the debt-service burden and think it is excessive, they may increasingly demand less aid with near-market conditions. Foreign military sales credit will most probably suffer the most assuming that recipient countries come to the conclusion that preparing for, and engaging in, international wars are a waste of resources. The maintenance of internal stability does not require enormous expenditure on arms. On the other hand, the willingness of the US to continue distributing aid will also depend on the continuing creditworthiness of recipient states.

Supplementary Explanations

The level and frequency of foreign aid to a recipient country also depend on such factors as the levels of intraregional conflict and superpower rivalry as well as perceptions of rival powers' regional intentions. For example, military aid flows to the Middle East are largely motivated by the level of actual conflict, and potential for conflict. The same is true of aid to India and Pakistan, Ethiopia and Somalia, or North Korea and South Korea. Because of the existence of highly conflictual and potentially conflictual subregions, the consequence has been the existence of a kind of foreign aid-giving race by donors and competitive aid demands by recipient countries. The Soviet provision of aid to North Korea, North Vietnam, Syria, Iraq, and Ethiopia is bound to trigger a similar US extension of aid to South Korea, Thailand, Israel, and Somalia.

Table 1.3 presents a summary of subregions where actual and potential conflicts exist and thus very likely to attract aid from rival donors.

Inspite of the hypothesized aid race and aid acquisition in regions of high conflict, it is nevertheless reasonable to assume that foreign aid allocation operates on the assumption of an overall resource constraint view on the part of donors because donors do not possess infinite resources. Based on a fixed aid budget, it is only expedient for the donor to give more aid to the 'most valued' political, military, and economic country in a region. In such a situation, the donor targets the highest valued objective in the recipient country until goal realization and consolidation are achieved. In addition, a political consolidation of aid distribution can be viewed in terms of a 'utility function' of foreign assistance for both donor and recipient. Since economic aid is usually associated with trade and investment issues, there is assumed to be allocation problems and competition among recipients for a finite amount of aid. Where the donor is concerned, the character of an influence relationship vis-a-vis the recipient nation is both a function of the terms of trade as well as the volume of trade. Moreover, it is also reasonable to assume that an influence relationship is more likely to result and be lasting if significant levels of commercial transactions exist between donor and recipient in which aid flows play a key role.

While foreign aid is generally expected to ensure meaningful political and military returns in terms of a reduction in recipients political vulnerability, gaining influence with 'large' and geostrategic countries, it is at the same time used in superpower rivalries as a controlled and manipulated foreign policy output to achieve the following:
(1) regional aid-giving parity with a rival donor;
(2) self-reliance and economic development of allies and friends, thereby decreasing their level of dependence; and
(3) limited aid commitments to recipients as a way of reducing overall foreign policy responsibilities. In their efforts to achieve these three goals, the US and USSR in

Table 1.3
Regions of Actual and Potential Conflicts

Region	Adversaries
Central America	El Salvador/ Leftist Guerrillas Nicaragua/ Contras
North West Africa	Morocco/Polisario/ Muritania
West Africa	Chad/Libya
Southern Africa	South Africa/SWAPO Mozambique/RENAMO Angola/UNITA Angola/South Africa
Central Africa	Zaire/Congolese Liberation Movement
East Africa	Ethiopia/Somalia
Middle East	Leban/PLO/Israel Iran/Iraq North Yemen/South Yemen Egypt/Libya
Asia	North Korea/South Korea Thailand/Vietnam India/Pakistan Afghanistan/USSR/Mujahadeen

particular strive to win as many friendly nations as possible with the smallest amount of foreign aid possible. The whole foreign aid process thus involves rivalries and counter-strategies that develop into a game of 'aid race' in conflictual and potentially conflictual regions.

In the final analysis, conflicts involving foreign aid flows basically reside on four levels: (1) the superpowers' level -- mainly political rivalries aimed at gaining influence over regional influentials; (2) intraregional level -- basically involves the superimposition of superpower competition on regional power rivalries; (3) North-South level -- involves conflicts over the transfer of resources from developed to developing nations, with donors usually adopting opposing views; and (4) superpower-small power level -- a conflict pitting a superpower against a weaker state in which the other superpower tends to be drawn on the side of the latter.

SUMMARY AND CONCEPTUAL UNDERPINNINGS

We have so far briefly examined how foreign aid distribution has developed into a key element in relations between the US and Third World Countries. The types of aid programmes have increased, the number of recipients has grown substantially, and enormous amounts have been transferred since 1947 when the Truman Doctrine was proclaimed.

As we have already noted at the beginning, this study explores international political economic relations between the US and Third World regions with a general emphasis on foreign policy and a specific focus on foreign aid flows. A detailed analysis of US foreign policy is beyond the scope of this book. However, this section tackles some key concepts of international political and economic relations and their applicability to foreign aid-giving within the context of foreign policy. Foreign policy behavior and international interactions provide conceptual tools to analyze interstate relations that contain elements of both politics and economics, and internal and external systemic factors.

Cold war and biopolycentrism

Reference to Superpower rivalries implies stages in interactions between the US and USSR in each of which aid-giving plays a key role. Under the Marshall Plan and Point Four, the US extended foreign aid to most of the colonies of the European powers and in forty independent Third World Countries. Between 1948 and 1952 over one-fifth of US aid was distributed to Third World regions. [29] The US foreign aid programme has evolved through a process that could be divided into two broad stages, roughly corresponding to changes in the international system and similar changes in regional power configurations. The period from 1945-1965 could be roughly categorized as a Cold War period in US - Soviet relations, whereas the period after 1965 to the present could be labelled as one of Bipolycentrism.

The use of the term Cold War in this analysis refers to a period and a situation. As a period it makes reference to roughly between 1945 and 1965 when the international system was dominated by a pattern of hostility and intense rivalry between the two superpowers. As a situation, it refers to the above pattern of interaction regardless of a time frame. For instance, we can refer to the situation in the Persian Gulf area as one of restrained Cold War. During the Cold War period bilateralism in aid distribution was the dominant pattern, with the US clearly the most significant aid-giver by all standards. Most aid-giving was also dominated by the advanced capitalist countries who later established the Development Assistance Committee (DAC). Between 1956 and 1960 bilateral aid from the DAC countries amounted to 89.7 per cent of total financing during this period. The US was clearly the most significant aid-giver with a portion of 67.6 per cent in 1956 and 60.5 per cent in 1960. [30]

In terms of volume and frequency of aid distribution the Sino-Soviet bloc was still far behind the US. The Soviets did not make their first commitment of economic aid to a noncommunist Third World Country (Afghanistan) until 1954. China made its own commitment in 1956. Although the 1950's were a period of US superiority aid-giving by the Sino-Soviet bloc created a stronger willingness on the part of the US to supply aid to Third World nations. By 1960, the USSR had made commitments to only thirteen countries, and China to only seven. [31] The competition signalled by Communist bloc aid motivated the US to urge the OECD (formed in 1961) countries to expand their own aid programme. As the OEEC most of its aid during the late 1950s went to donor overseas territories. By the early 1960s OECD countries were extending aid on a regular basis; however, three-fifths of bilateral aid from the advanced industrial countries was still donated by the US. Both economic and military aid during this period were justified on the basis of the Cold War rivalry but also later justified on the basis of 'development' criteria.

Bipolycentrism is used in reference to the loosening of the major Cold War rivalries and issues. It recognizes the continued existence of two rival blocs, the West and the East, each led by the US and USSR respectively. But at the same time bloc members exhibit more independence and self-interest in their foreign policies than during the Cold War bipolar period. There is an emphasis on the significant increase in the number of state and non-state actors since the early 1960s. States, guerrilla organizations, liberation movements, and terrorist groups are the motivation behind the distribution of economic and military assistance. The ushering in of the period of Bipolycentrism was marked by a relaxation of tensions between the US and USSR, the signing of the Nuclear Test Ban Treaty on September 1963, the installation of the hotline, and the US approval of a sale of 150 million bushels of grain to the Soviet Union. By the mid 1960s the newly independent Third World nations of Asia, Africa, and the Middle East had formed themselves into a Non-Aligned Movement (NAM), further helping to diffuse the rivalry between the two Superpowers. With the near recovery of Western Europe and Japan, and the existence of the NAM, the international system basically lost its immediate post-War configurations of power. With these changes in the international system multilateral aid began to gain in popularity. Bilateral aid began to decrease with the DAC total decreasing from 54.2 per cent in 1960 to 37.9 per cent in 1970. The growth in multilateral aid was a result of the creation of, in particular two affiliates of the International Bank for Reconstruction and Development (IBRD), the International Finance Corporation (IFC) in 1956 and the International Development Association (IDA) in 1960. Multilateralism was on the increase largely in response to Third World pressures for aid distribution to be free of political strings.

The changing international political system affected the conception of bilateral aid programmes through their redefinition, reorganization, and a need to make them more economic in orientation. In 1961 the Agency for International Development (AID) was established to reflect the new emphasis and to replace the MSA, the Foreign Operations Administration, and the International Cooperation Administration, all forerunners of AID. Furthermore, since the 1960s there has been a gradual decline in the importance of US bilateral aid, although the US is still the largest bilateral donor. However, in 1980, US aid totaled only 23.8 per cent of bilateral aid from DAC countries and 12.6 percent of all official aid in 1980. [32] The trend since the mid 1960s has been an Ex-Metropole and sphere of influence pattern of aid flows with Latin America receiving 89 per cent of their aid from the US in most of the late 1960s. In 1980 the top ten recipients of UK aid were all former colonies accounting for 61 per cent of Britain's total aid. France allocated 41.6 per cent of its aid in 1980 to nonsovereign overseas departments, with a significant portion of the remainder allocated to ex-colonies in Africa.

High-conflict regions

Since the post-World War II inception of foreign aid as a key component of foreign policy, distributional emphasis has focused on high-conflict nations. Israel, South Korea, Taiwan, and South Vietnam have been the targets of US foreign aid. Changing times and circumstances partly a result of Bipolycentrism have eliminated Vietnam from the priority list, but only to be replaced by Egypt and El Salvador starting with the late 1970s.

In the conduct of foreign policy certain regions and nations are considered actual or potential high-conflict zones. During the Cold War period Taiwan, the two Koreas, the two Vietnams, most of the Middle East, and the Congo would be included in this category by many analysts. Even after the Cold War the Middle East and the two Koreas are still part of this scenario. Other regions and nations have joined the ranks of the volatile and explosive. Central America, the Horn of Africa, Southern Africa, and the India-Pakistan area would be included in the category by many observers. Our definition of a high-conflict region is based on empirical evidence of: (1) the existence of civil or guerrilla wars spilling over and impacting on a wider area such as in the Horn of Africa and Central America; (2) the escalation of conflict between two or more actors such that it reaches the proportions of an international war; the Iran-Iraq War would fit into this definition, while the Chad-Libyan conflict and the Angolan-South African situation would follow closely behind; and (3) the existence of potential conflict. For instance, the potential exists for the eruption of another Arab-Israeli war, or a Nicaraguan-Honduran war because of the activities of the Contras operating from Honduran territory against Nicaragua.

Moreover conflicts and instability are not only an integral part of interstate relations in Third World regions, but they are also the nature of political and socioeconomic interactions within nation states. Irredentist movements, border clashes, antigovernment groups, regional conflicts, ethnic and religious rivalries often lead to a demand for external aid and a supply from an interested donor. The pervasive nature of the conflicts and instability in certain regions matured with the end of the post-War bipolar system which ushered in a period of bipolycentrism with characteristics of power diffusion, rival regional influentials like Ethiopia and Somalia, India and Pakistan, Angola and South Africa, among others.

Among these regional rivals the belief is prevalent that the acquisition of armaments and an increase in military forces are key elements of foreign policy. They also believe that military power, in particular relative military power,

Table 1.4
Historical Patterns in Foreign Aid Distribution

	Cold War Period (1945-1965)	Bipolycentrism (1965-1980's)
Type and Level of Conflict		
Intraregional Conflict	Very High	Low
Superpower Conflict	Very High	Low
Aid Distribution Strategy		
Selective	Very High	Low
Penetrative	Very High	High

could be increased through the demand for more military aid from donor countries. An increase in military power in turn enhances the regional leverage of a nation in regional politics. In other words, increased military assistance becomes necessary in the case of a plausible regional internal or external threat as well as its enhancement of military power for its own sake.

Furthermore, most nations in a region of high conflict sense some potential military threat even if they are not one of the combatants. They therefore ensure a steady source of arms supply, and maintain a large military force for protection. They also maintain armed forces that are large relative to the size of their populations and spend relatively large shares of their GNPs on the military. For example, in 1963 Israel spent 8.6 per cent of its GNP on defense and had 2.7 per cent of its population in the military. By 1968 the amount spent on defense had increased to 17.7 per cent of GNP and 3.4 per cent of the population in the military. Similarly, in 1963 North Korea spent 12.2 per cent of GNP on defense with 3.1 per cent of the population in the military, in 1968 it had increased to 17.4 per cent of GNP with still 3.1 per cent of the population in the military. [33] This trend is similar for other nations like Egypt, Jordan, South Korea, Syria, and so on who are also members of high-conflict regions.

Finally, the high conflictual level of certain regions has implications for aid distribution. It means that certain countries become priority targets of US foreign policy. For instance, between 1950-1975, South Vietnam, South Korea, Taiwan, and Israel were the US priority foreign policy targets. Because they are in regions of high conflict and feel threatened they were the recipients of 20 per cent of all US economic assistance and about 45 per cent of all military assistance excluding the maintenance of US forces in South Vietnam and South Korea.

Demand-supply factor

In the light of intra-regional conflicts as shown in Table 1.4 it is reasonable to assume that Third World nations like the Superpowers engage in an 'aid race' whereby the desire to attract more foreign aid such as new weapons systems or development projects sometimes becomes a foreign policy priority. For instance, in terms of military aid, the level of arms and degree of weapons sophistication of Israel are determined almost entirely by those of Syria and vice versa. Since their military aid suppliers are the US and the USSR respectively, there is a tendency to constantly demand more military aid from their donors. Their demands are enhanced by the fact that the regional foreign policies of the two

43

powers plus theirs are intricately linked together. A similar demand-supply relationship with the Superpowers could be applied to India and Pakistan, North and South Korea, Ethiopia and Somalia, and Thailand and Vietnam.

In terms of the more technologically advanced military aid recipients like Israel and South Korea the demand-supply process becomes part of a regional arms acquisition syndrome in which they express a desire to catch up or keep up with the new technological developments of their donors particularly in the area of fighter aircrafts, radars, and the like. The need to demand and acquire new weapons systems is largely strengthened by the IMET programme which inculcates in Third World military elites the bureaucratic pressures to attempt to expand their relative status by acquiring more modern military hardware and increase the size of their military. The realization of both objectives usually results in request for assistance from the US and other major donors. The same application could be done in the case of economic development aid as well with an emphasis on the desire for projects like hydroelectric schemes, chemical and fertilizer plants, and other infrastructural amenities.

In all instances, it is worthwhile to keep in mind that the demand-supply relationship and overall international political economic interactions are affected by the prevailing attitude of a donor or recipient toward an issue or event. The 1977-78 realignment of forces in the Horn of Africa was largely affected by the attitudes of both Superpowers and Ethiopia and Somalia with regard to regional events and the demand for aid. In addition, the scope and intensity of transactions often have a bearing on the ranking of a region as perceived by the major powers. Perception of economic and military salience may be explored through the establishment of an aid relationship in the case where none is in existence. As early as 1951, in Congressional hearings on the foreign aid programme the geostrategic and economic salience of Third World regions had been emphasized. Nelson Rockefeller underscored the salience of the Third World when he stated that: 'Clearly the success of the industrial mobilization plans of the North Atlantic Treaty Countries is contingent upon the increasing supply from underdeveloped areas of strategic materials as bauxite, chrome, copper, lead, manganese, tin, uranium, and zinc.' [34] The success of international political and economic relations with the Third World is largely enhanced by the supply of aid by the industrialized donor nations.

Selective and penetrative strategies

The finite nature of foreign aid has led to its

distribution being based on two strategies: (1) selective, and (2) penetrative. In a selective pattern of aid distribution the donor transfers aid to a recipient because the recipient has strong ties with the donor. For instance, it is often the case that the US provides a recipient with aid because the recipient is pro-American, anti-Soviet, and often threatened internally or externally by Communism; the recipient may also border a Communist country. United States foreign aid to Egypt, Israel, South Korea, and the Philippines among others fall in this category. In other words, a selective aid extension strategy has the element of significant transfers of resources to a few countries because of either their geophysical location or the fact that they are actually or potentially threatened by rival nations. In FY 1983, 52 per cent of all ESF aid went to Egypt and Israel. Eight other countries: Pakistan, Turkey, Lebanon, Sudan, Zimbabwe, Costa Rica, El Salvador, and Jamaica account for the rest of the ESF for FY 1983. [35] The ESF in particular provides economic aid to promote economic and political stability in areas where the US has special interests. The Middle East share in 1982 was 59 per cent or $1.6 billion. The key recipients of US military aid for 1959, 1970, and 1982 satisfy the characteristics of political salience to the US, location along the communist periphery, and actual or potential communist threat. Finally, in selective targeting there is usually recurrence of mostly the same countries as top recipients of aid from year to year. This recurrence is partially revealed in Table 1.5 which shows the top 10 recipients of US military aid for three randomly selected years: 1959, 1970, and 1982.

In a penetrative aid-giving strategy aid flows are used by the donor to break new ground in foreign policy and politico-economic interactions with a particular country. Aid is thus used as a diplomatic pathfinding instrument. The initial objective is to create a more positive relationship with the target country which may be susceptible to political influence. The country may be pro-Western but guided by a strong commitment to 'non-alignment' in foreign policy. A penetrative strategy may also be directed at a country espousing a rival political ideology. For example, in the case of China in particular, the aid relationship has spilled over into a trade relationship. First, in early 1980 the US granted the PRC most-favored-nation status, later followed by an agreement to transfer arms to the PRC. Between 1978 and 1985 US - Chinese trade grew steadily and now approximates or even surpasses trade turnover with the USSR. [36] Other examples of US aid such as to Poland, Romania, or Yugoslavia are expected to result in increased interactions that would enhance US foreign policy. In other words, aid and trade are instrumental in the process of normalizing relations with

Table 1.5
Top 10 Recipients of US Military Grant Aid,
1959, 1970, and 1982

	1959	1970	1982
1.	Taiwan	Vietnam	Israel
2.	Turkey	South Korea	Egypt
3.	Italy	Taiwan	El Salvador
4.	South Korea	Turkey	Turkey
5.	Greece	Cambodia	Sudan
6.	France	Laos	Portugal
7.	Iran	Thailand	Somalia
8.	Japan	Greece	Honduras
9.	Netherlands	Spain	Kenya
10.	Pakistan	Israel	Liberia

Sources: Fiscal Year Series, Department of Defense, 1982;
Presentation Document, Security Assistance, FY
1984.

Table 1.6
Purposes of Postwar US Foreign Aid Programmes

Period	Amount	Purposes & Types
1. Postwar Relief Period (1946-1948)	$12.5 billion	1. Focus on the relief and rehabilitation of war ravaged countries 2. Rebuilding of a new international economic system 3. About 50% of aid in the form of credits
2. Marshall Plan Period (1949-1952)	$18.6 billion	1. Reconstruction of pro-Western economies, primarily in Europe and Asia 2. Restoration of capital assets damaged during the war 3. Revitalizing the world economy
3. Mutual Security Act (1953-1961)	$24.1 billion	1. Shift in emphasis from economic aid to military aid 2. Military aid conceived of in terms of the Cold War 3. Shift in regional emphasis from Europe to Third World
4. Foreign Assistance Act Period (1962-1984)	123.1 billion	1. Emphasis on Third World development 2. Focus on improving the lives of the poorest citizens through basic needs 3. Substantial reliance on technical assistance and economic stability

Source: Adapted from US Overseas Loans and Grants and Assistance from International Organizations, 1985:4.

Note: Figures are nearest approximations of exact amount disbursed.

neutral or pro-Soviet nations.

In addition, it is worthwhile to note that both strategies carry the implication that foreign aid has specific purposes because it is often targeted at a particular foreign policy objective in the recipient country. For instance, aid can be used to revitalize a country's economy, or for military containment purposes, or simply for meeting basic needs. Table 1.6 shows the specific periods in the evolution of US aid programs and their avowed purposes. Finally, we would expect regional aid policies within the context of foreign policy to be a function of:

(1) the regional imperative in foreign policy; [37]
(2) attitudes to aid, perceptions of aid; and willingness to demand and receive aid;
(3) regional status of recipient state as well as the perceptions of the region by superpowers;
(4) intensity and frequency of foreign economic and military activities in the region; and
(5) the willingness of donors to engage in an aid competition in a region or toward rival recipient countries.

All of the above factors are in turn related to the associational pattern between the flow of aid and country, regional, and global events.

NOTES

[1] US, Department of State Publications, The Military Assistance Program, July 1949, p. 4.
[2] US, Department of State, International Security and Development Cooperation, Special Report 108, April 4, 1983.
[3] In some descriptions of US foreign aid programs, the ESF is included in the same category as other military assistance programs. However, the ESF may not be used to buy defense articles or services. For an examination of this program along with other military aid programs, see, Andrew K. Semmel, 'Evolving Patterns of US Security Assistance 1950-1980,' in Charles W. Kegley and Eugene R. Wittkopf (eds.), Perspectives on American Foreign Policy: Selected Readings (New York: St. Martins Press, 1983) pp. 79-95.
[4] US, Agency for International Development, Department of Defense, Defense Security Assistance Agency, 1970-1984, p. 5.
[5] US, Department of State Special Report No. 108 p. 15; Congressional Presentation, Security Assistance, FY 1984, pp. 6-9.
[6] US, Department of State, Internal Security and

Development Programme, Special Report No. 108, April 4, 1983, pp. 12-13.

[7] New York Times, May 18, 1986, Editorial Page.

[8] US, Agency for International Development, Statistics and Reports Division, US Overseas Loans and Grants and Assistance from International Organizations, July 1945-June 1983.

[9] US, Department of State, Conventional Arms Transfers in the Third World, 1972-1983.

[10] US, Department of State, The Mutual Defense Assistance Program, April-October 1951, p. 3.

[11] US, Department of State, Department of Defense International Cooperation Administration, The Mutual Security Program, Fiscal Year 1958, p. 38.

[12] US, Department of State, Conventional Arms Transfers in the Third World, 1972-1983.

[13] For an excellent analysis of the relational concept of influence see, Alvin Z. Rubinstein, 'Assessing Influence as a Problem in Foreign Policy,' in Alvin Z. Rubinstein (ed.), Soviet and Chinese Influence in the Third World (New York: Praeger, 1975) pp. 1-22.

[14] Congressional Presentation, Security Assistance Programs, FY 1984.

[15] A detailed examination of this influence strategy is found in, Robert B. Cialdini, Influence: How and Why People Agree to Things (New York: William Morrow and Co. Inc., 1984) pp. 29-65.

[16] See, for example, Arms Control and Disarmament Agency (ACDA) World Military Expenditures and Arms Transfers, 1969-1978, p. 2; and Stockholm International Peace Research Institute (SIPRI), Yearbook, 1980, p. 115.

[17] US, Foreign Aid, Report of the Special Senate Committee, 1957, p. 9.

[18] US, House of Representatives, Foreign Assistance Legislation for Fiscal Year 1975: Hearings Before the Committee on Foreign Affairs, First Session, part 1, p. 6.

[19] US, Department of State, Composition of US Economic Cooperation Programs from 1968 to 1984.

[20] US, Department of State, Nationalization, Expropriation and Other Takings of United States and Certain Foreign Property Since 1960. Research Study RECS-14 (mimeo), December 1971.

[21] For a detailed account of the investment battles see, Charles T. Goodsell, American Corporations and Peruvian Politics (Cambridge: Harvard University Press, 1972).

[22] Goodsell, American Corporations and Peruvian Politics.

[23] UN, Economic and Social Council, Committee on Natural Resources, Permanent Sovereignty over Natural Resources E/C. 7/53. January 31, 1975.

[24] See, Section 502B, Public Law 940329, 94th Congress.
[25] Julius Nyerere, Aid and Development: The Recipients Point of View (New Zealand: Institute of International Affairs, Wellington, 1974) p. 10.
[26] OECD, Development Cooperation: Efforts and Policies of the Members of the Development Assistance Committee, 1978-1982 reviews.
[27] US Congress, 1978 Amendment to the Foreign Assistance Act.
[28] Julius Nyerere, Aid and Development: The Recipients Point of View, p. 12.
[29] Economic Cooperation Administration, Eighth Report to Congress, and Thirteenth Report to Congress, 1950-1952.
[30] OECD, Development Cooperation: Efforts and Policies of the Members of the Development Assistance Committee, 1956-1960 reviews.
[31] US, Department of State, The Sino-Soviet Economic Offensive in the Less Developed Countries, 1958; it is sometimes published under the title of The Threat of Soviet Economic Policy.
[32] OECD, Geographical Distribution of Financial Flows to Less Developed Countries, 1977/78.
[33] US, Arms Control and Disarmament Agency (undated).
[34] Nelson A. Rockefeller, 'Widening Boundaries of National Interest,' Foreign Affairs 29, 4 July 1951, p. 527.
[35] Congressional Presentation, Security Assistance Programs, FY 1984.
[36] See, US, International Trade Commission, 1978-1985, and US, Bureau of the Census, 1985: Tables 5 and 8.
[37] The regional imperative refers to the geopolitical, strategic, military, and economic importance of a region that makes it compelling for the Superpowers to compete for power, influence, and leverage among its countries. For example, the Middle East has qualities that makes it imperative for the Superpowers to link its security with their overall national security.

2 Foreign Aid and Geopolitical Theories

Geopolitics is basically concerned about the spatial global power relationships between the key competing nations of various epochs. Evidently, the state-centric, regionally-focused analysis of modern global resource allocations constitutes a major element of the current geopolitical equation as evidenced in the existing superpower spheres of influence in Third World regions. Foreign aid is only one vehicle, among many, for the acquisition of spatial advantages, it has albeit been a powerful one in US-Soviet global power projection. Questions of strategies of resource allocation to obtain spatial advantages, as we shall see in subsequent chapters, are best understood within the context of changing configurations of power and influence in the international system.

This chapter will focus on a discussion of past and more recent geopolitical theories as prescriptions for global dominance in the multipolar international system of nineteenth and twentieth century Europe, and as indicative of a new trend in the vocabulary of current strategic competition relating to ideological differences, the nuclear arms race, concerns about resource scarcity, economic warfare, and the increasing political and economic assertiveness of Third World nations. The description and interpretation of past and current geopolitical writings will then be linked to foreign aid's articulation into the global US competition with the Soviets for spatial advantages.

The geopolitical theories of the early twentieth century and beyond, with their emphasis on global dominance, overwhelming maritime control by one power, have little relevance for our current international system where imperial conquest is no longer a systemic value. Nonetheless, the ongoing US-Soviet competition reflected in ideological conflicts, proxy wars, competition for overseas bases, and arms races, are all basically separate but interconnected elements of a strategic game of spatial competition for power and influence in anticipation of war.

Geopolitical theories of all decades are predicated on an endemic global power competition. The birth of geopolitics dates back only about a century, even though some scholars have traced its development well back into history. Just as there is no overwhelming consensus regarding its beginnings, so is there controversy surrounding its designation as to whether it is a science, pseudo-science, or another term for political geography.

Some scholars, writing about the concept point to a consensus among theorists in all epochs who view the importance of spatial and power relationships only in terms of major actors in existence at the time. [1] In ancient times, evidently, the world that mattered was geographically limited in extent, regional in focus, until the beginnings of European expansion into other continents. According to Saul Cohen, the regionally-oriented geopolitical perspectives of Christian Europe began to change with the Portuguese circumnavigation efforts of the fourteenth and fifteenth centuries. [2] This European outward expansion ushered in a new age and Weltanschauung characterized by the acquisition of colonial territories, the control over strategic sea passages and coastal trading posts.

It was in the nineteenth century that we started seeing the beginnings of the fine outlines of modern geopolitical theory in contrast to the hazy geopolitical portrayals of four centuries back when most geographic knowledge was based on erroneous Ptolemaic or Macrobian conceptions of the Indian Ocean and Southern Africa. [3] Ratzel's nineteenth century reference to the analogy of the state as an 'organism' with emphasis on the space it occupied was very relevant to the later themes in geopolitical theory. He was also perhaps the first to recognize the salience of the large continental land formations of Russia, North America, Australia, and South America in relation to political power. [4] At this point in the development of geopolitical thinking the tendency to link large continental areas with political power was already a key element in global thinking.

THE FOCUS ON LAND, SEA AND AIR POWER

As the evolution of geopolitical theory continued into the twentieth century the varying attributes of the importance of land, sea, and air power in relation to spatial location gained added relevance. The Englishman, Halford Mackinder, is considered by many to be the most renowned of the twentieth-century geopolitical theorists to underscore the importance of land in the struggle for world domination. 'The Geographical Pivot of History,' which he wrote in 1904 underscored the overwhelming importance of the Eurasian continental heartland and the inevitable competition between it and the rimland, which Mackinder termed the 'marginal crescent.' [5] This heartland-rimland dichotomy has apparently had a major influence on the strategic calculations of major powers, and has in addition been the motivation behind numerous theories on the heartland and rimland dimensions of global power projection.

Central to Mackinder's theory was the perception of inner Eurasia as the preeminent region of global politics. In order to achieve global domination control of this heartland was essential. In the tradition of Mackinder, other theorists have applied the factors of large geographic and population sizes to provide the basis for domination even though they, including Mackinder, never clarified what they meant by domination. Mackinder's basic thrust of a dominant Eurasia was a reflection of an age-old British concern about a continental coalition between Russia and Germany which could dominate Europe and change the balance of power at the expense of Britain, or by the possibility of military domination of the one by the other.

The basic focus of Mackinder's theory has been reflected over the seven decades in some of the most spectacular foreign policies: the theoretical underpinnings of German geopolitics and Nazi foreign policy largely responsible for the outbreak of the Second World War and the subsequent breakdown of the multipolar European international system; the immediate post World War II Soviet foreign policy with its spatial reference to a 'capitalist encirclement,' and for the past forty years in the mostly Soviet-Centric thrust of American foreign policy reflected in the term 'containment.' Some analysts, for example, claim that the United States playing of the 'China Card'--using ties with China to check Soviet expansionism -- is predicated on the heartland strategy. Robert Walters, arguing along the same lines, believes that the US strategic nuclear doctrine emphasizes its capabilities of mass destruction to counter-balance the Sino-Soviet advantages of military manpower and geographic size. [6] The American struggle for overseas bases and military allies is evidently going to be a continuous foreign policy objective and could be viewed as related mostly to the future contingency of an anti-American monolithic Sino-Soviet bloc.

In contrast to the Mackinderian emphasis on land power, Mahan's thesis, also at the early part of the century, stressed the historical supremacy of seapower. [7] Hence the Mahanian conception of geopolitics could be considered a major rival thesis, although its point of focus was also the Eurasian landmass. For Mahan seapower and the pervasive influence of dominant seapowers are indivisible. He claimed that global seapower projection is less costly compared to long distance overland transport. In order to achieve hegemony, according to Mahan, indivisible control of the sea is of primary importance, and control over strategically located land bases is a necessary condition. Mahan's thesis like Mackinder's was rooted in his reflection on the spectre of a confrontation between a potentially powerful Russian seapower and a weak rimland, which at the time he wrote was very vulnerable to domination by long range seapower. [8] Mahan made reference to an alliance between the US, UK, Germany, and Japan against Russia and China, almost a perfect forekowledge of the 1950s configuration of alliances, and virtually indicative of the rimland versus heartland spatial competition. The emphasis for Mahan, unlike Mackinder, regarding world domination, lay in control over the rimland littoral as reflected in the naval power projections of Britain and France, Holland, and Portugal over the large populations and land masses of India, China, and other territories.

Nicholas Spykman, the American, also contributed to the already existing corpus of geopolitical theories in his writings during the Second World War. [9] Inspired mainly by Mahan's thesis he developed an offshoot of the seapower-rimland strategies combined. His analysis was largely influenced by the fear of German aggression and the need to counteract it with a combination of Anglo-Saxon seapower and Soviet landpower. The strategic importance of Mackinder's marginal crescent was also emphasized in Spykman's analysis because of its focus on Maritime Europe, the Middle East, India, South-East Asia, and China especially in relation to their combined resources, populations, and interior sea lines. Moreover, for Spykman land-based airpower had become a key complementary element of seapower around the rimland and in the marginal seas. [10] Although very strategic in the geopolitical equation Spykman did not think that heartland airpower would take preeminence over the rimlands.

In addition to theories about land and sea dominance, there also exists within the traditional corpus of geopolitical writings, theories of airpower dominance. This last leg of the triad emerged only after the development of long range bombers and aircraft carriers during the interwar period. Airpower theory identified a new geostrategic area in the North Pole region and at the same time emphasized the vulnerability of both the Eurasian and Anglo-Saxon segments of the northern land mass across the Arctic. [11] Also identified as strategic were the trans-Arctic 'great circle routes' which formed the shortest air distances between the US and Soviet Union.

Among the airpower theorists, Douhet and Seversky in particular, did not consider overseas bases as a crucial component of airpower dominance. [12] Nonetheless, in reality transit bases, refuelling facilities, early-warning radar installations, and fighter bases would still play a crucial role in a war involving long distance battles. Moreover, the airpower geopolitical theorists view the heartland advantage conferred on the USSR as erroneous. According to John Slessor, one of its proponents, air power has made the open spaces of the USSR once a strong source of defense against Napoleon and Hitler, a source of vulnerability, one reason being it can now be attacked from almost all angles. [13] George Cressey, another geopolitical theorist, in fact claimed that 'The Heartland' might actually lie in North America instead of in Eurasia because of the former's central location, access to two oceans, compact shape, and above all technological dominance. [14] His conclusion was evidently based on the new post World War II reality in which technology had surpassed geostrategic location as a key determinant of global dominance.

GEOPOLITICS IN SOVIET-AMERICAN COMPETITION

Traditional geopolitical theorizing slipped into utter oblivion with the advent of the new bipolar international system. New technological developments in air, land, and sea weaponry and logistics, were believed to have contributed to the demise of an Eurasia-centered heartland theory. Furthermore, the emergence of a new international system, new configurations of power and influence, the increasing primacy of socioeconomic issues, the rise of modern guerrilla warfare and the existence of various liberation movements spelt the death knell of geopolitics as a field of inquiry.

Technological dominance, industrial production, among other factors, seriously challenged the traditional view of the relationship between size, location, and power, as evidenced in the post World War II arms races. Quality in industrial and scientific research became the emphasis; in terms of military technology this translated into effectiveness of firepower and delivery speed. By the late 1950s geopolitics as a field of inquiry had almost been overshadowed by issues of nuclear deterrence, arms races, limited warfare and counter insurgency in the discipline of international relations.

After almost three decades of dormancy, in the 1970s Geoffrey Kemp and Colin Gray began to resuscitate geopolitics as a field of inquiry. [15] Kemp pointed to developments in the 1970s which had given a new importance to geography in world politics; the global nature of arms transfers, increasing importance of access to critical raw materials, among others. He also emphasized the growing geostrategic importance of the sea lines of communication (SLOCs), especially those of the South Atlantic and the Southern Indian Ocean in the strategy of the Western maritime powers. Colin Gray in his analysis pointed to a Soviet strategy of 'hemispheric denial,' in Europe which can be effected through a blitzkrieg and control of the North Atlantic. He also applied the same thesis of a possible Soviet denial strategy in connection with Africa and Asia. Like Mackinder's thesis, the potential for global dominance is depicted in Gray's analysis and reflected in the idea of a 'Eurasian-African World Island.' [16]

The change from bipolarity to a more complex and multifaceted international system produced a rather still inexplicable resurgence of geopolitics. United States and Soviet politics of resource transfers and other elements of foreign policy have become increasingly underpinned by a perennial concern about spatial power relationships. Foreign aid has been used as a quid pro quo for maintaining political influence, gaining access to strategic bases and sources of critical minerals in Third World nations. Saul Cohen in his 1963 analysis of geopolitics seemed to lay emphasis on the inter-connectedness between geography, strategy, and politics. [17] In particular he claims that: geopolitical conceptions are a reflection of changing international political settings and man's interpretation of the nature of this change; and the concern, in large part, of geopolitics is with the identification of spatial frameworks that encompass interacting power entities.

Analyzing the concept at about the same time as Cohen, Harold and Margaret Sprout prefer to avoid the seemingly false pseudo-scientific aura which had surrounded the term, and focus instead on three 'geopolitical hypotheses:' (1) 'Those where the distribution of political power and influence in the world are explained mainly as a function of geopolitical configurations, i.e., the layout of continents, oceans, and connecting seas;' (2) 'Those in which political distributions are explained or predicted as functions of variations among nations in security of access to useful earth material, especially non-human sources of energy;' and (3) 'Those which see power and influence as functions of variations of climate.' [18] In their view these three have competed for primacy over the decades. The first and second of these hypotheses, as we shall see in subsequent chapters are related to the ongoing US-Soviet competition for military bases and strategic raw materials in which arms transfers and economic aid play a critical role.

The current informal use of the term geopolitics which is made in reference to the Unites States global projection of power in competition with the Soviet Union is a somewhat new departure from the historical focus of political geography. The traditional, historic conceptualization as we have already discussed emphasized grand strategy to cope with the endemic nature of global power struggle. The focus on grand strategy had as its objective to find answers about who might triumph and why in the essentially Hobbesian view of the world. The recent renaissance of geopolitics in indicative of a renewed struggle for spatial advantages in the pursuit of economic, political, and military influence in Third World regions.

A reflection of the current geopolitical thinking is evidenced in the polarization within the United States Foreign Affairs bureaucracy between geopolitical and regionalist orientations of the decision making elite. These two perspectives have been described in detail by Saaram Chublin in this way:

The differences between the Carter Administration and the Republican Administration preceding it were less basic than often appeared, but, as was the case with parallel polarization in academia between geopolitical and regionalist approaches to the Third World, the emphases were quite different. The debate about the merits of these two approaches is important because it contains what promises to be a continuing divergence in perspective about the sources of third-world instability and the appropriate responses to that instability.

The primary difference between the two schools lies in their assessments of the centrality of the competition with the USSR and the role of force. While the geopoliticians continue to see the world in these terms, the regionalists point to the expanded agenda of world affairs and the multi-polarity, complexity and diversity. The one therefore focuses on Soviet power, the importance of regional balances and allies and immediate American interests. The other, more relaxed about military power, seeks to avoid open-ended involvements while pursuing long-run world-order interests. The geopolitician seeks

57

to cultivate and reward allies, stressing American dependability and credibility; the regionalist emphasizes the compatibility (or incompatibility) of allies with the values of the United States and advocates dissociation. The former fears an eroding balance, divided allies and set-backs that reverberate to the global disadvantage of the United States; the latter fears entanglement, irrelevance and reflexive linkage. The geopolitician sees the risk of war increasing because of uncertainties created by regional retreat; the regionalist seeking a more limited definition of security, cringes at muscular machismo and at loose talk of 'credibility.' The one looks to military security, strong leadership and resilience as the key to world order; the other believes that world order is nurtured by adjustment, restraint, bargaining and moral example.

These views lead to quite different assessments of the function of military power and of its relationship with the exploitation of third world conflicts. The geopoliticians assert the continuing and inescapable centrality of military power, and they stress its importance in deterring the USSR. They demand American leadership of the Allies and seek to reassure friendly states in the Third World. It follows that regional military balances are therefore seen as especially critical, both because strategic parity encourages probing and because the United States is reluctant to become directly involved in defending her interests. In short, military power still determines the risk calculus of the opportunistic exploitation of third-world instabilities. The regionalists, on the contrary, are impressed by the limited utility of military power (which they expect that the USSR will also eventually understand), and they see regional successes as determined less by power than by local political conditions. The 'prevailing local winds' are the principal determinants of influence; the trick of diplomacy is to adjust to them and thus inhibit Soviet advances. The regionalists focus on the constraints operating on Soviet power (which, they emphasize, is one-dimensional), on the intractability of many problems to solution by military power, on the strength of indigenous nationalisms and on the costs of alignment with third-world states which face multiple threats and invariably fail to meet minimal standards on human rights. [19]

The new usage of the term geopolitics is cognizant of a bipolycentric international system where foreign policy is underpinned by the transfer of rewards (economic and military aid) and the cultivation of allies in order to maintain regional military balances and military security.

Finally, the modern usage of geopolitics as emphasized by Robert Harkavy cannot be theoretically pinned down because of its inclusion of traditional conceptualizations. [20] In addition geopolitics is currently used to mean any one or all of the following: (1) classical nineteenth century balance of power; (2) competition for spatial advantages, at times irrespective of ideological incompatibilities; (3) the sum total of tactics and strategies used to deal with the issues of territory, resources, war and diplomacy in the maximization of national power; (4) an umbrella term for power politics or reference to all of the concerns of international relations. Our use of the term geopolitics in subsequent analyses will include as many of the above meanings as possible, but particularly in relation to the spatial articulation of foreign aid programmes in the conduct of US foreign policy to maintain regional balances in its competition with the Soviet Union. In the contemporary international system measures of military-strategic value range from population size, territorial location, among others to the more recent superpower concerns about access to critical raw materials and military basing.

SUMMARY

The strategies of US power projection and containment over the years have been basically geographic and political in focus, prompting political elites to use the term geopolitics in reference to American global competition with the Soviets. The current US containment strategy has highlighted to the Soviets regions vital to American security which would be protected at all costs. In the late 1940s these regions included Great Britain, Germany and Central Europe, and Japan. The number and location of such territories were later to increase as the Third World emerged and the global configuration of power changed from multipolarity, bipolarity, to bipolycentrism. A key element of any effective and enduring containment of the Soviet bloc would ultimately be a massive programme of US economic and military aid given on a prolonged and extensive basis to forestall communist inspired revolutions and any political instability that could prove advantageous to the Communist bloc.

The recent resurgence of the term 'geopolitics/ geopolitical' in connection with arms transfers, military-strategic competition, or basing access in world politics is reminiscent of nineteenth and twentieth century emphasis on the heartland/rimland focus on land, sea, and air power.

59

It underscores the ongoing Soviet-American competition for influence over areas of large geographic and population sizes, critical spatial locations, and strategic resources. Moreover, geopolitical competition since the mid 1960s reveals changes in regional balances. The US geopolitical advantage of the 1950s characterized by a ring of alliances and an extensive basing network has been weakened by a Soviet network of client states in many parts of the Third World.

The policy pronouncements of the Reagan Administration during its first three years pointed to a willingness to compete for geopolitical advantage with the Soviets even in distant locations. The Reagan Doctrine with its promise to aid right-wing liberation movements in any part of the world, the existence of the Rapid Deployment Force, and the recent effort to extend the existing military basing network, among many other factors, are indicative of the US resolve to compete effectively for air, land, and sea dominance. This competition in relation to the distribution of economic aid, military aid, arms transfer, and other forms of resource allocation will be examined in the succeeding chapters. Regional conflicts and how their locational aspects (Middle East, Horn of Africa, Southern Africa, among others) structure trends and patterns in resource allocation will be a key element of scrutiny. Another equally important focus will be new developments in the foreign aid relationship between the US and recipient countries such as the level of reverse leverage wielded by them over the US in its pursuit of geostrategic access.

NOTES

[1]   See, for example, Saul Cohen, Geography and Politics in a World Divided (New York: Random House, 1963).
[2]   Saul Cohen, Geography and Politics, p. 32.
[3]   C.R. Boxer, The Portuguese Seaborne Empire 1415-1825 (New York: Alfred Knopf, 1969) p. 26.
[4]   Saul Cohen, Geography and Politics, p. 36.
[5]   See, Halford Mackinder, 'The Geographical Pivot of History,' in Halford Mackinder, Democratic Ideals and Reality (New York: W.W. Norton, 1962), pp. 241-264. Other works which have made reference to the marginal crescent are many and include, among other, Nicholas Spykman, 'Heartland and Rimland,' in his The Geography of the Peace (New York: Harcourt, Brace, 1944), pp. 38-41, and more recently Colin S. Gray, The Geopolitics of the Nuclear Era (New York: Crane, Russak, 1977), Ch. 2.; and Robert Harkavy, Great Power Competition for Overseas Bases (New York: Pergamon Press, 1982), Ch. 6.
[6]   Robert E. Walters, The Nuclear Trap (Baltimore: Penguin Books, 1974), Ch. 2 especially.

60

[7]   Alfred T. Mahan, The Influence of Seapower Upon History
        1669-1783 (Boston: Little, Brown, 1980).
[8]   Alfred T. Mahan, The Problem of Asia and its Effects
        Upon International Policies (Boston: Little, Brown,
        1900).
[9]   see, Nicholas Spykman, Geography of Peace; and Nicholas
        Spykman, America's Strategy in World Politics (New
        York: Harcourt, Brace, 1942).
[10]   Spykman, Geography of Peace, pp. 50-65, discusses the
        relative advantages of heartland airpower compared to
        the rimland in connection with an intra-rimland
        strategic conflict.
[11]   Robert Harkavy, Great Power Competition, p. 287, and
        Stephen   Jones,   'Global   Strategic   Views,'   The
        Geographical Review, 45, 4 (July 1955: 492-508).
[12]   Alexander P. de Seversky, Air Power: Key to Survival
        (New York: Simon and Schuster, 1950); and Edward
        Warner, 'Douhet, Mitchell, Seversky: Theories of Air
        Warfare,' in Edward Earle (ed.) Makers of Modern
        Strategy (Princeton; Princeton Univ. Press, 1941) Ch.
        20.
[13]   John Slessor, The Great Deterrent (New York; Praeger,
        1957) p. 500.
[14]   George Cressey, The Basis of Soviet Strength (New York:
        McGraw-Hill, 1945), pp. 245-246, and Stephen Jones,
        'Global Strategic Views,' p.497.
[15]   See, Geoffrey Kemp, 'The New Strategic Map,' Survival
        19, 2 (March/April 1977): 50-59, and Geoffrey Kemp and
        Harlan K. Ullman, 'Towards a New Order of US Maritime
        Policy,' Naval War College Review, Summer 1977, pp.
        99-113.
[16]   Colin Gray, Geopolitics of the Nuclear Era, Ch. 3
        especially.
[17]   Saul Cohen, Geography and Politics.
[18]   See, Harold and Margaret Sprout, 'Geography and
        International Politcs in an Era of Revolutionary
        Change,' in W.A. Douglas Jackson (ed.). Politics and
        Geographic Relationships: Readings on the nature of
        Political Geography (Englewood Cliffs, N.J.: Prentice
        Hall, 1964). The hypotheses are from page 42.
[19]   Shahram Chubin, 'The United States and the Third World:
        Motives, Objectives, Policies,' in Third World Conflict
        and International Security, Part II Adelphi Paper No.
        167 (London: International Institute for Strategic
        Studies), p. 22.
[20]   Robert Harkavy in Great Power Competition, pp. 273-274,
        outlined the varied uses of the term geopolitics which
        has produced implicit, explicit, overlapping, broad,
        narrow, and contradictory meanings as evidenced in
        newspaper articles, periodicals, and in speeches of
        foreign policy elites.

3 The International Political Economy Context

In Chapter One, we discussed how foreign aid programmes are not created out of, nor maintained in, a vacuum; rather they are motivated by realities in the global system which impact on US foreign policy. The issues that have dominated international politics for the past forty years could partially be attributed to the existing anarchic international system that has engaged the Superpowers in an institutionalized resource transfer to Third World regions in the pursuit of their objectives. The major focus of this chapter is to discuss how foreign aid programmes articulate and have broadly articulated into subregions, regions, and the global system to maintain geopolitical and economic balance. The nature of the international system is such that major powers cannot simply afford to ignore the idea of foreign aid distribution if they are to avoid losing their friends and jeopardizing their interests. The problem of state sovereignty and its corresponding anarchic tendency has made self-help and mutual help a strong justification for constantly making the effort to safeguard and promote vital national interests. This means that the foreign aid relationship comprising of economic and military assistance will remain a necessary component of international politics.

A proper understanding of foreign aid within the context of regional and subregional foreign policies could be grasped in connection with the national interest. The national interest, for the purposes of this analysis, simply refers to the sum total of geopolitical, strategic, and socioeconomic objectives pursued by the donor country in the process of transferring resources to recipient countries. Two aspects of the national interest are particularly relevant in this regard: the national interest at the aspirational level and the national interest at the operational level. [1]

The national interest at the aspirational level is primarily predicated on the state's history and political ideology and very often implies the vision and conception of the good life which the state would eventually like to realize given the opportunity either through an increase in the state's capabilities and/or a sudden favorable international systemic change. Frankel outlined seven major features of the aspirational national interest: they are long-term; grounded in history and ideology; they are underscored and emphasized by the opposition, and equally tolerated by the government and other political parties; they provide a sense of direction and purpose in policies; they may be conflicting and poorly articulated; they do not have to be seriously studied; and they are based on political will rather than on capabilities. Since the Cold War period to now the aspirational national interest has been expressed in the various Acts of the US Congress regarding the distribution of foreign aid. For example, the Mutual Security Act of 1951 emphasized the containment of the Soviet Union thereby providing a sense of direction and purpose in aid distributional efforts. Regions of high conflict become particular targets of selectivity and penetration with the ultimate aim being the protection of the sum total of objectives.

The national interest at the operational level comprises of eight main features: they are usually goals capable of realization in the immediate future, and therefore short term; they are often based on motivations of expediency and necessity; they are the pervading and daily concern of the ruling party; they are often couched in descriptive rather than in normative language; they are studied carefully to avoid contradictions in their implementation; they are susceptible to success and may be translated into policies that can be costly; capabilities rather than political will is the key factor in their determination; and they are made up of both maximum and minimum programmes with the former falling into the category of the aspirational national interest. In terms of foreign aid programmes the focus is on the right mix of economic and military aid to a recipient; or decisions as to which recipient should be given ESF or PL 480. Foreign aid to a region of high conflict requires careful study and proper implementation if short term goals like maintaining military bases are to be realized. Finally, the attitudes of recipients towards the aid should be taken into account if it is to be an effective foreign policy instrument.

SUBREGIONAL ENTITIES

The two types of national interests discussed above have a strong bearing on the role the US plays vis-a-vis threatened countries in the Third World. Threatened countries usually resist the hegemonic pretensions of a stronger regional power, either through diplomatic means or the use of force. In the attempt to protect the threatened nation the US enhances its own security by gaining a foothold in the region. Establishing a foothold first involves the penetrative strategy, followed by the selective strategy which is an indication of commitment to the threatened nation. Resource transfer is a significant component of both strategies. For example, in 1977 the Soviet response to Ethiopian requests for assistance resulted in the USSR gaining a new foothold in the Horn of Africa. In time, the other regional powers, feeling threatened and isolated by an alliance between a superpower and its regional opponent, would also request the other superpower to restore the regional balance through commitment and support. Somalia's behavior in the Horn of Africa in 1977 closely conformed to this pattern after the Ethiopian-Soviet alliance.

The consequence of regional penetration and subsequent alliance formation is fourfold: (1) the subregion's level of conflict undergoes change and may even intensify; (2) each of the Superpowers gain a foothold in the subregion primarily through the strategy of penetration made possible by the existing intraregional conflict; (3) the Superpowers' other regional and global rivalries are superimposed on the subregional conflict; and (4) through the commitment that develops towards the new regional ally the strategy of selectivity in treatment takes a firm hold such that the ally becomes an integral part of the Superpower's national security concerns. When most or all of these four conditions are satisfied, aid-giving in the region ultimately assumes the character of a 'differentiated approach' strategy. The USSR in the 1960s targeted most of its aid to countries perceived to be socialist or anti-Western in orientation. The US distributes as much as 85 per cent of its bilateral assistance to countries that are of the 'greatest interest.' [2] Table 3.1 is a presentation of the twenty top recipients of US military aid for FY 1983. The recipients are basically members of subregions of high conflict and thus are accorded a differentiated approach.

The dual strategies of penetration and selectivity in the conduct of foreign policy is better understood within the

64

Table 3.1
Twenty Top Recipients of US Military Aid, FY 1983

Country	Per Cent of Total Aid	Amount ($ millions)
Israel	30.4	1,700.0
Egypt	23.7	1,326.9
Turkey	7.2	402.8
Spain	7.2	402.5
Greece	5.0	281.3
Pakistan	4.7	260.8
South Korea	3.3	186.7
Portugal	2.0	111.2
Tunisia	1.8	102.0
Lebanon	1.8	101.7
Morocco	1.8	101.3
Thailand	1.7	96.2
El Salvador	1.5	81.3
Jordan	0.9	52.8
Phillipines	0.9	51.4
Honduras	0.9	48.3
Sudan	0.8	44.3
Somalia	0.5	30.6
Oman	0.5	30.1
Indonesia	0.5	27.4
Total (20 countries)	97.2	5,439.5
Total (all countries)		5,599.0

Source: AID, US Overseas Loans and Grants, 1945-1983.

context of regional subgroupings of states. For example, in dealings with Ethiopia in the Horn of Africa, Soviet interactions with that country has security implications for Somalia and the Sudan. Similarly, in the Southeast Asia subregion US security dealings with Thailand have significant implications for Vietnam, Cambodia, and Laos. Because of the importance of subregional groupings there are not many geostrategic issues that can be considered as purely bilateral. The increasing significance of regional clusters also means that Superpowers focus their foreign policy efforts at those clusters leading to either an increase in the level of intra-regional conflict or its potential. The ultimate consequence is the reproduction of Cold War environments in certain subregions. The perspective of subregions has a direct bearing on the balance of power approach to internaltional politics in which states are divided into one of three roles: aggressor states; status quo states; and balancer states. For example, it is believed that Vietnam in Southeast Asia is an aggressor state whereas Thailand is a status quo state, and China a blancer state. The Superpowers also play the roles of status quo and balancer states in regional politics. The common pattern of regional politics is when Superpowers and regional states align to check and balance each other.

In terms of both Superpowers and regional states the idea of regional politics is strongly linked to the concept of the national role. Political decision-maker's role conception of the state's goals and capabilities in the international and regional environment determine the state's actual role performance in international relations. In this regard and in relation to regional politics role theory comprises of four factors: (1) national role performance -- the overall foreign policy behavior of states; (2) the national role conception -- the decision-maker's image of appropriate direction of the state towards the international system; (3) the role presecription -- the impact on the state of the nature of the international system; and (4) status -- a measure of the state's prestige (ranking) in the international system. US role performance in subregions is strongly predicated on resource transfers to threatened friendly nations thereby enhancing its own security and prestige and those of the threatened nation.

The US is active in subregional contexts because of the increase in regional security threats since the mid 1970s. The growth is due to three factors: (1) the geographic expansion of Soviet military power; (2) the emergence of more aggressor regional states bent on regional hegemony and subversion such as Cuba, Libya, Ethiopia, and the like; and (3) increased political instability caused by poor global economic conditions. Within Central America Cuba is known to engage in efforts of destabilization of Guatemala, El Salvador, Honduras, and Costa Rica. There are at present about 6,000 Cuban technicians and military personnel in Nicaragua. The Soviet Union and Cuba significantly support Nicaragua through military aid and technical training. In the Horn of Africa the Soviets are supporting about 3,000 of their own and over 14,000 Cuban troops in Ethiopia. Partly as a consequence of the support Ethiopia is playing the role of an aggressor state in its effort to destabilize the government of Somalia. In the Southern subregion of Africa, Cuba has since 1975 maintained about 20,000 troops in Angola. [3] The troops are there to protect the Marxist regime against external aggression from South Africa and internal attacks by the UNITA rebel group. In the Middle East Syria is well armed by the Soviet Union and has as many as 4,000 Soviet personnel operating its weapons. In South Asia the refugee problem caused by the Afghan War poses a threat to Pakistan's stability. As a result of the threat the US between 1981 to 1985 provided Pakistan with a $3.2 billion economic and security aid package. In the Southeast Asia region Soviet military aid flows to Vietnam and enables it to continue its occupation of Cambodia. Thailand, a US ally in the region, has been drawn into the regional conflict as a result of the refugee problem caused by the conflict. In the Northeast Asia subregion North Korea with about 800,000 troops is viewed as a continuing threat to South Korea. The security of South Korea is guaranteed by the presence of about 40,000 US troops and the provision of substantial military aid to the government annually.

Table 3.2 is a presentation of purposes of military aid for FY 1982. The focus as is shown is purely subregional: the maintenance of subregional balances in the Middle East, Southeast Asia, Northeast Asia, and Central America. It is assumed that aggressor states like Cuba and Vietnam, and potential aggressor states like North Korea, Ethiopia, and Syria threaten not only US security but the security of its allies as well.

Foreign aid has been instrumental in furthering US objectives in regions of high conflict through the use of aid as 'Carrots' to penetrate the regional actors. For example, the thrust of foreign policy during the Carter years was to seek the moderation of an aggressor regime's behavior by using aid as a Carrot strategy to influence the regime and modify its behavior. After the Sandanista victory in Nicaragua in 1979 the Carter Administration concentrated on diplomatically penetrating the new regime. A $75 million aid programme was provided to attain three objectives: (1) moderate the Soviet-Cuban influence manifested in technical assistance to Nicaragua; (2) encourage the establishment of a pluralist society with an influential

67

Table 3.2
Purposes of US Military Aid, FY 1982

Purpose	Cost of Money Grants	Loans
1. Promote Mideast Peace Process (Israel, Egypt, Lebanon)	68%	51%
2. Recompense for US access and facilities (Spain, Greece, Portugal, Turkey, Phillipines, Kenya, Oman)	9%	29%
3. Support key regional balances (Korea, Thailand, Pakistan, Jordan, Sudan, Somalia, Tunisia, Morroco, Honduras, El Salvador)	14%	17%
4. Other	9% 100%	3% 100%

Source: Congressional Presentation, Security Assistance, FY 1984.

middle class; and (3) ensure that Nicaragua's foreign policy behavior toward El Salvador in particular is one of moderation.

US foreign policy toward Afghanistan during 1978 and 1979 also adopted the Carrot approach to a subregion of high conflict. Until February 1978 when the US Ambassador, Dubs was assassinated a policy of diplomatic access to the Marxist regime was actively pursued. The policy was aimed at diluting any tendencies towards establishing strong ties with the Soviet Union. In addition to frequent diplomatic contacts between Ambassador Dubs and the Afghan Foreign Minister, the existing foreign aid relationship was maintained. However, with the Soviet invasion in December 1979 and the advent of the Reagan Administration in 1981 a policy of wielding the stick replaced the policy of carrots.

In Southern Africa the Carter Administration was partially successful in efforts to settle conflicts in Zimbabwe and Namibia. Mozambique played an influential role in persuading Robert Mugabe to participate in British-administered elections that eventually produced a settlement in Zimbabwe. As a way of rewarding Mozambique's efforts and cooperation, in 1980 President Carter authorized the extension of aid to the government. In terms of the Namibian problem, closer ties developed between the US and Angola because of the latter's interest in resolving it. The result of negotiations between the two countries was agreement on compromise measures to be presented to South Africa. The Angolan cooperation in the issue made the Carter Administration to authorize the extension of $152.4 million in Export-Import Bank loans and guarantees as well as the encouragement of American business interests in the country. [4]

In each case of subregional conflicts the US response is conditioned by a geopolitical approach that accords top priority to its regional and global competition with the USSR. Regional regimes come in various forms: leftwing as in Nicaragua, fundamentalist as in Iran, or expansionist as in Libya. All these have the common underlying theme of stimulating superpower competition that takes the basic form of an aid race in which first a penetrative aid-giving strategy is followed by a selective aid-giving strategy.

INTERNATIONAL ECONOMIC RELATIONSHIPS

Implicit in the whole notion of foreign aid-giving is the idea that underdevelopment is integral to the Third World. The claim that underdevelopment was an original condition which needed to be eradicated through the injection of foreign policy outputs such as aid, was challenged by historic studies on Latin America and Africa. Economic-oriented analysts were more likely to argue that problems associated with underdevelopment such as political instability and authoritarianism could be alleviated by the infusion of capital, foreign aid, and modern technology into a recipient country.

Foreign aid's articulation into the donor-recipient relationship was particularly significant in the case of European Overseas Territories. The Marshall Plan aid particularly had an enormous impact on those territories. Substantial US aid to the metropoles was designed for disbursement to their colonies for the development of specific economic objectives in the colonies, one of which was the development of strategic materials. In the case of Britain and Belgium such aid from the US amounted to $113 million for the period from March 30 - June 30, 1951 only. Table 3.3 gives us an idea of the volume and objectives of the aid as of June 1951.

The European Cooperation Administration (ECA) which administered the ERP or Marshall Plan had more ambitious goals than merely addressing the recovery of Europe; it also concentrated on putting on a sound footing a triangular economic relationship between Europe, North America, and the Third World. The ultimate objective was to create a new international economic order based on Western economic principles from the ashes of the prewar economic order. The aid flows of the Marshall Plan were to help create and cement this triangular economic system. The breakdown of the prewar economic order that resulted in the incorporation of the Third World into the new economic system linked by an aid relationship are due to three main factors. First, the significant trade transactions between Western and Eastern Europe had declined tremendously by the late 1940s such that West European countries requested aid from the US to make up for the difference in lost revenue from former trade with Eastern Europe. The establishment of Communist regimes by the Soviet Union was largely responsible for the interruption of former trade ties. Second, the emergence of nationalism and expressions of national self-determination in overseas territories threatened the economic stability of the Metropoles. Colonies like Indochina, Indonesia, and Malaya were already in rebellion. This development had two consequences: the Metropoles were losing revenues from their colonies while at the same time spending money to contain their increasing nationalist agitations. Britain and France alone together maintained about 1.5 million troops overseas. [5] Third, the overseas colonies themselves were adversely affected by the bleak economic conditions caused by the War. The terms of trade for gold and rubber were already on the decline thereby creating a serious trade deficit between

Table 3.3
Marshall Plan Aid to European Colonies as of June 1951

Type of Aid	Amount ($ millions)
Foreign aid to metropoles for overseas territories	
France	286.8[a]
Netherlands	101.5[b]
United Kingdom	98.0[b]
Belgium	15.0
Portugal	0.7
Overseas development fund	63.8
Strategic materials development aid	24.5
Counterpart	22.5
Counterpart from European aid	140.3
Technical assistance for overseas territories	0.9
Total	754.0

Source: Economic Cooperation Administration, Eighth Report to Congress (March 31, 1950), p. 54, and Thirteenth Report to Congress (June 30, 1951), pp. 46-49.

[a] Aid for Indonesia only

[b] Quarter of March 30 - June 30, 1951, only.

European countries and the US.

As a result of the above problems, one of the immediate goals of the Marshall Plan was to incorporate the Third World counties into the aid programmes so that they would fill in the gaps that have affected the economic health of the Metropoles. They would be expected to replace the markets that have been lost in Eastern Europe; they would also be a source of strategic raw materials, and new investment outlets for US multinational corporations. This triple economic objective based on a triangular economic relationship has already been described by William Mallalieu in this way:

> The United States had anticipated that the restoration of Europe would help to bring about economic viability in the rest of the world. It was soon evident, however, that the converse was equally important. The complete success of European plans required progress in the less developed areas of the world. Only increased purchasing power in the underdeveloped countries of Asia, Africa and Latin America could provide adequate markets for European industry. [6]

A major component of the triangular trade pattern is the emphasis on the development of strategic raw materials in the Third World which would then be granted easy access to US markets so that the Third World could earn the foreign exchange necessary to engage in meaningful trade with European countries.

A significant step in creating a new economic order came when between 1948 and 1952 the ECA decided to extend aid programmes to other Third World nations besides the colonial territories. The programme was extended to include Taiwan, South Korea, Thailand, Indochina, Indonesia, and Burma. Before the Chinese revolution the Marshall Plan legislation also authorized aid in the amount of $463 million to China. Table 3.4 presents a summary of US foreign aid distribution to the regions of the Third World between 1948 and 1952. The totals are for countries that had already gained independence by 1952.

The primary role played by foreign aid in creating a new economic order and incorporating Third World countries into the triangular trade system indicates that the US was also instrumental in creating a favorable investment climate for multinational corporations. Apart from the transfer of funds through the ECA to developing countries, the US also established investment guarantee programmes that reduced the risks of nationalization and foreign exchange issues. Such measures are consistent with neo-Marxist lines of argument regarding the post-colonial period. Economic links with the Third World were viewed as a process in which the state

72

Table 3.4
US Foreign Aid to Third World Regions (Excluding
Overseas Colonies), 1948-52 ($ millions)

Region	Economic Aid	Military Aid	Total
1. Near East and South Asia	534.3	252.6	786.9
2. East Asia	1948.1	405.6	2353.7
3. Africa	17.7		17.7
4. Latin America	590.8	0.2	591.0

Source: US Overseas Loans and Grants and Assistance from
International Organizations, Obligations and Loan
Authorizations, July 1, 1945 - June 30, 1970.

Note: Figures exclude aid to Israel and include
Export-Import Bank loans.

directed the process of capital accumulation on behalf of powerful corporate interests. The state, in this case the US, was at times prepared to go beyond the mere creation of a healthy environment to intervention in cases where a critical raw material is involved and access to it is threatened by Communism. This was what transpired with oil in Iran. At the end of World War II Iran was both a major oil producer and also threatened by Soviet Communism. A dispute broke out between Iran and the British-owned Anglo-Iranian Oil Company. The Parliamentary Oil Committee chaired by Mohammed Mossadegh decided to nationalize the oil company because of disagreement over changes in the 1933 oil concession which gave Iran little royalty payments. By October 1951 the dispute had escalated to the extent that Iran had taken complete control of operations and all British technicians had left the country. [7]

The US became concerned about two things, first the external threat posed by the Soviets including Iran's internal political situation and second the continued access of the West to Iranian oil, although the increased production in other countries took care of this problem. The concern was that access would fall into the hands of the Soviets. In addition, the Mossadegh regime was perceived by the US to have communist influences. The coup of 1953 that overthrew Mossadegh was a consequence of US covert assistance motivated by the strong need to change the regime which was not doing much to help create a favorable investment climate for Western corporations. The US decision to intervene could be interpreted in three ways: (1) to continue to promote investments so that the consolidation of the new economic order is not disrupted in that region of the world; (2) to ensure Western access to Iranian oil so that the Soviets are kept out; and (3) to wipe out the Communist elements within the Mossadegh regime that threatened Western economic interests.

A second case in which US foreign aid was backed up by intervention was that of Guatemala in 1952. Generally the US does not intervene through the use of force in corporate matters. But as in the case of Iran, the Guatemalan situation also had two interrelated elements that threatened US investments. These were the threat to Western investments and the communist problem in the county. The US in 1954 supported the overthrow of Jacobo Arbenz in Guatemala by Guatemalan rebels that had been trained by the CIA in neighboring Honduras. The explanation given for such support is that he had nationalized 234,000 acres of land owned by United Fruit Company. [8] This threat to direct investment was supported by a US perception that his other actions such as his support of labor legislation that undermined entrepreneurial incentives would result in Communist

74

influence in Guatemala. Other actions of Arbenz also contributed to the US suspicion that he was furthering the Communist cause. In 1952 Arbenz legalized the Communist Party and in 1954 Guatemala's arms imports came from Czechoslovakia. In domestic politics he was increasingly drawing his support from Communist elements in the Congress and in the peasant and labor unions. The perceptions of US officials were overdrawn because there was no evidence of any imminent Communist takeover in the country. The Guatemalan case is one example in which the US as the parent state of US corporations intervenes on the side of the corporation to maintain the corporate link with a Third World country.

During the Cold War period the objective of establishing and consolidating the new economic order was carried out primarily by the ECA. In the period of Bipolycentrism the ESF plays a significant role in the goals of maintaining the economic order and its triangular trade and investment pattern. To adapt to changing times and new demands, the International Security Assistance Act of 1978 created the ESF to replace the name Security Supporting Assistance. The ESF conjures in no unclear terms the economic objectives of the programme thereby distancing it from military assistance. Its economic salience in a period of global economic disruption derives from its capacity to protect and maintain threatened political and economic institutions in recipient countries. Its very essence lies in part on its flexibility in extending both nonproject and project aid to countries critical to US foreign policy interests. The balance-of-payments and other structural problems faced by many weak Third World economies are alleviated in the short run by nonproject aid which is very responsive to such short term difficulties. Most development assistance is extended in the form of project aid. Thus, the two elements of nonproject and project aid contained in the ESF invests it with a wider utilitarian value. The provision of commodity imports, the financing of specific projects, and the reduction of budget deficits are some of the valuable functions performed by the programme. In the 1980s, an increasing portion of ESF has been directed to poorer countries. Table 3.5 shows the top 15 recipients of ESF for FY 1982. The short term problems solved by the nonproject element of the ESF are critical to the long term maintenance of the existing international economic order.

In the Cold War rivalries period foreign aid was instrumental in strengthening the trade and investment links between Western countries and the Third World; in the Bipolycentric period of the 1970s and 1980s that process has been completed and has resulted in the external reliance of the Third World on Western donors. The case of PL 480, in particular, has been emphasized by critics as producing dependence by the recipient countries on the US. The

Table 3.5
Top 15 Recipients of ESF, FY 1982

Country	ESF ($ millions)	Per Capita GNP (1980)
Israel	806	4,500
Egypt	771	580
Turkey	300	1,470
El Salvador	115	660
Pakistan	100	300
Sudan	100	410
Jamaica	91	1,040
Zimbabwe	75	630
Dominican Republic	41	1,160
Honduras	37	560
Liberia	35	530
Spain	22	5,400
Portugal	20	2,370
Somalia	20	155
Costa Rica	20	1,730

Source: AID, US Overseas Loans and Grants; World Development Report, 1982, The World Bank, Oxford Press, 1982.

argument is made that the provision of food assistance will result in depressing the price of local agricultural produce and lead to a disincentive on the part of the recipient government to stimulate its domestic production. Dependence is the consequence when the recipient government becomes dependent on the local currency proceeds of the food and expresses the wish to prolong the programme. A second aspect of the food programme that is dependency producing is when the food aid changes consumption patterns thereby leading to demands for food that the recipient countries cannot produce locally. Third, food assistance as a form of aid may transform a recipient government into the key importing and marketing agent in a country and undermine private initiatives. In the long run the very idea of promoting the Western economic system will itself be stifled with adverse effects on the recipient country's own overall economic development.

Unlike foreign aid, trade concession programmes do not per se involve the transfer of funds, but they have been instrumental in maintaining the present economic system. The trade concessions that improve access by Third World countries to the US market are in fact designed to repair the existing economic order by assisting the economies of recipient countries. One such trade promoting programme is the Generalized System of Preferences (GSP) which ensures that certain products from recipient countries are exported to the US duty free. Although the goods under GSP status are not substantial, nonetheless the programme represents an important tool of incentive for Third World countries to continue as members of the Western economic system.

Another trade programme that performs the function of encouraging international trade is the market access provided under Items 806.30 and 807 of the US Tariff schedules. [9] Under this programme, dutiable goods entering the US that contain US components are charged duty only on the non-American origin of their value. This legislation has a dual purpose: to encourage the use of American materials by foreign producers and to stimulate production in the producing countries by offering them a ready market for the finished product. For example, in Latin America 806/807 arrangements account for a substantial amount of the total exports to the US. For the US the whole arrangement is trade enhancing and beneficial to its economy because the content of US materials in the Caribbean Basin's exports is 65 per cent and 50 per cent for all developing countries.

Finally, the procurement-tied aspects of resource transfers have had a substantial economic articulation in to the US foreign aid programme. Aid-tying is the most common and prevalent form of donor export promotion and constitutes a requirement, sometimes an integral part of the aid programme, by which the recipient country obtains goods and services financed by an aid package from the donor country. During the period 1948-1959 about three-fifths of US official aid was in the form of grants, one-fifth was in loans, and the other one-fifth financed net sales of surplus agricultural commodities. For most of this period the tying of aid to domestic procurement was not an underlying requirement for the distribution of aid. By the late 1950s, Congress was pressured to the idea of tying US foreign aid dollars to domestic procurement primarily because of the increased deficit in the US balance of payments and the threat of unemployment. The period 1960-1969 could best be described as the period of the Eisenhower Procurement Policy. It included the latter part of the Cold War period and the early part of Bipolycentrism. It was during this period that the political economy of aid distribution shifted its emphasis on loans instead of grants. It was a period characterized by: (1) the extension of long-term loans with low interest, to be repaid with hard currency; (2) renewed focus on technical assistance in the areas of health and education, with little emphasis on technical know-how; and (3) the attempt to involve private domestic (US) groups in the aid programmes through trade and investment activities.

Procurement-tied aid became the underlying justification in the foreign aid programme and by 1969 US aid distribution was 99 per cent procurement-tied, an increase of 32 per cent from 1959 when it was 47 per cent of all AID-financed commodities. [10] Procurement was viewed as central to easing the US balance of payments and creating equilibrium in the US trade balance. In terms of the economic aspect of aid flows procurement-tied aid also performs the following functions: (1) increase the power of the US vis-a-vis the recipient; (2) acquire more leverage for the US on political and economic questions within the regional context; (3) increase the dependence of the recipient state so that the possibility of finding alternative sources of aid will be significantly reduced; and (4) drastically reduce the power and influence of vital donors within the recipient state or region.

During the 1960-1969 period 81 per cent of US aid was used to purchase commodities in the US. Approximately three per cent of annual US exports or the equivalent of $8.2 billion were the result of the procurement decade. By 1964, however, international political and economic realities had changed with the emergence of many Third World countries on the global scene. At UNCTADI in 1964 the procurement policy was assailed by Third World countries. They called for increased extension of aid through multilateral agencies. The arguement was made that recipients should be allowed to spend their aid dollars in countries that would allow maximum usage, that is where the purchase of needed goods and services are the lowest. In addition to claims of a more rational use of aid dollars, untied aid would ensure the following: (1) the decrease of donor leverage over recipients; (2) the reduction of a recipient's degree of aid dependence on the donor; and (3) the prevention of the development of donor hegemony over a particular region.

The outcry of the Third World had an impact on US aid policy, it led to President Nixon announcing in 1970 to end procurement-tying if other Western donors would do likewise. Ending procurement has two consequences: (1) aid being divested of its donor identity; and (2) stripping donor identity for the goods and services provided by the aid programme. The condition attached to Nixon's speech has geopolitical and economic implications. The call for an end to procurement-tying was a threat to the newly-acquired US power over Third World regions. The US had to make sure other countries would adopt the same policy so that its actions would not result in a unilateral loss of power, influence, and leverage over Third World recipients.

Despite the reluctance of other donors to implement the procurement-free policy, the US in 1969 unilaterally untied procurement of AID loan dollars to the Latin American region. The US chose Latin America as the first region to implement the policy because of the traditional ties between them. Second, the degree of Latin America's dependence on the US was strong enough to still guarantee US influence in the region regardless of the procurement policy. Third, Latin America because of its US sphere of influence status would serve as an appropriate testing ground for the new policy. Almost one year later, on September 15, 1970, the US extended the new policy to include most lower income countries. However, the refusal of some donors to go along with the procurement-free policy led the US to prevent purchase of goods and services in those countries with US aid dollars. Grants distributed by AID were not included in the untying process. In addition, aid flowing through the Food for Peace Programme and the Export-Import Bank (EXIMBANK) remained untied, because by their very nature they were set up to finance the net sales of surplus US commodities.

Within the US foreign aid programme, the main example of aid-tying that is essentially trade promotional in orientation is the US Trade Financing Facility (TFF). It is designed to assist US exporters in the packaging of competitive credit terms for the purchase of American products. It has two primary conditions: first the US cash bidder must be the lowest in a recognized international tender issued by a recognized entity within the recipient country; and second, the external competitor must offer a financing package with an effective interest rate below 10 per cent and made up of mixed credits. The TFF is not yet a common US trade promotional strategy and is currently limited to Egypt, although it may be provided for any recipient of ESF aid, even though ESF is not officially designated as a trade promotion program. A second example of trade promotion in the US foreign aid programme is the US Trade Development Programme. It is designed as a specific trade promotional activity which is carried out by AID-financed feasibility studies carried out for the promotion of US exports financed outside the AID programme itself.

In the whole process of trade promotional activities, PL 480 occupies a central place. While it has several purposes, Title I PL 480 is particularly trade promotional because of its function of developing markets for US agricultural resources. It extends long term credit at low interest to recipient countries to assist in the procurement of US agricultural commodity products. The regions of Asia and Africa are large recipients of Title I/III food aid. Africa in particular has increasingly received such aid because of reduction in supply to Asian countries. In 1975 only two African countries received Title I/III food aid, in 1981 a total of 17 countries received the aid worth $183.4 million. [11]

'Mixed credits' constitute another form of trade promotion that is essentially procurement-tied. It refers to any loan extended to a recipient country that is a combination of concessional assistance, and private bank loans. Because of this special blend such loans are not as 'hard' as loans at the market rate. Mixed credits make funds available for development purposes and they are also trade promoting in orientation. In the short run, the export promotion function of mixed credits have a penetrative function, in particular market penetration. The concessional element of mixed credits can facilitate the introduction of products in a market where they are still unavailable so that a new market for the product is opened up. In the long run after the market is consolidated and the penetration is complete the product can then be sold at the regular market rate. In addition, the trade promoting aspect of mixed credits also performs the function of market preemption. This is where mixed credits are extended to finance exports to discourage another donor from successfully penetration the market. Furthermore, market promotion is another trade promotion strategy. This is where the donor offers mixed credits to protect their acquired markets against losses resulting from mixed credit competition from other countries. The idea of mixed credits is used along with the EXIMBANK, although it is a device rarely employed by the US. Other DAC countries are more in the habit of using it as a strategy of penetration. While mixed credits are trade promoting they foster imperfect competition among donors. They are criticized and believed

80

Table 3.6
Tied Percentages of Bilateral ODA, 1981

	Grants		Loans	
	Tied	Partially Tied	Tied	Partially Tied
France	47.2	4.8	53.4	24.6
W. Germany	35.4	0.0	16.3	0.0
Japan	59.1	7.6	33.9	27./
Sweden	16.1	0.0	0.0	0.0
United Kingdom	78.3	1.4	75.4	2.8
United States	54.7	17.0	72.4	13.2
CMEA	100.0		100.0	

Source: OECD, Development Cooperation, 1982 Review.

by the US to distort international trade and certain aspects of comparative advantage.

The TFF, Trade Development Program, Title I/III PL 480, and mixed credits are all instruments that are basically commercial in orientation, and because they are specifically donor export oriented in nature they are procurement-tied. Table 3.6 shows the percentages of tied bilateral grants and loans for the US and other DAC countries for 1981. The US hardly uses mixed credits whereas Britain, France, and Japan use them more frequently.

In the arguments of recipients tied aid may: (1) slow the expansion of trade within a region because of the requirement to purchase aid-financed goods and services in donor countries; (2) increase the obligations of recipients to the donor; and (3) result in undue donor political influence over the recipient. Since credit for aid projects and programmes tends to spillover into political alignments and obligations, tied aid is said to be characterized by both political and economic articulation into foreign policy. Political aspects include: (1) the desire by the donor country to be recognized as the brain-child of successful programmes and the initiator of development projects; and (2) within the aid process, aid allocations can be more easily defended because aid funds are spent within the donor country, thereby helping to ease the problems of the domestic economy. Economic aspects include: (1) facilitating the full use by the donor of idle domestic resources, including industrial capacity; and (2) the expansion of exports which helps balance of payments problems in donor country.

HUMANITARIAN DIMENSIONS

Within the context of altruism, the rationales for giving can be divided into three types: a pervading desire to benefit others; a generalized feeling of social obligation; and a reaction to the social needs of known recipients as in the case of responses to earthquake or flood victims. Altruism as a response to the needs of others is in fact charity. As charity, it is also strongly linked to the notion of social contracts. The donor is motivated to give because of the concern that if he breaks the contract, then others may also decide to break the contract in his own hour of need by refusing to extend any aid whatsoever.

Foreign aid distribution that is based on humanitarianism is viewed as contributing to the eradication of malnutrition, illiteracy, high mortality, and the like. In the broader context of US foreign policy, the humanitarian approach has been emphasized by both theorists and politicians. Even before World War II the administrations of Theodore Roosevelt and Woodrow Wilson espoused altruism in their relations towards Latin America in particular. President Truman, during the Cold War period, vividly expressed the humanitarian concern when he said:

> We must embark on a bold new program for making the benefits of our scientific advances and industrial progress available for the improvement and growth of underdeveloped areas. [12]

Later on towards the cooling off of the Cold War rivalries, President Kennedy's Alliance for Progress was punctuated by the recurring themes of the concern for the development of the Third World and improved living standards. Foreign aid as altruism is the genuine attempt by rich, powerful states to alleviate the perennial problems of underdevelopment by raising the standard of living in poor counties.

Just like other forms of foreign assistance, US humanitarian aid is motivated by the imperatives of a superpower status. As a Superpower, the US views its role in terms of the dual factors of interests and responsibilities. The giving of aid during times of disaster arises out of a sense of responsibility that is based on the fact that an affluent and prosperous nation ought to reach out and share its bounties with others. The feeling of noblesse oblige which motivates a rich powerful nation to help in reducing the misery of other nations is widely accepted by the American people. In connection with the issue of hunger, former Secretary of State, Henry Kissinger addressing the 1974 World Food Conference referred to US agricultural bounty as a 'global trust.' In the same address he stated that 'the American people have a deep and enduring commitment to help feed the starving and hungry.' In addition, a 1979 public opinion survey on US attitudes to world hunger conducted by Potomac Associates and the Gallup Organization revealed that 80 per cent of the people surveyed favored the extension of more assistance to reduce world hunger, with 38 per cent favoring budgetary increases in programmes designed to alleviate misery and want.

The current US foreign aid programme that is specifically designed to address the problems of hunger is the PL 480 food assistance. Altruism is essentially an underlying rationale for the PL 480 programme. The programme itself is divided into three components: Title I, Title II, and Title III. The Title I is a concessional sales program that offers long term credit at low interest to recipient nations to assist in the financing of agricultural commodity imports. Its major objective is to increase the overall availability of food within the recipient country. The Title II programme provides for food assistance with emphasis on nutritional goals.   This type of aid is usually administered by US private voluntary organisations and the World Food Programme of the UN. The rationale for this aspect of the programme is that improved nutritional level of mothers and children contributes to the development of human capital and health conditions.   More recently the developmental aspects of the programmes have been underscored.   The third component, the Title III (Food for Development) programme is similar to Title I because of its focus on self-help measures and balance of payments support.   It is much more ambitious in design because it is primarily targeted at rural and agricultural development programmes through reform and policy change.   In 1984, Bangladesh, Egypt, Sudan, Senegal, Bolivia, and Honduras had become recipients of Title III programmes.

The whole idea of disaster relief as an aspect of humanitarian aid has gained increased prominence since the 1970s.   A succession of bad harvests first hit many developing countries in 1972 and 1974; these were followed by financial crises triggered by the sharp increase in oil prices.   These problems coupled with natural disasters made it very difficult for the poorest developing countries to recover economically.   The instability of the international food market of the 1970s which resulted in domestic price rises, and the agricultural slump of 1976 triggered the Third World nations to call for a New International Economic Order (NIEO).   These events led the US Congress to enact the New Directions, basic needs foreign aid legislation in order to preserve the aid relationship and the stability of the existing international economic order, especially after the call for a NIEO by the Third World nations.

During the Cold War, humanitarian aid was basically viewed as aid that is motivated by benevolence.   However, with the increasing emphasis on, and shifts in foreign aid objectives from security concerns to, basic needs in the 1970s, certain aspects of humanitarian aid have assumed the character of a human right.   For example, disaster relief as human right should not be denied any country regardless of political and economic ideology.   It has been argued that just as all countries have a right to develop and provide basic human needs for the people within their boundaries, so should all countries share the responsibility and the obligation to make sure that humanity's basic needs are satisfied.   The question of basic needs as human right and their linkage with the more traditional foreign policy goals was vividly expressed by President Carter in this way:

> The world is still divided by ideological disputes, dominated by regional conflicts, and threatened by the danger that we will not resolve the differences of race and wealth without violence or without drawing into

84

combat the major military powers. We can no longer separate the traditional issues of war and peace from the new global questions of justice equity, and human rights. [13]

Humanitarian aid to the poorest countries could be viewed as a form of wealth distribution. It is common knowledge that countries that are most affected by the inequitable distribution of wealth are those that are most prone to disasters and their impact. The poverty of these countries means they cannot adequately plan against disasters.

Although disaster relief and other forms of humanitarian aid are increasingly viewed as a right and not as charity, many disaster relief programmes run into political problems. This phenomenon in foreign assistance was very well captured by former Secretary of State Cyrus Vance in his Law Day Speech on Human Rights and Foreign Policy in 1977:

> Second, there is the right to the fulfillment of such vital needs as food, shelter, health care, and education. We recognize that the fulfillment of this right will depend, in part, upon the stage of a nation's economic development. But we also know that this right can be violated by a Government's action or inaction -- for example through corrupt official processes which divert resources to the elite at the expense of the needy, or through indifference to the plight of the poor. [14]

This observation by Cyrus Vance is true of a war-torn county like Ethiopia, where the relief efforts of 1985 were hampered by Ethiopian governmental obstruction and indifference. It is also the case in the Sudan at the moment.

A key component of the humanitarian aid programme is carried out by Private Voluntary Organizations (PVOs). These are entities whose membership is made up of private citizens formed for the purpose of achieving philanthropic goals. They engage in foreign aid activities that include famine relief, refugee aid, disaster aid, and economic development activities. They are funded primarily by contributions from individuals and they are are also recognized by the AID while an estimated 400 have some type of programme in Third World regions.

The developmental role of PVOs is especially important with regard to the entire US food aid programme. Title II of the Agricultural Trade and Development Act of 1954 authorized the donation of food aid to voluntary groups for distribution overseas. In this way, the aid relationship between the US and Third World regions also came to include PVOs. [15] The contribution of these agencies to development is based on the belief that school feeding and maternal child health programmes contribute to the development of human capital and increased labor productivity in the long run. In 1973, the Foreign Assistance Act further strengthened the role of PVOs in the US foreign aid programme. As a response to the emphasis on basic needs and a 'New Direction' in aid-giving, the Act authorized assigning a greater role to the private sector and private institutions in the effort to achieve the objectives of food production, health and education. The support of PVOs in reaching the poor majorities has been reiterated since 1973.

In one way, the PVOs are pioneers in the slow growth of a foreign aid constituency in the US. They mobilize private financial and human resources to enhance the foreign aid programme. They are constantly informing the American public through television of areas of need in recipient countries. In addition to encouraging monetary and in-kind contributions and professional and semi-professional volunteer services, they also stimulate public interest and educate the public both in the US and in the recipient country on the role of foreign aid. As shown in Table 3.7, PVO activities in recipient countries work in the areas of nutrition, health care, rural water supply, rural cooperatives, other infrastructural development activities and the provision of specialized services such as malaria eradication.

Thus, in addition to overseas sales of US surplus agricultural products under PL 480 by the US government itself, PVOs also use PL 480 for relief of victims of famine, flood, or other natural disaster. Through their branches abroad, these agencies, Catholic Relief Services, Church World Service, CARE, Lutheran World Relief, to name only a few, complement the activities of the official US foreign aid programme. Those that are registered with AID and are recognized by the agency receive AID funds. In the mid-1970s their grant programme was worth $23 million and by 1980 it had risen to $72 million. Table 3.7 also shows the trend in AID funding of PVO activities since 1978 with the Sahel as an integral part of the field-oriented part of the programmes.

SUMMARY

In the above analysis, we have attempted to examine the fact that foreign aid programmes are subject to regional imperatives that are structured by the donor's national interest, international economic relationships, and humanitarian objectives. In time, the interests, commitments, and obligations of donors like the US and USSR coupled with the existence of regional conflicts tend to produce cold war environments reflected in local arms races. Such situations have increased since the 1970s as evidenced

Table 3.7
Sectors of PVO Activities and AID Funding
Trends ($ millions)

Sector	FY 1978	FY 1980	FY 1982	FY 1983
Agriculture, RD and Nutrition	29.6	34.3	38.1	41.0
Population Planning	48.6	46.5	70.4	74.2
Health	5.9	13.1	13.4	11.5
Education and Human Resources	18.7	26.3	28.1	23.7
Selected Development Activities	33.8	35.2	32.7	27.5
The Sahel	3.9	4.9	3.8	5.6

Source: AID, Office of Food and Voluntary Agencies (FVA).

by the conflicts in the Horn of Africa, Southern Africa, Central America, and the Afghanistan crisis, among others. The competitive arms demand and supply process that is produced leads to three outcomes: (1) an ever-present need to maintain geopolitical balance among rival regional influentials; (2) the occasional heightening of regional tensions that may escalate into crisis situations; and (3) the unintended establishment of military dictatorships that undermine the progress of democracy and human rights in recipient countries.

In US foreign policy, the political (ideological) imperative, which will be discussed in detail in Chapter 8, provides a good deal of logic and structure to the foreign aid relationship, such that political considerations often outweigh economic considerations in the US response to nations that nationalize US corporations. Generally aid is denied to a country only after it has completely adopted a Marxist-Leninist ideology. American foreign aid distribution which is basically selective in orientation takes three forms: (1) country targeting such as aid to Egypt or Israel; (2) a regional focus such as aid to the Caribbean Basin, or the Alliance for Progress towards Latin America; and (3) the non-state actor concentration or aid to liberation movements or guerrilla organisations. Through a process of diplomatic signals, and the promise of future economic and military assistance the United States maintains relationships with politically hostile nations.

Finally, the focus on utilitarian and need approaches to aid distribution underscores the multidimensionality of foreign policy behavior. Non-political activities such as trade and investment between donor and recipient assume increasing importance such that they spill over into the purely geopolitical concerns of foreign policy. Instead of the quest for political power taking precedence over economic penetration of recipient states, it is economic targeting in the form of aid, trade and investment that lays the foundation for the political and military access to the recipient states. Similarly, altruistic concern for a recipient state is important in establishing the environmental milieu within which economic and political activities can thrive. The transfer of basic needs in the form of personnel-intensive aid is believed to foster cultural understanding in the foreign policy relationship and also create a favorable image for the donor.

NOTES

[1] For a further analysis of the concept, see, especially J.N. Rosenau, 'The National Interest,' in J.N. Rosenau, The Scientific Study of Foreign Policy, (New York: Free Press, 1971; and J. Frankel, The National Interest, (London: McMillan, 1970).

[2] See, US Department of State, The Threat of Soviet Economic Policy, 1961.

[3] See, US Department of State, Communism in Africa, Statement of Under Secretary of State for Political Affairs David D. Newsom, Subcommittee on Africa of House Committee on Foreign Affairs, October 18, 1979, Current Policy Series, no. 99.

[4] See, Cyrus Vance, Hard Choices (New York: Simon and Schuster, 1983).

[5] See, for instance, Thomas G. Peterson (Ed.), Cold War Critics (Chicago: Quadrangle Books, 1971); and David Baldwin, Economic Development and American Foreign Policy: 1943-1962, (Chicago: University of Chicago Press, 1966).

[6] William C. Mallalieu, British Reconstruction and American Policy (New York: Scarecrow Press, 1956), p. 196.

[7] For a detailed account, see Stephen Longrigg, Oil in the Middle East: Its Discovery and Development. (London: Oxford University Press, 1968).

[8] See, US Congress, House, Committee on Foreign Affairs, Expropriation of American-Owned Property by Foreign Governments in the Twentieth Century, Committee Print, 88th Congress, 1st Session, 1963.

[9] US Department of Commerce, Bureau of the Census. Concentration Ratios of Manufacturing, 1981, Census of Manufactures, Special Report Series MC81, 1983.

[10] OECD, 'Development assistance: Efforts and policies of the members of development assistance committee,' (Paris: 1971).

[11] US, Department of State, Composition of US Economic Cooperation Programs, 1975-1981.

[12] President Truman's inaugural address in January, 1949 contained a four-point statement on foreign policy. It is the fourth point that is quoted above from Documents on American Foreign Relations, 1949, pp. 7-12.

[13] President Jimmy Carter, Speech on Humane Purposes in Foreign Policy (1977) delivered at the Commencement Exercises of the University of Notre Dame, also in Walter Laqueur and Barry Rubin, The Human Rights Reader (New York: Meridian, 1979), p. 307.

[14] Cyrus Vance's Law Day speech on Human Rights and

Foreign Policy in 1977 contained a definition of human rights. It is the second part of the definition that is quoted above from The Human Rights Reader, p. 300.

[15] See, for example, Report of the Council on Foundations 1982; and AID Policy Paper on Private Organisations, 1982.

4 Third World Regions and Resource Allocations

In the preceding chapters, we analysed the geopolitical and socioeconomic rationales on which specific aid programmes are based, the overlapping functions of economic and military aid, recipients' attitudes to foreign aid, the politics of subregions and the role of aid in maintaining the existing economic system. In this chapter, we shall discuss the geophysical characteristics, resource endowments, and socio-economic issues of regions and how these factors are related to the phenomenon of foreign aid and foreign policy. Our focus will be on a broad and flexible use of the concept regions to refer to Africa, Asia, Latin America, and the Middle East. The inclusion of only the Third World regions is based on three reasons: first they are the recipients of most US foreign aid dollars since the end of the Cold War; second, they are the primary targets of the sum total of geopolitical, strategic, and economic objectives pursued by the US and USSR in foreign countries; and third, they are also the primary focus of four fundamental US interests: preventing the spread of Soviet power and influence; safeguarding the independence and territorial integrity of friendly countries; ensuring the free flow of trade and investment; and strengthening political ties with foreign countries to enhance national security. By focusing on each region individually, we can identify the specific geopolitical, economic, and social factors that make that region unique and thereby motivating a specific US foreign policy response.

Geophysical factors, resource endowments, and strategic location weigh heavily in US foreign aid distribution and the overall pursuit of foreign policy objectives. It has long become a consistent pattern of US foreign policy to buttress friendly states that border the Communist bloc. In addition, the goals of acquiring and protecting military bases, resupply lines, and overhead flights are some of the geostrategic policies vigorously pursued by the US on a regional level in its competition with the USSR. This means that strategically located countries like Ethiopia, the Philippines, Egypt, and Iran are the perennial targets of US-USSR geopolitical competition. Similarly, heavily resource-endowed states like Brazil, Zaire, India, and Saudi Arabia become primary targets in the competition to achieve trade and investment objectives.

To say that geopolitical factors are significant in the process of selective targeting of countries in foreign policy is to invoke a formidable principle of geostrategic thought that the politico-military impact of armed might is in 'inverse proportion to the distance from its source.' [1] Minimizing such a distance or relationship becomes a prime concern of a Superpower's foreign policy. A region becomes a priority target in world politics partly as a result of the status (ranking) of its states in relation to the states of other regions in terms of the values of power, wealth, and prestige. Because communication lines, and critical raw materials are so significant in contributing to a nation's power and influence, Superpowers have since the end of World War II competed to ensure easy access to and control of these facilities in Third World regions. The struggle for access to sea lanes, canals, straits, gulfs, ports, channels, and critical raw materials tends to result in open and restrained regional cold wars.

Superpower regional rivalry becomes more complex when a region is plagued by liberation movements, guerrilla organizations, terrorist groups, and international war. Ensuring regional peace and stability is a priority for US foreign policy because international and domestic political crises have a strong impact on the level of economic activity within regions. For example, the ongoing guerrilla warfare in the Central American republics affected the level of outputs of mineral industrial activities in the subregion. Similarly, the war between Iran and Iraq affected their regional production of oil and other minerals for six years. The Iran-Iraq war was even more threatening to economic activities because of its potential for spilling over into the entire Gulf region and complicating the present US-USSR geopolitical conduct in the region.

With the onset of decolonization in the late 1950's, Africa was gradually dragged into the East-West conflict. The withdrawal of Portugal from Angola in 1975 and the emergence of radical nationalism in Ethiopia in 1977 were two developments that effectively opened the way for superpower political struggle in the region. The region itself is one of ethnic and cultural diversity that has experienced increased intra-regional and international conflicts. The potential for ethnic irredentism is high in states like Ghana, Chad, and Zaire. International clashes have occurred between Uganda and Tanzania, Ethiopia and Somalia, and Angola and Zaire, among others.

One area of conflict in Africa is in the Horn, whose internal problems are complex and have deep historical roots. They revolve around three problems: (1) the attitude of the Ethiopian government; (2) the Eritrean, Tigre, and Oromo opposition and secessionist movements; and (3) the Ethiopian-Somali conflict over the Ogaden. The present Ethiopian government of Colonel Mengistu has stubbornly refused to share power with other nationalities. The Provisional Military Administrative Council, or the Derg is still composed of elites largely drawn from the Amharic ethnic group. The attitude of the government is strengthened through Soviet support, making it very hard for the national aspirations of people demanding self-determination in some parts of the country to be realized. The Eritrean Liberation Front (ELF), the opposition umbrella of the Eritrean people has been waging its struggle since 1962. In that year, Emperor Haile Selassie abolished the federation with Eritrea and incorporated the territory into Ethiopia as a province. The struggle between the government and the ELF resulted in a flow of refugees to Sudan which by 1982 numbered up to 500,000. [2] In 1970 a splinter group of the ELF had been formed, the Etritrean Peoples Liberation Front (EPLF) which is militarily stronger than the ELF because of its administrative efficiency and better understanding of the political, and socioeconomic aspirations of the majority of the people.

In addition to the struggles of the ELF and EPLF against the government, there are two other groups opposing the government: the Tigrean Peoples Liberation Front (TPLF) and the Oromo Liberation Front (OLF) both formed in 1975. The former movement is resisting the idea of a central Ethiopian state, while the latter also representing the struggle of the Oromo people against the central government is largely motivated by opposition to seizure and redistribution of their land among other Ethiopians. It is the liberation organization of the most populous minority group.

The existence of actual and potential conflicts in the region has resulted in an increasing involvement of the Superpowers. Between 1977 and 1978 there occurred a realignment of forces transforming Somalia -- for long a Soviet ally -- into a US ally and Ethiopia into a Soviet ally. The events that led to the realignment caught the US by surprise because of the perception that the Emperor, Haile Selassie was in effective control of events in Ethiopia. Before the Ethiopian-USSR alliance, the Derg had carried out significant economic reforms -- nationalizing the major banks, insurance companies, and major industries -- that are obviously opposed to US foreign policy objectives. The fear by the Derg of US disapproval of its reforms accelerated the alliance with the USSR. The immediate reasons for the shift in alliance were the subsequent suspension of US foreign aid coupled with the decision by the Eritrean guerrillas to intensify their secessionist moves, and the preparations by Somalia to launch an offensive in the Ogaden and annex that region. Beset by wars on two fronts the USSR was the only country readily available to provide the economic and military support needed to contain the internal and external threats. With about $2 billion in military assistance and the help of about 14,000 Cubans, the Derg was able to contain the two threats. [3]

In the past, the subregion has been the selective target of US foreign aid dollars. Ethiopia, the most strategic nation in the Horn, received about $279 million in US military aid between 1953 and 1977, with nearly 4,000 Ethiopian military personnel trained under IMET programme. [4] The aid relationship resulted in the use of the Kagnew Communications center in Asmara which was central to US communication objectives. It was used for gathering intelligence on the Middle East, the Indian Ocean, and parts of Africa. Its importance declined gradually due to the US presence in the Indian Ocean and the development of satellite communications technology.

The US still continued to distribute aid to Ethiopia even after the overthrow of Haile Selassie because it was believed that aid would continue to guarantee friendly relations between the US, Ethiopia, and Israel; and prevent any alignment of Ethiopia with the radical Arab forces in the area. Moreover, with the continuation of the aid relationship, it was believed that Ethiopia would still maintain its pro-American stance, an idea considered beneficial for US perception in the entire continent. Furthermore, with the existence of the aid relationship, Ethiopia would be helpful in maintaining the subregional balance in the Horn because Somalia was still aligned to the Soviets. However, with the continued ties between the Derge and the USSR the aid relationship was finally ruptured.

Human Rights violations were cited by the Carter Administration as the reason for terminating the flow of foreign aid. The response of the Derg was to close all US military installations in April 1977. The US eventually shifted its support to Somalia and Sudan. The Treaty of Friendship signed by Ethiopia and Moscow in 1978 with provisions for military aid was a motivating factor in the signing of the US-Somali military agreement of 1980. This was followed in 1982 by an expenditure of about $24 million for port and airfield expansion and refurbishing. In the same year it was proposed to extend $20 million in development assistance, and $25 million in PL 480 food aid. [5]

A second area of conflict in the region of Africa is in the Southern subregion. The Reagan Administration expressed concern for East-West tensions in the area. Summing up the major concerns of the US in the region in 1981, the Assistant Secretary of State for African Affairs, Chester A. Crocker declared:

> First, South Africa is a region of unquestionable importance to the United States and Western economic and strategic interests . . . . Second, this region has the tragic potential of becoming a magnet for internationalized conflict and a cockpit of East-West tension . . . . It is imperative that we play our proper role in fostering regional security, countering Soviet influence and bolstering a climate that makes peaceful change possible. [6]

The fear is that the Soviet Union might establish military bases in the region or gain control over strategic minerals. Upon President Reagan's election, the long-standing restrictions on US-South Africa relations were reversed. The US outstripped Great Britain to become South Africa's leading trading partner in both imports and exports, a 50 per cent increase over 1980. [7] In addition, US foreign direct investments increased by 13.3 per cent, and loans to South Africa were increased after a substantial drop during the Carter years. The reversal of policy under Reagan led to growing US foreign aid to the Southern African subregion, which by the mid-1980s, reached approximately 25 per cent of the total bilateral US aid to all sub-Saharan African countries.

In the past, the US has found it beneficial to steer a middle course rather than condemn or side with the apartheid regime of South Africa. The rapid and frequent changes in governments in the region made it dangerous to support one side. The revolutions in the late 1970's in Angola, Mozambique, and Zimbabwe, were perceived as a threat to the white minority in South Africa. Actions by the Pretoria government since that time have been geared to undermining the governments in these countries. One outcome of the competition between South Africa and the neighboring states was the formation of the Southern African Development Coordination Conference (SADCC). The SADCC grew out of an increased cooperation between the states bordering South Africa in the struggle for the independence of Zimbabwe. The member states -- Angola, Botswana, Lesotho, Malawai, Mozambique, Swaziland, Tanzania, Zambia and Zimbabwe -- hope to reduce their dependence on South Africa by improving their transport systems and promoting investment in their countries.

US foreign policy in the subregion is plagued by contradictions. One such contradiction was inherent in the policy towards Namibia. After World War II, Namibia (South West Africa) was made a protectorate of South Africa by the United Nations under an agreement that Namibia would be given independence in accordance with the League of Nations Mandate system. South Africa for a long time refused to obey the United Nations, including the UN Security Council Resolution 435 which provided a timetable and a date by which South Africa should withdraw from Namibia. After four decades of sanctions, resolutions, and negotiations, the Namibian independence plan is finally being implemented.

United States policy towards Angola also totters between an appearance of alignment and nonalignment with South Africa. While the US had acted as a seemingly neutral broker between South Africa and Angola in talks for the withdrawal of South Africa and Cuban soldiers, it has actually been supplying foreign aid to insurgents in Angola along with and via South Africa. In fiscal year 1986, Congress voted to extend $15 million dollars in covert aid to the National Union for the Total Independence of Angola (UNITA), a group led by Jonas Savimbi fighting against the Marxist Angolan government. [8] The government has received up to $4 billion dollars in aid from the Soviet Union to help contain both South African and UNITA aggresion.

Another contradiction in US policy in the subregion has to do with the fact that trade and investment ties are maintained with the Marxist government in Mozambique and the pro-Soviet government in Zimbabwe. In September 1985, the late Mozambiquan President Samura Machel visited the United States. Mozambique receives aid from both the West and the Soviet bloc nations. In 1986-87, the US extended $3 million in military aid to Mozambique to help them fight off the attacks by the South African supported guerrilla group, RENAMO. [9]

While political events in the African region contribute significantly to Superpower competition, strategic materials

96

endowments also contribute to such rivalries. The region is recognized as an important source of supply for five strategic minerals: chromium, cobalt, manganese, platinum, and vanadium. The existence of these minerals has resulted in the region coming under two types of leverages: an economic leverage exercised by the multinational corporations, and a political leverage exercised by the Superpowers. The Reagan Administration in 1980 declared its policy of 'resource warfare' against the USSR, with Southern Africa targeted as the theatre of the warfare since most of the minerals listed below are concentrated in that subregion.
┼Strategic materials always have a tremendous impact on the geopolitics of regions. They have both a politico-military and economic articulation into foreign policy. While they are useful for the nuclear and armaments industries of the Superpowers, they are also a motivating force in the investment activities of multinational corporations. Minerals such as cobalt, chromium, manganese, platinum, titanium, and uranium are significant in both military and economic terms such that they are referred to as 'strategic' -- critical to military and industrial activities.

A significant portion of US direct investments in Africa is in the extractive industry of minerals. Consequently, a substantial portion of foreign aid is targeted towards developing mineral industries and consoldiating those that are currently in existence. The region is very salient as a source of US strategic minerals: (1) 78 per cent of US ferrochrome is obtained from South Africa and Zimbabwe, with both countries controlling 98 per cent of known non-Communist reserves; (2) Gabon controls 40 per cent of US manganese supplies; (3) 42 per cent of US cobalt comes from Zaire; and (4) the US gets its supply of platinum from South Africa. Most of these minerals are found in the Soviet Union, but for political and strategic reasons the US prefers to get them from Africa.

The existence of strategic materials in the region has led the Reagan Administration to support particular states in some subregions. The US backed up the efforts of Belgium and France during the guerrilla attacks on Shaba in 1977 and 1978. The indirect support was aimed at protecting and maintaining the Zairean regime from overthrow by the Front National Pour la Liberation du Congo.

Generally, Africa assumed some geostrategic importance in the past decade because of Soviet expansionist goals in the Southern and Eastern subregions. The USSR maintains strong relations with Angola, Congo, Ethiopia, and Mozambique, all of which are naturally endowed with critical raw materials and also strategically located. Cuban and Eastern bloc civilian and military advisers assist in cementing Soviet relations with these countries. The US response to Soviet

Table 4.1
Africa - Strategic Materials[A]

	Number of Strategic Materials
South Africa and Nambia	21
Zaire	16
Zimbabwe	16
Zambia	10
Madagascar	8
Nigeria	8
Ghana	5
Ethiopia	4
Ivory Coast	4
Kenya	4
Mozambique	4
Sierra Leone	4
Gabon	3
Guinea	3
Uganda	3
Cameroon	2
Central African Republic	2
Congo	2
Niger	2
Ruranda	2
Angola	1
Botswana	1
Burundi	1
Chad	1
Lesotho	1
Mali	1
Burkina Fasso (Upper Volta)	1

Sources: Adapted from, Rae Weston, Strategic Materials: A World Survey. London: Croom Helm, 1984; and US Department of the Interior, Bureau of Mines, Minerals Yearbook. Washington, DC: Government Printing Office.

[A] Includes the following strategic materials: Antimony, Beryllium, Cadmium, Chromite, Cobalt, Columbium, Germanium, Hafnium, Indium, Lithium, Manganese, Mercury, Molybdenum, Nickel, Platinum group metals (platinum, palladium, rhodium, iridium, ruthenium, osmium), Rhenium, Selenium, Tantalum, Tellurium, Titanium, Tungsten, Vanadium, Zirconium; also includes aluminum metal or ore (bauxite), Petroleum (crude) and/or natural gas, Gold, Diamonds, Silver, Copper, Tin, Zinc, Ruby, Uranium, and Sulfur.

expansionism in the entire region is still inadequate in terms of military and economic aid flows. This lack of strong response is due to the region's low ranking in terms of geopolitical and economic salience to the Superpowers in comparison to other regions. It is viewed basically as a secondary source of military resources and as a springboard to the more salient regions of the Middle East, Indian Ocean, and Asia.

Africa's low geopolitical ranking is reflected in its low ranking on US economic aid from 1946-1977 as shown in Table 4.2. No country in the region ranks among the top 10 recipients during that period, with only 7 countries falling in the category of upper middle recipients. Most of the states in the region fall in the category of lower middle recipients with rankings between 70 and 124 out of 135 countries. During the period covered by the rankings total US economic aid amounted to $100.565 billion to all regions. Africa received the least amount $5.588 billion among the major regions.

Table 4.3 is a presentation of rankings on US military aid from 1946-1977. Out of 84 countries covered, again no African country ranks among the top 10 recipients. Only two countries, Ethiopia and Zaire fall in the category of upper middle recipients with rankings of 29 and 36 respectively. Most countries in the region fall within the category of either lower middle and bottom 10 or do not receive any US military aid. Again, Africa received the least amount of foreign military aid ($752 million) out of a total of $75.727 billion distributed during 1946-1977.

It is the sea routes around Africa that attract more strategic interests than the interior of the region itself. Because of Soviet moves in the Southern, Central, and Eastern subregions the US has become more active in the region. Militarism and military intervention have become significant in the conduct of US foreign policy in the region. [10] The immediate reasons for militarism in the northern, eastern, and southern parts of the region is the emergence of socialist-oriented or 'closed' economies operating protectionist policies.

The dual strategy of intervention and militarism is intended to safeguard US interests. US presence in the east and north of the region is particularly significant. The US Central Command (formerly known as the Rapid Development Force) is responsible for policing and safeguarding vital interests in the region. Out of more than thirty bases in the region about half of them belong to the US. Kenya, Sudan, Somalia, and Mauritius are strategic countries in the region with US bases.

United States geopolitical behaviour can also be viewed as a backup to the roles played by the ex-Metropoles -- Britain,

99

Table 4.2
Africa - Country Ranking of Total US Economic Aid,
1946 - 1977

Top 10 Category

Rank (out of 135)	Country None	Amount ($ million)

Upper Middle Category

Rank	Country	Amount
35	Zaire	489.1
41	Nigeria	392.9
45	Ethiopia	310.1
48	Liberia	248.5
51	Ghana	236.7
60	Tanzania	190.0
64	Kenya	163.1

Lower Middle Category

Rank	Country	Amount
69	Sudan	120.9
71	Guinea	112.0
74	Mali	89.7
76	Somalia	82.2
79	Senegal	81.8
80	Niger	79.8
83	Upper Volta	65.3
85	Sierra Leone	57.2
87	Botswana	45.7
89	Cameroon	43.7
90	Chad	42.2
91	Uganda	42.2
93	Ivory Coast	36.0
94	Lesotho	35.9
95	Togo	34.0
98	Mauritania	31.7
99	Malawi	31.2
102	Benin	19.2
103	Mozambique	17.5
104	Madagascar	17.2
105	Mauritius	16.5
106	Rwanda	15.7
107	Burundi	13.9
108	Cape Verde	12.7

Source: Adapted from, The Book of World Rankings by George
Thomas Kurian, Facts on File, INc. 1979, pp. 64-65.

Table 4.3
Africa - Country Ranking of Total US Military Aid, 1946-1977

Top 10 Categories

Rank (out of 84)	Country	Amount ($ million)
	None	

Upper Middle Category

29	Ethiopia	285.3
36	Zaire	127.2

Lower Middle Category

44	Kenya	50.7
57	Liberia	14.1
61	Senegal	10.9
66	Gabon	4.0
67	Mali	3.5
71	Nigeria	1.5
73	Sudan	1.1
74	Guinea	1.0

Bottom 10 Category

75	Ghana	0.6
78	Cameroon	0.5
80	Ivory Coast	0.2
81	Benin	0.1
82	Niger	0.1
84	Upper Volta	0.1

Source: Adapted from, The Book of World Rankings, by George Thomas Kurian, Facts on File, Inc., 1979, p. 79.

France, Italy, and Portugal. The backup function is done through cooperation and joint tasks in military and economic issues in particular. In this context, the foreign policy strategy of militarism is usually manifested in joint exercises between the US, its European allies, and friendly states in the region. The 1981 'Bright Star' operations involving troops from the US, France, West Germany, Britain, Egypt, Somalia, Sudan, and Oman is one of the most significant of such exercises.

In implementing its policy of militarism the US targets pro-Soviet states in the region and effectively opposes them. In 1983, for instance, after France dispatched 2,500 troops into the Chad conflict, President Reagan backed up France's efforts by donating $100 million of military aid to Hissen Habre. The decision by France to intervene was said to be due to pressure from the US and repeated allegations by the White House that Libya was giving significant support to the interests of the Soviets in the region.

Finally, while militarism involves both economic and military aid, it also includes covert operation or intervention. In the Chadean conflict, for instance, the CIA admitted to aiding Hissen Habre overthrow Goukouni Wade, the OAU recognized president. In 1975 the FNLA mercenaries in Angola are alleged to have received aid from the CIA. With regard to the North-West African conflict, in February 1985, the Polisario Front claimed that Moroccan and US military exercises were staged in an area contiguous to the SADR.

ASIA

Within the entire Asian region, the South-East subregion presents a rather complex case of alliances and conflicts among the states. The involvement of the US, USSR, and the PRC makes the configuration of power assume the form of tripolarity patterned by a restrained Cold War. Vietnam's drive for regional power status is opposed by the PRC because of the former's client relationship with the USSR. Moreover, Vietnam's alliance with the Soviets is viewed by the PRC as an encirclement.

In addition to the Sino-Vietnamese conflict, Vietnam is also opposed by Thailand and Malaysia in the regional power politics. This opposition is evidenced in the support given by Thailand and Malaysia to the Khmer Rouge forces fighting the Hanoi-supported regime in Cambodia. Furthermore, the region is also the hotbed of protracted guerrilla wars involving Thailand, Malaysia, Burma, Cambodia, Laos, and the Philippines. It could be considered one of complexity and contrast for the following reasons: (1) the co-existence of prosperous states like Singapore, Taiwan, and Hong Kong with others that are not; (2) the existence of states like Vietnam and Indonesia with objectives of regional hegemony; [11] and (3) the presence of regional influentials like India and the PRC that defy any easy classification by virtue of their size, military strength, and cultural diversity.

The complex and fluid nature of coexistence in the region is reinforced by traditional rivalry between India and Pakistan on the one hand, and India and the PRC on the other. Other traditional rivalries are those between the USSR and the PRC, Vietnam and the Khmers, and Thailand and Burma. These traditional enmities are given added significance because of superpower involvement. Generally, the regional struggles tend to take the form of restrained Cold War rivalries between the US and the USSR on the one hand, and the PRC and the USSR on the other.

Three significant potential and actual geopolitical conflicts are those between the two Koreas, in Indochina, and in the Philippines. The US is strongly committed to the defense of South Korea. Since the Korean War in the early 1950's, South Korea has had to contain a significant North Korean force at the 38th parallel as well as a regime determined to reunify the country at all costs. A tripolar power relationship is the consequence of this potential conflict, with both the PRC and the USSR supporting reunification, thereby pitting the US against the two communist powers on the Korean question. The PRC also exploits the strained relationship between North Korea and the USSR by developing strong ties with the former. United States-South Korean ties have remained significantly strong because of both ideological and military threats to the territorial integrity of the latter. The subregion could thus be considered one of restrained Cold War rivalries, a fact which motivates the US to give significant economic and military support to South Korea. Various types of foreign aid: grants, military sales credits, military education and training, and excess defense articles, have been extended to South Korea, such that between 1953 and 1978 the US had disbursed about $8 billion in military aid. [12] The external threat posed by North Korea led President Reagan to decide not to withdraw the 40,000 American troops in that country. North Korea receives about 90 per cent of its military aid from the USSR. This makes it all the more important for the US to preserve the present geopoliticla and military balance in the region. Both Superpowers are aware of the delicate balance and are accordingly careful not to supply military aid that would trigger an overreaction of the potential adversaries.

The level of intraregional conflict in Indochina spread rapidly by the 1970's. It started with North Vietnam using Cambodian territory to transport troops for the war in South

Vietnam. After Prince Sihanouk's overthrow, General Lon Nol tried to contain the fighting along Cambodia's eastern border, but by 1975 the conflict escalated resulting in an influx of thousands of peasants into Phnom Penh fleeing for their lives. At the same time, the Khmer Rouges under Pol Pot exploited the chaos along the borders and after the withdrawal of US forces from Cambodia in April 1975 succeeded in taking over the Cambodian government with the help of North Vietnam. Despite Hanoi's assistance in Khmer Rouge victory, by 1976 the regime in Phnom Penh began to undermine the existing good relations between the two regimes by maintaining friendly relations with the PRC, a competitor of Hanoi in the region.

The continued shift of the Khmer Rouge away from Vietnam's regional goals resulted in its invasion of Cambodian territory in late 1978. Phnom Penh fell to the Vietnamese in January 1978. By late 1979 the Khmer Rouge-Vietnamese conflict had escalated into a guerrilla war that spread through the country resulting in thousands of Cambodian refugees fleeing into Thailand to escape the continuing violence in Cambodia. It is estimated that between 1975 and 1979 after the Vietnmaese invasion nearly 34,000 Cambodians fled into Thailand. [13] Vietnam believes that maintaining influence over the Cambodian regime is essential to its regional security and has vowed to occupy Cambodia until all resistance to the present regime ceases. Cambodia continues to be a country of high conflict because of the numerous groups fighting against the Vietnamese-backed Heng Samrin regime. In 1985 the conflict widened and for the first time since 1979 the Vietnamese troops pursued the opposition forces into Thailand thereby directly carrying the conflict into Thai territory. This resulted in direct confrontation with Thai forces. These incursions into Thai territory by Vietnam has required a US response in the form of increased military aid and immediate airlift of artillery pieces, ammunition, and tanks.

The Philippines assumes special importance because of the strategic importance of the two military installations: the Clark Air Force Base and the Subic Naval Base. The two together contain 15,000 US troops. The Clark air base is the largest aerial port in the Western Pacific, large enough to be used by just about all US military planes. The Subic Naval base, which is considered to be one of more importance than the air base, is the largest US naval installation outside the United States. It has the largest ship repair facilities in the Western Pacific and performs about two thirds of the ship repair work on the US Seventh Fleet. It has a naval supply depot that can supply every ship in the US fleet including Polaris ballistic-missile submarines. [14] It also has training for nearly every type of naval warfare.

The Philippines lies adjacent to vital sea lanes which link sources of important supplies to other parts of the world. Having US naval forces in the Philippines allows for the protection of these lanes so these supplies can be delivered to friendly nations. The Western Pacific subregion of which the Philippines is an integral part is economically important. The US trades more in this region than in any other part of the world, constituting 30 per cent of all US foreign trade.

In addition, the Philippines is part of the location that lies right next to the vital Western Pacific sea and air lanes and at the gateway from the Pacific to the Indian Ocean. The Philippines also lies close to the Soviet installations in Vietnam, and is within four flying hours, or five sea days, of Korea, Singapore, Japan, or Australia.

There are US concerns with the balance of power between communist and democratic governments. The Soviet military capability in the Asian-Pacific region is increasing every year. Besides their naval buildup, the Soviets have also increased their air and ground forces in the Far East. Because of the Soviet presence in the region US policy in the Philippines in particular has emphasized security and stability rather than democratic values.

Security and stability have been pursued through military aid in particular. Under the Nixon and Ford Administrations, military aid increased steadily, but dropped drastically under the Carter Administration. However, President Carter, a strong advocate of human rights who opposed the Marcos regime, recognized the importance of US security interests in the face of a growing Communist insurgency in the Philippines. Towards the end of his administration, he too, resumed the normal, steady increase of military aid.

With the Reagan Administration there was a sharp increase in the amount of military aid given to the Philippines. Two factors contributed to the increase in aid: first, the alarming growth rate of the communist New Peoples Army (NPA), and second, the importance President Reagan placed on American security. [15] The advent of the Aquino regime has coalesced more support for the Philippines because of its restoration of democratic ideals which had completely disappeared during the Marcos years. Congress, the State Department, and the President all agree that the US should firmly support the Aquino government in its reforms. To this end an additional $150 million in bilateral economic and military aid was initiated, $300 million in ESF was extended to help invigorate the economy, and for FY 1987 an additional $200 million in economic assistance was promised the Aquino government. [16]

The Association of South East Asian Nations (ASEAN), the regional association comprising of Thailand, Malaysia,

Singapore, Indonesia, and the Philippines has major economic ties with the US. Excluding Japan, Asian states overall account for over 12 per cent of US manufactured imports and exports, and 18 per cent of US agricultural exports. US exports to the East Asian subregion amounted to $41.7 billion in 1982. This total includes trade with Australia, New Zealand, South Korea, and Taiwan, and is equal to about four-fifths of the volume of US exports to the EEC. Table 4.4 shows that the region is also rich in strategic minerals most of which are concentrated mostly in India, South Korea, Malaysia, Indonesia, Thailand, and the Philippines.

The geopolitical salience of the Asian region has made it the recipient of massive amounts of US foreign aid since the end of World War II. Table 4.5 reveals that four countries: South Vietnam, South Korea, India, and Pakistan, are among the top 10 recipients of US economic aid from 1946-1977 out of a total of 135 recipient states. Out of a total of $100.565 billion the East Asian subregion alone received $23.087 billion. In the rankings most of the other nations in the region fell in the category of upper middle recipients. Similarly, in the area of US military aid for the period 1946-1977, five regional nations rank among the top 10 recipients out of a total of 84 countries. Out of a total of $75.727 billion, the East Asian subregion received $35.442 billion the highest among all subregions. In the entire rankings many of the other regional nations fall into the category of upper middle recipients as in the case of economic aid.

Finally, every subregion of Asia is central to the interests of the major powers. The northeast area is geopolitically important to the US, USSR, the PRC, and Japan because of the commercial and military intersection of their interests. In the Southeast subregion, the area is very volatile and explosive because of the recurring offensives and counter offensives involving Vietnam, Cambodia, the PRC, and the numerous operations of guerrilla movements. The Southwest Pacific and the Indian Ocean are a foreign policy focus of the US because they contain vital sea lanes such as the Malacca and Singapore straits the passages for a huge amount of seaborne commerce bound to and from Japan in particular. The Soviet invasion of Afghanistan and the India-Pakistan conflict are two problems that have resulted in a US foreign policy response. Events in that area have assumed the nature of a mild bipolar rivalry in which India and Pakistan have become the allies of the USSR and the US respectively. Massive amounts of friendship treaties have become part of the scenario thereby investing the area with an atmosphere of a mild Cold War rivalry structured by an institutionalized aid-giving competition among the major powers.

Table 4.4
Asia - Strategic Materials[A]

	Number Strategic Materials
India	21
South Korea	12
Malaysia	12
Indonesia	11
Thailand	11
Philippines	10
Burma	9
Taiwan	8
Pakistan	7
North Korea	7
Vietnam	3
Bangladesh	3
Sri Lanka	3
Brunei	2
Hong Kong	1
Nepal	1

Sources: Adapted from Rae Weston, Strategic Materials: A World Survey. London: Croom Helm, 1984; and US Department of the Interior, Bureau of Mines, Minerals Yearbook. Washington, DC: Government Printing Office, 1982.

[A]Includes the following strategic materials: Aluminum group metals, Antimony, Bismuth, Cadmium, Chromium, Cobalt, Colombium-tantalum, Cooper, Gold, Iron and Steel, Lead, Manganese Ore, Mercury, Nickel, Platinum-group metals, Silver, Tin, Titanium, Tunsgsten, Uranium, Vanadium, Zinc, Zirconium concentrates, Asbestos, Barite, Diatomite, Sulfur, Coal, Natural gas, Petroleum.

Table 4.5
Asia - Country Ranking of Total US Economic Aid, 1946-1977

Top 10 Category

Rank (out of 135)	Country	Amount ($ million)
1	South Vietnam	6,457.1
2	South Korea	5,550.0
3	India	5,436.9
4	Pakistan	4,123.2

Upper Middle Category

13	The PRC and Taiwan	1,936.5
14	Indonesia	1,838.0
15	Japan	1,685.4
16	Philippines	1,652.0
21	Bangladesh	1,098.6
23	Laos	899.4
26	Pacific Islands	823.2
29	Cambodia	768.2
33	Afghanistan	496.4
47	Sri Lanka	292.4
55	Nepal	205.8

Lower Middle Category

84	Malaysia	61.2
86	Burma	53.6
88	Hong Kong	43.8
101	Albania	20.4
125	Singapore	2.8

Bottom 10

133	Papul New Guinea	0.3

Source: Adapted from, The Book of World Rankings, by George Thomas Kurian, Facts on File Inc., 1979, pp. 64-65.

Table 4.6
Asia - Country Ranking of Total US Military Aid,
1946-1977

Top 10 Category

Rank (out of 84)	Country	Amount ($ million)
1	South Vietnam	16,424.1
2	South Korea	6,933.7
6	PRC and Taiwan	4,101.2
9	Laos	1,606.8
10	Thailand	1,557.4

Upper Middle Category

12	Cambodia	1,281.6
14	Japan	1,204.9
20	Philippines	866.6
21	Indochina (undistributed) (represents regional aid programs)	731.5
23	Pakistan	704.7
28	India	127.2
41	Burma	88.7

Lower Middle Category

43	Malaysia	78.6
60	Singapore	11.4
64	Afghanistan	5.4
68	Sri Lanka	3.2
70	Nepal	2.0

Bottom 10 Category

None

Source: Adapted from, The Book of World Rankings, by George
           Thomas Kurian, Facts on File Inc., 1979, p. 79

Historically and in the present, the US has vigorously defended its hemispheric objectives. Defense of such objectives takes the form of direct and indirect military interventions. Instances of intervention include Guatemala 1954, Cuba 1961, the Dominican Republic 1965, Chile 1973, Grenada 1983, and Nicaragua still in progress since 1981. Most of the US interventions in the region could be described as 'benevolent' -- designed to maintain the status quo by militarily and economically aiding the regime in power -- and aimed at maintaining the historical sphere of influence relationship with the rest of the region. Factors such as civil wars, political vulnerability of a regime, and general social instability are significant predictors of the propensity for a US intervention.

The region's strong economic links with the US has not led to a decrease in social upheavals especially in the Central American subregion. The existence of a conflictual atmosphere in Central America started in the late 1970's with the unstable Nicaraguan regime under Anastasio Samoza. His alienation of the middle class coupled with increased internal repression increased the revolutionary fervor of the Sandanista revolution and its insurrectionist style changed the whole picture of politics in Central America and even inspired the insurgents in El Salvador and Guatemala.

The lesson was not lost on insurgents in El Salvador and Guatemala that the success of a revolution is largely based on a war of attrition conducted from the countryside. While guerrilla forces focus their efforts on the peasantry, the government forces in turn extend their operations in rural areas. Government repression is then targeted at peasant populations accused of sheltering guerrillas. The repression triggers anti-government feelings and radicalization of the peasantry. The governments of El Salvador and Guatemala conduct counter insurgency campaigns designed to intimidate the rural people thereby resulting in more conflict, violence, and casualties. The ongoing clash between right-wing groups, government forces, and left-wing guerrillas has created a climate of terror in the Central American territories.

Casualty rates increase in El Salvador, Guatemala, and Nicaragua with the rise in the level of conflict among opposing forces. Within El Salvador and Gauatemala, ardent followers of opposition parties have either been killed or forced into exile. Increased military operations are conducted in the rural areas that result in intimidation, destruction of peasants' property suspected of helping guerrilla groups. The domestic violence in individual countries is complicated by the increase in interstate hostilities especially between Nicaragua and Honduras. The use of Honduran territory as the staging ground for Contra attacks into Nicaragua has resulted in occasional raids by the Nicaraguan military into some areas of Honduran territory. The decision by the US to dispatch military advisers to Honduras for joint training exercises with the Honduran military was a strong indication that the Central American conflict had assumed the proportions of an East-West confrontation. This is also reflected in first the rapid and continuing increase in US economic and military aid to El Salvador, Honduras, and Guatemala in particular. Second, the resolve of the Reagan Administration to overthrow the Sandanista regime through Contra and CIA operations. The Soviet Union and Cuba for their part have responded by gradually strengthening their relations with Nicaragua through technical assistance.

Since 1981 President Reagan reemphasized the transfer of military aid for counterinsurgency purposes. Regional guerrilla threats have been underscored with strong accusations of Cuban and Soviet involvement. The US objective with Latin America in general is to provide arms credits at concessionary rates so that they would enhance the security of nations in the region and help deter internal aggression. In the subregion of Central America the total amount of MAP grants, FMS credits, and ESF loans and grants for Central America rose from $145.9 million in 1981 to $476.2 million in 1983. [17] The determination of the Reagan Administration to overthrow the Sandanista and eliminate the Soviet-Cuban menace resulted in the National Security Council (NSC) under Admiral Poindexter to violate Congressional authority barring official funds to the Contras. The matter, now referred to as the Iran/Contra affair is currently under Congressional investigation.

In the entire region of Latin America, Brazil is clearly the most populous, economically dynamic, and resource endowed of the states. The region itself is greatly endowed with substantial resources. The oil producing states are Mexico, Venezuela, and Ecuador. Venezuela is at times perceived as an average regional power because of its geostrategic location, and oil wealth which supports only a sizable population. Mexico and Argentina have not qualified as regional powers like Brazil because of the severe economic disruptions and overpopulation plaguing both countries. Overall, the region is regarded as having a much higher socioeconomic level of development than much of Africa and Asia. Other countries in the region like Peru, Chile, Bolivia, and Jamaica are endowed with strategic minerals in varying amounts. Table 4.7 presents the number of strategic materials possessed by nations in the region.

Apart from the Central American subregion the region is

Table 4.7
Latin America - Strategic Materials[A]

	Number of Strategic Materials
Brazil	22
Mexico	20
Argentina	17
Chile	15
Bolivia	11
Colombia	9
Venezuela	9
Dominican Republic	6
Cuba	5
Ecuador	5
Guatemala	4
Trinidad and Tobago	3
Nicaragua	3
Jamaica	3
Bahamas	2
Barbados	2
Haiti	2
Costa Rica	2
Guyana	1
Surinmae	1
Uruguay	1

Sources: Adapted from, Rae Weston, Strategic Materials: A World Survey. London: Croom Helm, 1984; and US Department of the Interior, Bureau of Mines, Minerals Yearbook. Washington, DC: Government Printing Office, 1982.

[A] Includes the following strategic materials: Aluminum group metals Antimony, Bismuth, Cadmium, Chromium, Cobalt, Colombium-tantalum, Cooper, Gold, Iron and Steel, Lead, Manganese ore, Mercury, Nickel Platinum-group metals, Silver, Tin, Titanium, Tungsten, Uranium, Vanadium, Zinc, Zirconium concentrates, Asbestos, Barite, Diatomite; Sulfur, Coal, Natural Gas, Petroleum.

generally not one of high levels of conflict. It is also not an arena of East-West geopolitical rivalry compared to the Middle East or Asia. Moreover, it has always been regarded as a US sphere of influence since the proclamation of the Monroe Doctrine in 1823. Because of these factors the region has never been one of foreign aid-giving competition. Table 4.8 shows the ranking of regional recipients in US economic aid for the period 1946-1977. Unlike the Middle East and Asia, no country falls in the category of top 10 recipients. Out of a total of $100.565 billion in aid distributed during the period, the region received only $12.748 billion, about 50 per cent of the amount received by Asia and the Middle East. Seventeen recipients fell in the category of upper middle recipients out of a total of 135 countries in the entire ranking. Similarly, in terms of US military aid, the region ranks lower than the Middle East and Asia. Out of a total of $84.7 million in aid distributed during 1946-1977 no country in the region ranks among the top 10 recipients out of a total of 84 countries in the entire ranking. For the whole period the region was the recipient of only $1.782 billion, far less than one per cent of the amount received by the Middle East and Asia. Of the 21 regional countries included in the ranking only 8 fall in the category of upper middle recipients.

Since the late 1970's the region has been showing increased signs of change tending toward more instability and assertiveness of nations. There exists the baffling question for successive US Administrations, whether political agitations are primarily nationalistic or communist inspired. What is becoming certain is that the US sphere of influence status is increasingly under attack. The US has had to reckon with the increasing independence and assertiveness of states in the region. They have made continued efforts to maintain wider trade ties with the USSR and East European countries. While some states still willingly support US regional security policies, still many others have withheld their endorsements. The whole process of assertiveness and increased independence is aimed at strengthening their bargaining power vis-a-vis the US in political and economic matters. Brazil the only regional power has diversified its political and economic ties to include the Eastern bloc and many Third World countries. Recently, it announced its intentions of resuming normal diplomatic relations with Cuba.

United States response to assertiveness and increased independence has had two implications: political and economic. The foreign policy of interventions is considered primarily political. Different Administrations perceived the domestic instability and assertiveness of regional nations to be part of a wider communist strategy of exporting revolutions. Thus the Reagan Administration like others in

Table 4.8
Latin America - Country Ranking of Total US Economic Aid,
1946-1977

Top 10 Category

Rank (out of 135)	Country	Amount ($ million)
	None	

Upper Middle Category

Rank (out of 135)	Country	Amount ($ million)
12	Brazil	2,049.2
22	Colombia	1,078.6
24	Chile	893.0
32	Bolivia	655.2
37	Dominican Republic	457.1
40	Peru	393.2
43	Guatemala	351.4
44	Panama	326.3
50	Nicaragua	244.0
53	Ecudaor	212.9
54	Mexico	210.8
56	Honduras	205.1
58	Costa Rica	198.2
59	Haiti	197.5
65	El Salvador	144.8
67	Jamaica	131.7
68	Paraguay	128.5

Lower Middle Category

Rank	Country	Amount ($ million)
70	Uruguay	119.4
73	Venezuela	100.5
77	Guyana	82.1
81	Argentina	78.9
92	Trinidad and Tobago	40.5
116	Belize	8.1
121	Surinam	5.0
123	Cuba	4.0

Bottom 10 Category

Rank	Country	Amount ($ million)
126	Barbados	2.2
132	Bahamas	0.3

Source: Adapted from, The Book of World Rankings, by George
Thomas Kurian, Facts on File Inc., 1979, pp. 64-65.

Table 4.9
Latin America - Country Ranking of Total US Military Air, 1946-1977

Top 10 Category

Rank (out of 84)	Country	Amount ($ million)
	Upper Middle Category	
26	Brazil	511.8
30	Peru	197.0
31	Argentina	190.3
32	Chile	172.7
33	Colomiba	159.5
39	Ecuador	94.5
40	Bolivia	92.6
42	Uruguay	84.7
	Lower Middle Category	
48	Dominican Republic	41.0
49	Venezuela	36.1
50	Guatemala	34.4
51	Nicaragua	30.6
52	Paraguay	30.0
53	Honduras	22.7
55	Cuba	16.1
56	El Salvador	15.1
58	Panama	13.1
62	Mexico	9.9
63	Costa Rica	7.0
65	Haiti	5.4
72	Jamaica	1.1

Bottom 10 Category

None

Source: Adapted from, The Book of World Ranking, by George Thomas Kurian, Facts on File, Inc., 1979, p. 79.

the past did not ruled out direct military intervention to restore the status quo. United States foreign policy behavior also takes the form of economic sanctions and indirect covert intervention. In Chile, the means used to disrupt the Chilean economy and render the government politically vulnerable were primarily economic. The US effectively blocked the extension of loans to the Chilean regime, and made it more difficult for the government to refinance its debt obligations. In other words, interventions and economic sanctions which include withholding foreign aid were instrumental in containing communism and protecting trade and investment.

Finally, just as in other regions, the South American, Central American, and Caribbean subregions possess sea passages that transport commercial imports for the US. The Caribbean route provides passage for about 60 per cent of US crude oil imports and 70 per cent of refined oil imports. The South Atlantic sea routes handle about 50 per cent of US crude oil imports, 75 per cent of Western Europe's petroleum imports, and from 20 to 85 per cent of various critical minerals imported from the US and Southern Africa. These sea lines of communication are strategic to the defense planning of NATO because of their usefulness as lines of resupply and reinforcement in the event of a crisis. The importance of Central America and the Caribbean was underscored by President Reagan in 1982 when he outlined a programme of special assistance to those countries. The programme known as the Caribbean Basin Initiative (CBI) resulted in a $14.1 billion appropriations Bill after undergoing a series of political battles between Congress and the White House.

THE MIDDLE EAST

The Middle East has developed into a volatile, explosive, and at times dangerous region because of its geostrategic characteristics and resource endowments. It is now undoubtedly considered the most conflictual region in the international system. As a geographic unit, it lies at the crossroads of East and West thereby enhancing its commercial and military salience. Both Superpowers have long been aware of the geopolitical significance of the regional influentials as well as the critical passages that are essential to navigation and commerce. The Soviet Union has sought to make its presence known in the region since the 1950's. First, the Soviets depend on waterways like the Mediterranean and the Suez Canal for military access and shipping particularly since they are close to the Soviet Union. Second, the Soviets are serious about increasing their influence in the region because of their ongoing ideological competition with the US. Their goal in this regard is to strengthen alliances with the anti-Western regimes and more radical states in the region. [18] Although it has lost Egypt, Moscow still maintains strong ties with Syria and South Yemen.

The Arab-Israeli conflict has been the longest and will undoubtedly be the most enduring in the region. It started with the 1948 conflict which led to the creation of Israel and also marked the beginning of the existing Arab hostility against Israel. Since 1948, four other wars have been fought. In the 1956 Suez Crisis, Israel and Egypt battled each other. This was followed in 1967 by the Six-Day War in which Israel and Egypt were both on the offensive. In 1973 under the leadership of Egypt the Arab countries attacked Israel resulting in the Yom Kippur War. Finally, in 1982 Israel led an offensive in Lebanon which resulted in a war between Israel and the PLO.

While the Arab-Israeli hostility is primarily based on Israeli occupation of Palestinian territory, it was not until 1982 that the Palestinians themselves, the primary focus of the conflict, directly confronted the Israelis in a full-scale war. Since the PLO defeat the Arab states have not been willing to confront Israel militarily on the Palestinian question. The Palestinians for their part have resorted, as they have always done, to occasional acts of terrorism directed either at the US or Israel.

However, the seemingly dormant Arab-Israeli conflict does not mean the potential for war is non-existent. The lack of unity among radical Arabs from whom one might expect an offensive against Israel was strongly related to the Iran-Iraq War. The war constituted a source of Arab disunity. The radical states -- Syria, Libya, and South Yemen -- threw their support behind Iran, whereas the more moderate states: Egypt, Jordan, and the Gulf principalities favoured Iraq. Syria and Libya were very overt about their support, such that Syria closed the Syrian port of the Iraqi oil pipeline in April 1982; and both supplied military aid in the form of tanks and SS missiles. Iraq which used to belong to the radical camp of Arab states is now aligned with the moderates. The regional realignment and enmity that emerged from the Iran-Iraq War introduced a lull in the traditional Arab-Israeli conflict.

The region is generally a theatre of both intrastate and interstate conflicts. Some of the more notable interstate disputes have been those between Egypt and Syria after the breakup of the United Arab Republic, Egypt and Libya in connection with their 1977 border war, North and South Yemen in 1972 and 1979, and currently between Algeria and Morocco over the Western Sahara. During the time of Sadat, strong hostilities were directed at Egypt by other Arab states because of the peace treaty concluded by the former with

Israel. [19]

In addition to the more traditional interstate conflicts, there exists the issue of separate nationalisms and parochial loyalties such as emphasis on a Druze identity, Palestinian unity, or a Libyan distinctivenss. In other words, the idea of pan-Arabism is relegated to a secondary role thereby polarizing both domestic and international relations within the region. The existence of parochial nationalism is complicated by an increase in Islamic fundamentalism with its revolutionary orientation. The region is generally characterized by conservative religious movements around which politics revolves. Islamic fundamentalism in particular has contributed to regional instability. The Sunni-Shia rivalry presently makes Saudi Arabia very suspicious of the Shia Iranian revolution. The Sunni-Shia split is also a potential source of instability over the Kurdish question in many parts of the region. Because of this split, the continued cohesiveness of Syria where a Shia minority is running the government appears threatening. The resurgence of fundamentalism with its attendant fanaticism may exacerbate the internal divisions within each religious sect as well as between them.

Regional conflicts are also sparked by interventions such as the many years of Egyptian interventions in the domestic affairs of other Arab states. Iranian intervention in Iraqi affairs via the Kurdish problem and vice versa are other cases in point. Part of the scenario of both intrastate and interstate conflicts has to do with the struggle for regional hegemony. The exporting of revolutions and the destabilization of rival regimes become favored methods in trying to achieve such an objective. Egypt and Iran have respectively used Islamic revival and pan-Arabism as instruments to achieve regional hegemony.

Middle Eastern politics and power configurations can be volatile and ephemeral resulting in profound changes from time to time. The Central Treaty Organization (CENTO) created in 1955 suffered a heavy blow in July 1958, because of the revolution in Baghdad which also served as headquarters for the organization. CENTO died a natural death with the Iranian revolution in 1979. By 1975 Iran and Iraq maintained good diplomatic relations, but with the fall of the Shah, Iraq invaded a portion of Iran resulting in the Iran-Iraq War which has been going on for seven years.

The geopolitics of the region is brought into sharper focus because of the potential threat posed by the USSR-Cuban connection. Indicators of such a threat are Soviet successes in Ethiopia, the Peoples Democratic Republic of Yemen (PDRY), and Afghanistan. These successes are menacing to Saudi Arabia, the Sudan, and North Yemen. The US reaction has been to increase its militarism in the gulf Region through the RDF

118

which patrols the area. While the conflict in the Horn of Africa may be viewed as primarily an African problem it in fact has a strong bearing on the Gulf region because of its geographic proximity to the Middle East and the superpower competition involved.

A significant factor that makes the Middle East a target of superpower rivalry are its geopolitical and resource endowments. First, the region is strategically located as the midpoint of three continents. It offers the shortest sea routes from West to East. Second, the region is the most important source of the most widely-used strategic resource, oil. Furthermore, the geopolitical, military, and economic salience of the region has resulted in the emergence of two relationships: (1) patron-client relationships such as those between the US and Israel, and the USSR and Syria, and (2) shifting and unstable alliances between regional members and the Superpowers such as those between the USSR and Egypt in the late 1950's and the US and Iran before the Iranian revolution.

The region is even more salient in geostrategic terms because it is endowed with five-eighth's of the world's proven oil reserves outside the communist world. Table 4.10 presents the strategic materials found in the region. Up to 70 per cent of the industrialized countries oil supply comes from the Middle East, including 80 per cent for Japan and 32 per cent for the US. A top priority in US foreign policy thus becomes the protection of oil supplies by limiting Soviet influence and promoting regional stability.

The Arab-Israeli conflict assumes such enormous priority in US foreign policy that the Middle East has been a key recipient of US foreign aid in the attempt to maintain peace and stability. The importance of Egypt and Israel in US foreign policy in the area puts them among the top 10 recipients of US economic aid to the region from 1946-1977. Out of a total of $100.565 billion in economic aid for the period, the Middle East and a few neighboring countries mostly from South Asia received $23.768 billion, more than any other region. Many countries in the region do not however fall in the category of upper middle recipients as shown in Table 4.11. This is an indication that in the Middle East US economic aid is skewed in favor of a few key recipients. Similarly in US military aid two countries-- Israel and Turkey fall in the category of top 10 recipients of aid out of 84 countries for the period 1946-1977. Out of a total of $75.727 billion the region ranks second with $16.403 billion in aid after Asia. Table 4.12 shows the figures and rankings of individual country recipients.

Finally, the Middle East has emerged as the new theatre of a silent US-Soviet geopolitical competition in the last decade in particular. The recent Soviet interest in the

Table 4.10
The Middle East - Strategic Materials[A]

	Number of Strategic Materials
Turkey	13
Morocco	10
Iran	9
Algeria	8
United Arab Emirates	8
Iraq	7
Israel	6
Libya	6
Egypt	5
Sudan	5
Tunisia	5
Kuwait	5
Cyprus	4
Mauritania	4
Saudi Arabia	4
Afghanistan	3
Bahrain	3
Oatar	3
Oman	2
Syria	2
Jordan	1

Sources: Adapted from Rae Weston, Strategic Materials: A World Survey. London: Croom Helm, 1984; and US Department of the Interior, Bureau of Mines, Minerals Yearbook. Washington, DC: Government Printing Office 1982.

[A]Includes the following strategic materials: Aluminum, Antimony, Bismuth, Cadmium, Chromium, Cobalt, Colombium-tantalum, Copper, Gold, Iron and Steel, Lead, Manganese Ore, Mercury, Nickel, Platinum group metals, Silver, Tin, Titanium, Tungsten, Uranium, Vanadium, Zinc, Zirconium concentrates, Asbestos, Barite, Diatomite, Sulfur, Coal, Natural gas, Petroleum.

Table 4.11
The Middle East - Country Ranking of Total US Economic
Aid, 1946-1977

Top 10 Category

Rank (out of 135)	Country	Amount ($ million)
7	Egypt	2,924.7
9	Israel	2,664.7

Upper Middle Category

11	Turkey	2,061.2
19	Jordan	1,131.1
30	Morocco	674.4
31	Tunisia	670.6
38	Iran	457.1
42	Syria	361.2
57	Libya	204.1
62	Algeria	188.6
66	Lebanon	135.2

Lower Middle Category

72	Cyprus	102.3
75	Yemen Arab Republic	83.0
96	Iraq	33.6
100	Saudi Arabis	27.5
122	South Yemen	4.5

Bottom 10 Category

127	Bahrain	2.0
128	Oman	1.4

Source: Adapted from, The Book of World Rankings, by George
Thomas Kurian, Facts on File, Inc., 1979,
pp. 64-65.

121

Table 4.12
The Middle East - Country Ranking of Total US Military Aid, 1946-1977

Top 10 Category

Rank (out of 84)	Country	Amount ($ million)
3	Israel	6,102.0
4	Turkey	4,756.7

Upper Middle Category

19	Iran	896.2
25	Jordan	621.3
34	Morocco	136.3
37	Tunisia	106.0

Lower Middle Category

45	Iraq	50.0
46	Lebanon	49.0
47	Saudi Arabia	41.6
54	Libya	17.6

Bottom 10 Category

77	Yemen Arab Republic	0.5
83	Syria	0.1

Source: Adapted from, The Book of World Rankings, by George Thomas Kurian, Facts on File, INc., 1979, p. 79.

Persian Gulf area and the presence of some 40,000 Cuban and Eastern bloc civilian and military advisers scattered in different parts of the region has resulted in a US foreign policy response by way of the Rapid Deployment Joint Task Force (RDJTF) to police the Gulf subregion in particular as a deterrent to Soviet intentions. In the past twenty years both Superpowers have in fact gradually shifted their focus to the region by distributing massive amounts of economic and military aid to their client states. The states of Syria, Iraq, South Yemen, and Afghanistan have been the priority recipients of some $42 billion in Soviet military aid over the past twenty-five years. With the shift from Vietnam the US targeted Israel, Egypt, and Saudi Arabia as the priority recipients of its military aid such that in 1982 Israel was the largest recipient of the Economic Support fund amounting to $806 million, followed by Egypt with $771 million, and Turkey $300 million.

SUMMARY

Since the mid 1950s Third World regions have been the recipients of most US foreign aid. In this period of bipolycentrism they have also developed into the main focus of the ongoing Soviet-American foreign policy concerns. Third World regions are characterized by pockets of restrained 'cold wars' between the superpowers and between rival regional recipients of aid caused by radical nationalisms, ethnic irredentism, civil wars, and international wars. Restrained cold wars are especially commonplace in volatile and explosive regions like the Middle East or in parts of Africa. The most enduring and pervasive feature of US aid programmes is that they have almost totally been rationalized on geopolitical and cold war terms.

The demand-supply relationship in resource allocations tends to be more influenced by the donor if the recipient does not occupy a strategic location and lacks critical raw materials, and the like. On the other hand, the recipient will be in a position to exercise more leverage in the demand-supply relationship if it occupies a geostrategic position and possesses critical raw materials for which there are no easy substitutes, and is also prone to switch donors regardless of political ideology. This line of argument in the resource allocation process will be pursued in greater detail in subsequent chapters, and especially in Chapter nine.

The degree of foreign policy outputs received by a subregion is in direct proportion to its qualities in terms of critical resources, geostrategic location, and command of important sea passages. Strategic minerals such as chromium,

123

uranium, vanadium, oil, and the like are central to the regional focus in US foreign policy. Besides, minerals have assumed added priority because of the recent theorizing of a 'resource warfare' whereby a rival power tries to deprive the other of materials essential to the other's military and commercial industries. Theorizing about such warfare ranges from issues about outright resource denial to a blockade of strategic waterways through which the materials are shipped. Thus the Straits of Hormuz, the Cape of Good Hope, the Suez Canal, and similar other critical sea passages become central to US-Soviet geopolitical rivalries.

In addition a regional focus in foreign policy is also underscored because of the pervasiveness of US multinational corporations doing business in Third World regions. Although MNCs tend to pursue a policy independent of US foreign policy, they nonetheless need occasional protection and intervention on their behalf by the US government. As disseminators of American values and products they are an integral part of a longterm US foreign policy. Their contribution to the short term goals of American policy is even more significant because of their engagement in the extraction of critical raw materials useful in the arms industry of the United States.

The involvement of recipient states in regional geopolitical competition produces a relationship of mutual dependence between the Superpowers and regional influentials because: (1) the superpower and the allied regional influential have compatible regional interests; (2) the compatibility or convergence of interests is structured by common perceived threats to their national security; and (3) a perception of mutual dependence bolsters the prestige of the recipient in the region thereby making it more interested in the relationship and in the furtherance of the superpower's foreign policy goals.

A perusal of Third World regions reveals that the US has friendly states in every region although the degree of alliance varies from country to country. In Africa the US has not developed as close ties as in other regions primarily because of the fluid political situation in the region. South Africa which could have been a stable ally happens to be a pariah state because of its inhuman apartheid system. Other regions tend to offer more promise. Latin America as a US neighbor is full of pro-US military and civilian regimes. In the Middle East Israel is a formidable US ally. The US-Israeli relationship has also developed into one of mutual dependence in geopolitical and military issues, although Israel is heavily dependent on the US for economic and military assistance. In the Asian region, South Korea is comparable to Israel in the Middle East. It has developed into a strategic client that receives over 2 per cent of all

US arms sales and about 10 per cent of US military aid since 1950. Although rather unstable it nonetheless serves US interests in the area such that a relationship of mutual dependence has also developed between the two in geopolitical, strategic, and even economic issues.

NOTES

[1] Nicholas J. Spykman, America's Strategy in World Politics (Hamden, CT: Archon, 1970) p. 65.
[2] See for example, Bereket H. Selassie, 'The American Dilemma on the Horn,' in Gerald J. Bender, James S. Coleman, and Richard L. Sklar (eds.) African Crisis Areas and US Foreign Policy (Berkeley: University of California Press, 1985) pp. 163-177.
[3] Central Intelligence Agency, Communist Aid Activities in Non- Communist Less Developed Countries 1978, ER 79-10412U, September 1979, p. 20.
[4] United States, Department of Defense, Foreign Military Sales, Foreign Military Construction, and Military Assistance as of 1981, Washington, DC 1981.
[5] See, for example, US Agency for International Development, 'PL 480, Title 2, Africa: Historical Trends.'
[6] Chester Crocker, prepared statement before the Subcommittee on Africa, Committee on Foreign Affairs, US House of Representatives, hearings on 'United States Policy Towards Southern Africa: Focus on Namibia, Angola and South Africa,' Sept. 16, 1981.
[7] UN Commission Against Apartheid, Notes and Documents.
[8] Christian Science Monitor, April 7, 1987, p. 8.
[9] For a discussion of the impact of destabilization efforts by South Africa on the SADCC countries, see William Minter, 'South Africa: Straight Talk on Sanctions,' in Foreign Policy, No. 65, Winter, 1986-87.
[10] Militarism is distinct from military interventions because it is limited to the conduct of joint military exercises between the US and client or friendly states as well as the presence of US bases and fleets in a subregion. Military intervention involves either direct US military action or indirect military action such as the supply of arms, furnishing of intelligence, and covert action aimed at realizing a specific political goal in a state.
[11] Indonesia has made territorial interventions on Moluccas, 1950-52, New Guinea, 1961-62, and East Timor, 1976-77. It is also believed to have designs on North Borneo. For other details, see Gerard Chaliand and

Jean-Pierre Rageau, Strategic Atlas: A Comparative Geopolitics of the World's Powers (New York: Harper and Row, 1985).

[12] US Agency for International Development, Overseas Loans and Grants, July 1, 1945 - September 30, 1978.

[13] United States, Committee for Refugees, Cambodians in Thailand: People on the Edge, Issue Paper, December 1985, p. 7.

[14] See, for example, Richard Nations, 'Subic and Clark,' FEER, May 9, 1985, p. 42.

[15] House of Representatives, Hearings Before the Subcommittee on Human Rights and International Organizations, Human Rights in the Philippines, 1983, p. 17.

[16] US Department of State, The Philippines and the United States, by Under Secretary of State Michael H. Armacost, 1986 pp. 2-3.

[17] Congressional Presentation, Security Assistance, FY 1984, pp. 6-9. Department of State Special Report No. 108 p. 15.

[18] Organisation of the Joint Chiefs of Staff, United States Military Posture for FY 1983. (Washington, DC: Government Printing Office, 1982).

[19] New York Times, March 25, 1979, 'On Eve of Treaty, Guns Pour into the Mideast.'

5 Distributional Trends and Global Priorities

In chapter one, we briefly and in the most general terms touched upon the distributional trends in the foreign aid programme in terms of the level of flows, regional shifts, and stages in its evolution. In a way, we gave the reader an insight into the dynamics and fluid nature of the foreign aid-giving phenomenon. The dynamism and fluidity of the aid programme are particularly related to the changing geopolitical, economic, and social conditions, as well as the dissatisfaction with the results of specific programmes on the part of US government officials. These two factors, among others, have always structured the flow of aid to Third World regions no matter which President is elected to the White House. In this chapter, we hope to analyze in more detail the political-economic march of foreign aid since the end of World War II by focusing on: (1) the relative distribution between military and economic aid in relation to international systemic changes; (2) the regional shifts in terms of priority regions; and (3) the policy changes that are a reflection of new goals for aid and in terms of regional and international geopolitical and economic changes. In other words, the analysis will involve an examination of the systematic linkage between US foreign aid distribution trends and foreign policy priorities.

The present international system which has been in existence for about forty years is a consequence of the destruction of the German and Japanese military regimes. In addition, the power of Great Britain, France, and Portugal as the dominant colonial powers was diminished through the decolonization process. These two factors, among others, largely precipitated the emergence of the US and USSR into positions of leadership in the Western and Eastern blocs respectively. The changed international environment also ushered in the political independence of several new nations constituting a Third World with a strong need for both economic and military aid. The intense immediate post War rivalry between the two superpowers gave a strong justification to the use of foreign aid for containment purposes. The US immediately embarked upon a policy of mutual defense and economic aid with other countries based on the belief that the fragility of many Third World regimes created opportunities for Communist subversion.

The first policy of mutual defense adopted by the US took the form of an aid act that involved Greece and Turkey in 1947. This particular act constitutes the inauguration of US economic and military aid to countries threatened by armed domestic and external groups. The Inter-American Treaty of Reciprocal Assistance of the same year was instrumental in cementing the political and economic ties between the US and the Latin American region. A few years later other mutual multilateral defense policies followed in this order: the North Atlantic Treaty Organization (NATO), 1949; the Australian-New Zeland-US (ANZUS) Treaty, 1951; and the South-East Asia Collective Defense Treaty, 1954. Bilateral Defense Treaties were those with Japan, 1960, South Korea, 1953, and the Philippines, 1951. [1] These policies of mutual defense were predicated first on the need to contain the Soviet threat, and second on the convincing need for economic and military aid to the new nations of the Third World.

MILITARY SECURITY AID FLOWS

The contemporary conduct of US foreign policy is filled with instances of security problems that elicit a US 'military' response. The Korean question in the early 1950's; Indochina in the 1960's and early 1970's; the Middle East in 1967, 1973, and 1982 involving the Israelis and Arabs; in the Horn of Africa between 1977-78; in Central Africa (Shaba Province of Zaire) in 1978; and currently in Central America.

In the distribution of military aid there are discernible trends that provide clues regarding the relative US regional priorities, interests, and commitments underlying US foreign policy. For most of the three decades (1950-1980), Security Assistance has been concentrated mainly in Asia and the

Middle East, for the simple reason that superpower rivalries have been more intense and concentrated in those regions. Table 5.1 is a presentation of the major recipients of Security Assistance and in all categories Middle Eastern and Asian Countries top the list. Other countries receiving continuous military aid since 1950 or independence are Morocco, Tunisia, Zaire, Kenya, Somalia, Oman, and El Salvador. Egypt received significant increases of such aid starting with 1978. Figure 5.1 shows more recent shifts in percentage of military aid by geographic region. Recent shifts in the flow of military aid and in overall US foreign policy attention have concentrated on the Persian Gulf area. The sensitivity of the region is based on the fact of oil as a strategic material to the economies of the West. In 1981 the region produced over 30 per cent of the world's crude oil and supplied more than 56 per cent of the Western world's oil including Japan. Its geostrategic importance is further underscored by the fact that it is at present endowed with over 60 per cent of the world's proven oil reserves. The undisputed strategic importance of the region led the US to establish, as early as 1949, a Middle East Force, based in Bahrain. In 1966, as a way of strengthening its presence in the region, it obtained access to British facilities at the island of Diego Garcia. United States naval presence in the region was further enlarged in 1979 because of the Iranian revolution. The increasing and continuous USSR naval presence in the region has resulted in an enlarged US presence so much so that by the Spring of 1982 the US Middle East Force was five ships strong.

The MAP dominated the US military aid programme for the entire Cold War period until the mid 1960's. In Europe and Third World regions military aid-giving was basically a process of disposing of surplus and scrap weapons from World War II. The US including Great Britain had produced many aircrafts in preparation for a long war against Japan which never materialized. While some weapons were scrap they were also in unused condition. Since it was the period of the Cold War, weapons were distributed on easy terms and often as grants to nations that demanded them and professed to be anti-Soviet. By the early 1950's the grant element of military aid was about $4.5 billion in current dollars. [2] In 1955 the FMS was started and involved making money available to recipient countries for purchase of US military hardware, training, and services. The FMS credit program grew in popularity until the emergence of Bipolycentrism in the mid 1960's. Southeast Asia and the Middle East became the priority regions of the FMS credit program during this transitional period in US foreign policy.

During the transitional stage from Cold War thinking military aid flows were still very significant. In 1965, for

129

Table 5.1
Security Assistance: World Totals and Major
Recipients, 1950-80 (billions of dollars)

	ESF		FMS		IMET		MAP
World Totals	28		22		2		54
Israel	4.0	Israel	12.0	S. Vietnam	0.3	S. Vietnam	14.8
Egypt	4.0	Egypt	1.5	S. Korea	0.2	S. Korea	5.3
S. Korea	2.0	S. Korea	1.2	Turkey	0.1	France	4.0
Turkey	1.0	Greece	1.0	France	0.1	Turkey	3.1
Jordan	0.9	Turkey	1.0	Thailand	0.1	Taiwan	2.6
		Taiwan	0.5	Iran	0.1	Italy	2.0
		Iran	0.5				
		Spain	0.5				
		Jordan	0.4				
		Brazil	0.3				

Source: Atlas of US Foreign Relations US Department of
State Bureau of Public Affairs, Washington, DC June
1983.

130

Figure 5.1

Regional Shifts in Percentage of Military Aid,

1970-1983

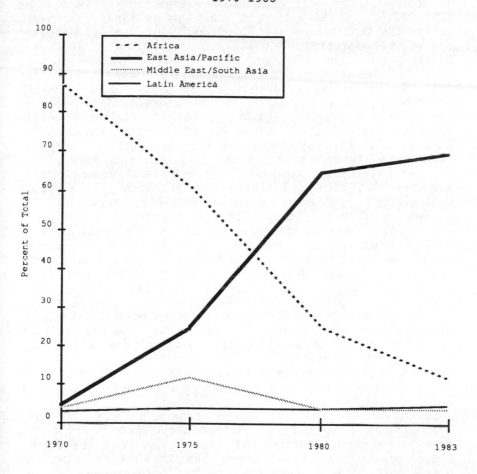

instance, military aid still amounted to $1.325 million. [3] More than 50 per cent of the military aid for that year was extended to the Far East, with Vietnam and Laos receiving 50 per cent of the Far Eastern portion of the aid. Table 5.2 reveals the regional AID commitments for FY 1965. Countries in the Asian and near East regions together received about $300 million of the entire military aid package. Moreover, during the same period the Third World bloc of Asia and the Middle East was being given a substantial amount of low-level military aid as an instrument of influence. The Soviets were by this time strong competitors having started their own military aid-giving programme as early as 1955. The US distributed aid mostly to allies in Southeast Asia, whereas the Soviets aided Cuba, Egypt, Syria, and Vietnam as their priority nations. Military aid-giving even during this period (1965-70) was basically for geopolitical purposes because of its significant grant element. Both superpowers were also reluctant to supply sophisticated weapons mainly for fear that they would fall into the hands of the enemy. Most weapons transferred by the US were often post-World War II surplus from the Korean conflict and the early post-War rearmament of Western Europe. In the Middle East, most of these weapons were used by Israel to fight the Six-Day War of 1967, and in Asia many of such weapons were used in the India-Pakistan War in 1971. The aid transfers were still basically under MAP or FMS credit programs. This, first stage of Bipolycentrism was marked by a rise in the number of state, and non-state actors: guerrilla movements, liberation organizations, and terrorist groups. Many new regimes were experiencing for the first time, political instability and threats to their authority. There was already a high level of intra-regional conflict in the Middle East, and the storms of conflict were gathering in other regions such as Southeast Asia.

By 1972 the military aid programme was becoming increasingly commercial in nature such that by 1974 the credit programme surpassed the grant element in the entire programme. This period which was the second stage of Bipolycentrism was characterized by increased demand for weapons and military services, the emergence of the nouveaux riches oil-importing countries, and seemingly ever present and widespread intra-regional conflicts. Extending from 1970-1980's it was a period in which the US had become embroiled in the Indochina regional conflict. United States aid was concentrated on the Southeast Asian subregion while at the same time aid was being reduced to other regions because of the impact of inflation on the US economy.

The FMS credit sales program increased significantly while the MAP progressively declined together with the Military Assistance Service Funded account (MASF), which provided

Table 5.2
Fiscal Year 1965 Regional AID Commitments
(Millions of Dollars)

Region	Devel. Loans	Tech. Asst.	Support Asst.	Contin-gency Fund	TOTAL
N. East/S. Asia	605.5	49.9	38.5	----	693.9
Latin America	441.5	78.6	35.7	32.3	588.1
Far East	69.4	39.2	326.2	15.0	449.9
Africa	46.1	80.7	37.0	.1	163.9
Total	1,162.5	248.4	437.4	47.4	1,895.8

NOTE: Totals may not add due to rounding.

Source: The Foreign Assistance Programmes: Annual Report to the Congress, Fiscal Year 1965 (Washington: US Government Printing Office, 1966), p. 12.

sizable grant military assistance to five Asian countries allied with the US during the Vietnam conflict. One of the main reasons for the increased demand for military supplies and aid was due to two interrelated factors: the highly conflictual nature of the Middle East and the OPEC price increases. The recurring and ever-present Arab-Israeli conflict had erupted again in October of 1973. The October War was so internecine in character that Israel, Egypt and Syria lost about one-third of their armor and aircraft in the early days of the War. The nations of the region were quick to learn that any state that wants to have the capacity to engage in a prolonged war should guarantee itself a steady supply of weapons from some major supplier. Another way to ensure enough weapons to fight a prolonged war is to stockpile them so that they could be used during a war while negotiating for a steady resupply as the conflict unwinds.

Second, the new found wealth of OPEC nations in a region of high conflict resulted in the use of their money to buy more weapons. The Middle East OPEC members (Saudi Arabia, Libya and others) are characterized by relatively small populations but vast amounts of oil money. In addition, other states like Iran and Iraq have pretensions of regional hegemony and view an increase in military power as one factor towards achieving that goal. Furthermore, by the 1970's the advanced industrial countries were battling with inflation, unemployment, and a recession made worse by the Arab oil embargo and so responded to the increased demand for military aid by shifting the emphasis more to cash and credit sales while de-emphasizing the grant element. The cash and credit sales would help the export sectors of the US to generate more foreign exchange which could help in defraying some of the cost for petroleum imports and assist in 'recycling petrodollars' to help the Western economies recover from their slump.

Table 5.3 is a presentation of the gradual shift in US foreign aid policy from grant aid (MAP and MASF) to foreign military sales and credit agreements for the period 1950-1980. The US, according to the totals at the bottom of the table, made FMS agreements with Third World recipients approaching nearly $80 billion and distributed grant military aid totalling $31.83 billion out of a combined aid package of $111.28 billion. Most of the amount in military agreements and contracts was extended during the 1970's while a substantial part of the grant aid was distributed during the 1950-1970 period and most during the Cold War period. Thus the emphasis from grants to cash and credit sales took hold after the transition from Cold War competition to Bipolycentrism in the international politics of the Superpowers. The shift in aid-giving focus was partly a consequence of the sudden emergence of economic issues which assumed the proportions of high politics. The maintenance and repair of the US economy as a result of the impact of inflation, unemployment, oil prices, and the general recession threatened the economic security and the very foundation of the nation's well-being. The shift was an adaptation to changing times and issues in which simple cold war patterns of interaction were relegated to a secondary role.

Another aspect of US military aid programmes that is worth discussing are the regional trends in distribution. The US military aid package during the Cold War period of 1950-1965 overwhelmingly favoured Western Europe. But the US also gave military aid to South Korea as part of its initial decision to extend the regional emphasis of the containment policy to other regions. Aid during this period was selectively targeted at forward-based recipients, or countries that are in close proximity to the USSR. A substantial shift in the regional scope of aid distribution came by the mid 1960's with the start of Bipolycentrism. Southeast Asia became a significant recipient of aid because of the Vietnam conflict. Aid was no longer just concentrated on countries (allies) bordering the Soviet Union but it was also distributed to those far away (friends). The East Asian subregion was the primary recipient of military grant aid between 1950 and 1980 because of the Vietnam conflict which resulted in the transfer of grants to South Vietnam, South Korea, Cambodia, Laos, and the Philippines particularly during the period 1966-1975.

The regional shift in the concentration of aid was also a result of the US need to assume new roles in the Middle East, the Persian Gulf, and Africa because of the European pull out of these regions. The British, French, Belgians, and Portuguese in the 1960's and 1970's were withdrawing from such strategic areas as Indochina, Central Africa, Southern Africa, and the Suez. The fear was prevalent that the USSR would exploit the power vacuums created by such withdrawals. Foreign military aid was viewed as an effective instrument to signal US readiness to defend the status quo in those areas.

Finally, Table 5.4 shows military aid transfers by programmes and regions covering the Cold War period and a substantial part of the period of Bipolycentrism. The strategic importance of the Middle East and Asia to US foreign policy and their high intra-regional conflictual nature have made them the dominant recipients of US military assistance. In the case of the Middle East its traditional Arab-Israeli conflict has made Egypt and Israeli the key recipients of the grant element in US military aid in the 1980's. The oil wealth of the region has also made it the region with the highest level of arms imports. Latin America and Africa have never been the recipients of large

Table 5.3

Military Aid: Sales[1] and Grants[2] ($ billions)

	FMS Agreements			MAP and MASF		
	1950-1970	1970-1980	Total	1950-1970	1970-1980	Total
East Asia Pacific	$1.44	$10.24	$11.68	$15.87	$12.90	$28.77
Middle East South Asia	2.70	63.00	65.70	1.71	0.46	2.17
Africa	0.01	0.68	0.69	0.17	0.04	0.22
Latin America	0.41	0.97	1.38	0.63	0.04	0.67
Totals	$4.56	$74.89	$79.45	$18.38	$13.44	$31.83

[1]Sales Agreements (includes cash and credit sales)

[2]Grants include both the MAP and MASF

Source: Department of Defense, Defense Security Assistance
           Agency. Foreign Military Sales and Military
           Assistance Facts, 1980.

Table 5.4
US Military Aid by Regions, 1946-1976
(Current dollars, in millions)

Region	MAP Grants 1950-76	FMS Credits 1950-76	Excess Items 1950-76	IMETP Grants 1950-76	Sec. Supp Assist 1946-76	Total 1946-76
East Asia, Total	28,302.7	1,283.8	3,737.3	792.7	11,259.3	45,375.8
Africa, Total	307.4	293.4	56.8	53.5	448.5	1,159.6
Latin America, Total	665.3	833.0	230.4	175.5	664.5	2,568.7
Middle East and South Asia, Total	6,628.0	7,663.1	1,473.4	278.7	5,123.4	21,166.6
Totals	35,903.4	10,096.4	5,497.9	1,300.4	16,995.7	70,293.8

Note: Excess Items are deliveries of 'surplus' US arms. Sec.
Supp. Assist are subsidies provided under the Foreign
Assistance Act to threatened pro-American regimes.

Source: US Defense Security Assistance Agency, Foreign
Military Sales and Military Assistance Facts, 1976.

137

quantities of military aid basically because of their low conflictual nature compared to Asia and the Middle East. In the case of the Middle East the regional concentration of aid reflects US concerns about the political and military stability of the region and the West's uninterrupted access to oil resources. Generally, from 1950 to the 1980's, the US military aid programme has selectively targeted three foreign policy priorities: (1) the security of Western Europe and NATO (1950-1965); (2) the Vietnam Conflict (1966-1975); and (3) peace in the Middle East which involves guaranteeing the security of Israel and the continued flow of Middle Eastern Oil (1974-1980's). Perhaps a fourth foreign policy priority of the 1980's is the US concern about Soviet gains in Central America.

ECONOMIC AID DISTRIBUTION

By 1953 President Eisenhower was already committed to the idea that direct American conflict with the forces of Communism as in Korea should be avoided. In other words US servicemen should if possible, be prevented from fighting directly in the containment of Communism. It was officially believed that a policy of development embracing the Third World would be one way to discourage Communism in those regions. President Eisenhower himself expressed the new emphasis in economic development aid in this way:

This government is ready to ask its people to join with all nations in devoting a substantial percentage of any savings achieved by real disarmament to a fund for world aid and reconstruction. The purposes of this great work would be: To help other peoples to develop the undeveloped areas of the world, to stimulate profitable and fair world trade, to assist all peoples to know the blessings of productive freedom. [4]

In order to enhance the scope of economic development aid, Congress in 1954 started by passing the Agricultural Trade Development and Assistance Act which established the Public Law 480 food aid programme. Initially the PL 480 programme was created not from concern about the Third World but because of a domestic problem of an increasing government agricultural commodity stock of about $5.8 billion in 1954. [5] Title I PL 480 was designed to extend surplus agricultural commodities in return for local currency of recipient nations as payment. It was also aimed at extending loans or grants with the proceeds going to strengthen economic development programmes.

Economic development aid received its next significant

138

emphasis in the early 1960's during the Presidency of John Kennedy. On March 1, 1961 the Peace Corps was established by executive order and on March 13 he launched the Alliance for Progress as a $1 billion 10-year programme of cooperation with Latin America. The emphasis on development aid was based on three rationales: (1) a realization that the existing foreign aid programmes were unsuited to the demands of the 1960's; (2) a recognition of the link between the growth of the Third World and the enhancement of US national security; and (3) the view that the US was facing a unique opportunity to help LDCs towards self-sustained economic growth. The idea of more economic aid had caught on since the Eisenhower era, such that in 1960 alone the US provided almost 60 per cent of total multilateral economic aid to Third World regions through the DAC. [6] India, Pakistan, and Africa received expanded US aid as a consequence.

Economic aid like military aid should be viewed in the context of the changing international environment starting with 1947. The idea of the Cold War first developed and matured in Europe, then Korea, and afterwards in the LDCs. Each change in the geopolitical locus of the rivalry resulted in a fresh evaluation of foreign aid programmes. It was during the third reappraisal of aid policies after Europe and Korea that in 1954 the Cold War was officially shifted to the Third World nations. Europe was almost recovered and the Korean conflict had ended making it possible for the geographic locus of East-West competition to be shifted to Latin America, Asia, Africa, and the Middle East.

Besides, by 1954 US policy-makers had also injected a longterm perspective into the East-West struggle in which economic aid would play a key role because by this time the Third World regions were made up of countries where annual per capita incomes were often below $150. Because of the belief in the linkage between underdevelopment and communist insurgency foreign aid programmes were to be targeted at longterm goals in LDCs. Moreover, the primary recipients of foreign aid were now the emerging Third World Countries. Finally, countries like Taiwan, Korea, Vietnam, Turkey, and Thailand because of their geophysical location near the Sino-Soviet bloc were to be accorded selective targeting in the distribution process.

In 1958 in particular there was an expansion in the foreign aid programme with the bulk of the emphasis on economic aid. Military aid dominated the aid package between 1950 and 1954 but in 1958 total military aid was $2.4 billion whereas total economic aid was $2.9 billion. By the end of the Cold War period and the beginning of Bipolycentrism in 1965 military aid had decreased to $1.3 billion, while economic aid had increased to $4.9 billion. Tables 5.5 and 5.6 show economic aid figures by regions. In Table 5.6 except for Israel and

Table 5.5
Economic Aid: US Grants and Loans: 1948-1980
By Regions

Middle East and South Asia:
$35.1 billion

Africa: 9.0 billion

Country	Amount	Country	Amount
Egypt	7,921.6	Morocco	778.9
Israel	6,369.7	Tunisia	752.1
India	5,777.2	Zaire	606.2
Pakistan	4,158.8	Sudan	489.9
Turkey	2,654.0	Liberia	405.1
Bangladesh	1,698.2	Nigeria	382.5
Greece	1,566.4	Kenya	372.1
Jordan	1,412.9	Ethiopia	328.8
Syria	544.8	Somalia	313.8
Iran	440.6	Tanzania	306.7
Other Nations	2,560.7	Ghana	301.1
		Libya	204.1
		Other Nations	3,740.5

Far East: $24.4 billion

Latin America: 10.9 billion

Country	Amount	Country	Amount
Vietnam	6,457.4	Brazil	1,807.7
S. Korea	5,540.5	Colombia	963.4
Indonesia	2,448.6	Bolivia	730.5
Philippines	2,034.6	Chile	725.3
Taiwan	1,879.6	Dominican	
		Republic	629.3
Japan	1,684.4	Peru	587.6
Laos	902.6	El Salvador	524.5
Cambodia	822.9	Guatemala	429.8
Thailand	716.5	Panama	375.4
Burma	66.3	Nicaragua	358.6
Other Nations	1,834.1	Other Nations	3,733.1

Oceania: $0.9 billion

Aid not allocated by region $29.5 billion

Total US Economic Aid $130.2 billion

Source: US News and World Report, December 13, 1982. Copyright 1982, US News and World Report, Inc.

140

Table 5.6
Changes in the Regional Emphasis of US Bilateral
Aid ($ millions current)

Region	Development Assistance[a]			Security Assistance[b]		
	1977-1980 Avg.	1983	Percentage Change	1977-1980 Avg.	1983	Percentage Change
Sub-Saharan Africa	397.0	518.4	+31%	137.8	402.9	+192%
Middle East &[c] N. Africa	117.3	141.5	+21	602.9	1147.1	+90
Israel and Egypt	193.0	255.1	+32	3685.4	4561.9	+24
East Asia	395.2	237.3	-40	364.1	422.5	+16
South Asia	527.5	559.4	+6	1.0	161.3	+4,603
South America	151.0	194.7	+29	34.5	10.2	-70
Central America[d]	232.5	417.8	+80	21.7	639.1	+2,845
Other	56.8	38.0	-33	450.5	827.1	+84

[a]Development assistance includes bilateral development assistance, PL 480, and other bilateral development programmes.

[b]Security assistance includes all military assistance programs and the ESF.

[c]Excludes Israel and Egypt.

[d]Includes Central America, the Caribbean, and Mexico.

Source: AID, US Overseas Loans and Grants, various issues.

Egypt, and North Africa and the Middle East the average amount of development aid is higher in all regions than the average amount of military aid as measured in current dollars for the period 1977-1980.

By 1965 there had also been a shift in favor of more loans as opposed to grants. The shift was due first to the reduction in military aid which almost always was in grant form during the period 1950-1965. The reduction resulted in more loans because the loan category of the aid package was not reduced. In addition, Congress had earlier expressed the desire in 1946 to place economic aid under loan conditions. However, at the end of 1967, Congress was getting disenchanted with the aid programme and was asking for further justifications in terms of goals and programmes. Donor fatigue, as the prevailing attitude came to be called, was manifested in the hostile posture of Congress towards foreign aid. National public opinion was also at this time strongly against the Vietnam War and with it the distribution of aid which was viewed as instrumental in America's interventionist foreign policy.

In 1967 and 1968 the foreign aid package was cut to its smallest level in ten years. In 1969 President Nixon requested the lowest level of economic aid $2.6 billion in 20 years. [8] He transferred the burden of Third World economic development to private organizations and resource transfers. However, with the recommendations of the Peterson Commission in 1970 it was suggested that the continuous decrease in US development aid be reversed. Another look at Tables 5.5 and 5.6 reveals that US aid distribution during the 1970's underwent marked geographic shifts. As aid inflows to Vietnam ceased as a result of the end of the war, distributional emphasis significantly shifted to Israel and Egypt in support of the efforts at an Arab-Israeli peace settlement.

Furthermore, during the late 1960's and 1970's a new focus was introduced into economic aid: the satisfaction of 'basic needs.' In 1973 the reappraisal of the foreign aid programme resulting in the recommendation to target the poorest countries through the extension of food aid, emphasis on population planning and health, and education and human resources. All this was a result of the Foreign Assistance Act of 1973 which introduced the idea of 'New Directions' of which basic needs is an integral component. New Directions emphasized long-term development aid implemented through local level projects targeted at the poorest of the people. In line with basic needs satisfaction, in 1975 there were further changes in the foreign aid programme. Through the International Development and Food Assistance Act Congress combined the food aid programme with the development aid bill and authorized that about 75 per cent of the Title I PL 480

funds be distributed to the 'poorest countries.' [9]
Congress also shifted to an emphasis on grants instead of
loans for the poorest countries. All along, multilateral
channeling of foreign aid was also being emphasized. For
example, in 1965 only two per cent of US aid was channeled
through the multilateral development banks, but by the mid
1970's an average of about 23 per cent was being channeled
through those banks.

In more recent years military aid is becoming comparatively
more important than economic aid. Reference to Figure 5.2
supports this observation as seen in the rising trend of
military aid. With the Reagan Administration the 1982
economic aid bill dropped significantly. There has since
been a trend to underscore the security aspect of US economic
aid and its role as a vehicle of foreign policy. Aid is used
to pursue short term political objectives especially with the
designation of ESF as non-military aid. Significant amounts
of ESF have been extended to Egypt and Israel to encourage
their cooperation in the Middle East peace process.
Recipient Countries UN voting patterns are indexed to US
aid-giving. Moreover, aid-giving has assumed a more
selective orientation because of its concentration on
troubled spots and liberation movements.

Finally, the annual level of foreign economic aid has grown
only modestly since 1949 because of a combination of donor
fatigue, poor global economic conditions, and the policy
orientation of the Reagan Administration. When aid
allocations are indexed to population growth, we find that
per capita aid receipts have actually dropped. Measured in
constant dollars, US aid between 1946-1955 is nearly two
times that for the 1976-1985 decade. Furthermore, just as in
the early Eisenhower years, the Reagan Administration changed
the character and pattern of aid-giving by its de-emphasis on
concessional aid and a renewed emphasis on private aid, trade
and investment.

THE ROLE OF PRESIDENTIAL ADMINISTRATIONS

A detailed historical and current analysis of the US aid
programme is definitely not the objective of this book. The
above examination of regional, programme, and policy trends
has been at best very selective and purposefully geared to
buttress our exploration of the interplay between
geopolitical realities, regional politics, systemic changes,
and US foreign policy with emphasis on the articulation of
foreign aid in the whole process. In order to fill in the
gaps that may still exist, as well as supplement the above
analysis, this section of the chapter will highlight the
major issues within each US administration from Truman to

Figure 5.2

Trends in U.S. Economic and Military Aid, 1977-1984

(billions of dollars)

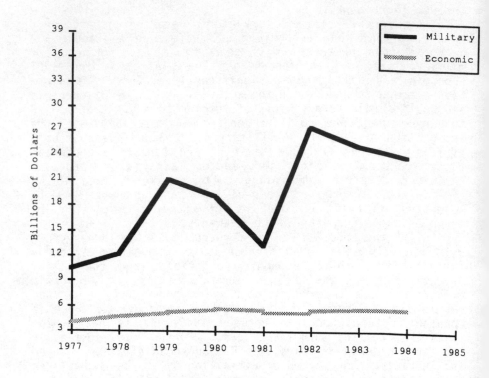

Source: Adapted from U.S. <u>Overseas Loans and</u>
            <u>Grants and Assistance from</u>
            <u>International Organizations</u>, 1985:4;
            and <u>Military Assistance Facts</u>, 1985:2.

Reagan, that have had a direct bearing on developments in the foreign aid programme.

The Truman Administration was the turning point in US foreign policy with the overall shift from the isolationism of the interwar years to active international engagement. The 'strategy of containment' which resulted, with its focus on a global network of military bases, alliances, and foreign aid relationships differed significantly from US policy during the interwar years and the era of President Franklin Roosevelt. Africa, Latin America, the Middle East, and Asia would emerge in later administrations as the theatre of competition between the US and USSR. By the time of the Eisenhower Administration the policy of containment had become a bedrock of post-World War II US foreign policy and found its first direct military application in the Korean conflict. The Korean conflict is significant in overall US foreign policy because it marked the first East-West military confrontation in the Cold War rivalry, and also signalled the difficulty the US would later encounter in the Asian region in pursuit of containment. Experience would reveal that geopolitical and strategic realities and circumstances differ regionally and over time and profoundly affect US ability to effectively use foreign resources to achieve foreign policy goals.

In August 1953 the US signed a security treaty with the Republic of Korea thereby setting in motion the signing of similar other treaties extending from Northeast Asia to the Middle East region. In continuation with the Truman Administration, Eisenhower supported France in Indochina. The importance he attached to the region is due to his realization of its geostrategic location and salience as a source of raw materials. United States support of the region was strengthened because both Eisenhower and John Foster Dulles subscribed to the Domino Theory, implying that the fall of Indochina would inevitably lead to the loss of all Southeast Asia.

To guarantee the viability and survival of the Indochina states -- Laos, Cambodia, Vietnam -- the Eisenhower Administration in 1954 included them in a military alliance, the South East Asia Treaty Organization (SEATO). Great Britain, France, Thailand, the Philippines, Australia, New Zealand, and the US were the other members of the organization. Although seemingly ambitious, it did not include some of the most important regional powers: Indonesia, Burma, and Malaysia. As a military alliance it was not as viable as NATO.

With the decline of British and French influence in Third World regions, the US had emerged as the most influential Western actor, and it was in the Middle East that the US played one of its most significant backup role for Britain and France. The resurgence of radical nationalism and anti-colonial sentiments between 1953 and 1958 resulted in the US having to fill the vacuum created by gradual British and French withdrawal from the region. Beginning with the 1950s the US was faced with the formidable and delicate task of trying to reconcile Israel's desire to survive and Arab demands in the region.

The US was not only regionally involved but at times intervened internally in its goal to influence events. In Iran due to Premier Mohamed Mossadequ's seeming vulnerability towards the Communist groups, the US supported the Shah in the domestic power struggle. Domestic Iranian conflicts eventually came to an end when Mossadeq was overthrown by the Iranian military forces. The Shah was installed as ruler and the Eisenhower Administration extended about $85 million in economic aid to Iran between 1953-1954. The oil dispute between Iran and Britain which was the major issue was eventually settled.

The priority task for the US in the Middle East increasingly became the frustration of Soviet objectives. In order to at least achieve the goal of reducing Soviet influence, President Eisenhower in January 5, 1987 proclaimed the Eisenhower Doctrine. [10] The Doctrine was a two-fold request: extension of military aid and $200 million in economic aid to help safeguard the independence of countries in the region, and second, authorization to use military force in the event of direct aggression by the Soviets and its clients against any countries in the region.

The Eisenhower Doctrine is significant because the US had come to recognize and accept the fact that the Middle East is a geopolitically important region in terms of US foreign policy. Through the Doctrine the foundation for the extension of aid to recipients in the region had been laid. The Doctrine and its emphasis on aid marked the beginning of an aid race between the two Superpowers in the region. It was also a reaction to significant extensions of Soviet aid to Egypt in response to a request from President Nasser. In addition to being an ally of the Soviets Nasser was also waging a strong campaign against moderate and conservative regimes. Jordan was so threatened by Nasser's Campaign that the US extended a grant of $10 million to it in 1957. Moreover, the Sixth Fleet was moved to the eastern Mediterranean in support of Jordan because of the campaign waged against its regime by Nasser.

Furthermore, it was during the Eisenhower Administration that the first rumblings of regional instability began in Latin America and the Caribbean. These agitations were not confined to that region alone but were in fact the start of a phenomenon sweeping over all Third World regions. This phenomenon sometimes referred to as 'the obsession to catch up' is an integral part of the 'revolution of rising expectations' that has produced violent revolutions in certain Third World Countries. The Soviet Union is viewed by the US as exploiting the agitation of Third World regions through appeals to the Marxist-Leninist ideals of social equality.

The US has always been determined to maintain its influence over Latin America and the Caribbean. This determination was manifested in the overthrow in April 1954 of the Arbenz regime because it enocuraged pro-Communist groups, and its replacement with the anti-Communist regime of Castillo Armas. The Eisenhower Administation also effectively checked the inflow of Eastern-bloc arms to Central America and the entire region. Increased foreign aid was extended to the region through multilateral institutions like the IFC, the IDA, and the Inter-American Development Bank. Overall, the distribution of both private and governmental aid increased from $232 million in 1953 to a peak of $1.6 billion in 1957. [11]

In the region of Africa, the decolonization process was just getting underway, and the US had few vital interests to safeguard in the region. The eventual US backup role was limited and still in its earliest stages. In the Congo crisis, the Administration supported UN multilateral action by providing airlift and supplies for a peace-keeping force made up mostly of Moroccan and Tunisian troops. Thus, the US assumption of European responsibilities vis-a-vis their former colonies first started with the Eisenhower Administration. The increasing backup role that the US would have to play was dictated by power vacuums created as a result of the decolonization process.

The Eisenhower presidency came to an end leaving the overall impression that it had not been dynamic enough in pursuing the goal of containing Communism. This impression specifically had a bearing on the loss of Cuba. Instead of an active containment policy, the administration was viewed as conducting a reactive one particularly regarding Cold War issues.

President Kennedy came to power with the aim of improving on the past administration's achievements. In order to do this he emphasized the role that foreign aid can play in alleviating Third World political instability. Thus, his focus was on improving the quality of life in Third World regions. The programmes that had been designed to help farmers sell their surplus crops abroad were renamed and put under the category of Public Law 480, 'Food for Peace.' An average of nearly $1.5 billion yearly was shipped to Third World regions that were particularly threatened by starvation.

Greater attention was focused on Latin America which had

been neglected by the Truman and Eisenhower Administrations due to their preoccupation with Europe and Asia. Because of its proximity to the US, the foundation for a closer cooperation between it and the US had already been laid in the past. Franklin Roosevelt's Good Neighbor Policy was part of the structure of such a foundation, in addition to the binding role of the Organization of American States (OAS). Kennedy's new emphasis on the region is summarized in the following passage from his inaugural address:

> To our sister republics --- we offer a special pledge: to convert our good words into good deeds, in a new alliance for progress, to assist free men and free governments in casting off the chains of poverty. But this peaceful revolution of hope cannot become the prey of hostile powers. Let all our neighbors know that we shall join with them to oppose aggression or submission anywhere in the Americas. And let every other power know that this hemisphere intends to remain the master of its own house. [12]

The OAS was one of the instruments used by Kennedy to isolate pro-Communist oriented states like Cuba and to check the spread of revolution to other parts of the region. In addition Peace Corps were sent to various parts of the region and increased amounts of Food for Peace shipped to the impoverished segments of the population.

The Kennedy Administration increased US role in Africa because by the early 1960's the decolonization process was fully under way. This period saw the increased extension of the Cold War to the region and the administration tried to dissuade some African leaders from their pro-Marxist tendencies. Sekou Toure of Guinea and Kwame Nkrumah of Ghana were two such leaders. In a dispute between Toure and the Soviets, the Soviet ambassador was eventually expelled from Guinea. Kennedy was able to seize upon the subsequent deterioration in relations between Guinea and Moscow. Toure was removed from Soviet influence with offers of aid and assistance from Peace Corps. Although Nkrumah was reluctant to sever links with Moscow, the Kennedy Administration still approved the allocation of aid funds to Ghana for the completion of the Volta Dam project.

In the case of Portugal and her colonies geopolitical realities and geostrategic expediency tended to supersede political matters like the granting of independence or the political orientation of a leader. For this reason, Kennedy ended up supporting Portugal in the UN regarding the issue of Angolan independence. Opposing Portugal may have led to the loss of the Azores base thereby jeopardizing NATO needs. Similarly, in trying to persuade Nasser to abandon his regional imperialist goals for internal economic development, the US increased the flow of PL 480 food aid to Egypt.

In conformity with past administrations, the Johnson presidency focused its attention on containing Soviet expansionist tendencies. On May 2, 1965 the Johnson Doctrine was proclaimed particularly with regard to Latin America and read: 'The American nations cannot, must not, and will not permit the establishment of another Communist government in the Western Hemisphere.' The Doctrine was proclaimed mainly because of the Dominican crisis and subsequent US intervention to forestall chaos and communist gains in the region.

In the Middle East Johnson was faced with the problem of balancing US foreign policy between the radical states (Algeria, Iraq, Syria, and the United Arab Republic) and a more conservative group of states (Morocco, Tunisia, Lebanon, Jordan, Libya, Saudi Arabia, and the Persian Gulf Sheikdoms). United States relations with the latter group was mostly cordial and strengthened by the extension of military aid to many of its members. The former group made up of radical socialist oriented regimes received aid mostly from the USSR. The US thus found itself in the dilemma of trying to balance its relationship to both groups as well as to Israel. All Arab states condemned the US for extending economic and military aid to Israel. The US often used its aid as a weapon to punish or apply leverage in disputes between radical and moderate states. In the Egyptian-Saudi conflict over Yemen the US in June 1966 refused to renew the agreement to ship food to Egypt under PL 480 because of Egyptian refusal to pull out its troops from Yemeni soil.

With regard to the Southeast Asia region, the Kennedy Administration bequeathed the Vietnam crisis to Johnson. Subscribing to the Domino Theory of Eisenhower, Kennedy had supported the provision of advisers, trainers, equipment, supplies, and other types of resource transfer to Vietnam. Johnson thus became a captive of this policy of commitment aimed at keeping the country and by extension the subregion, free of communism. It was in fact during the Kennedy Administration that the US became politically and militarily committed to Vietnam. This commitment was reinforced by the massive flow of economic and military aid which accelerated the escalation sequence of the crisis until the transfer of foreign aid amounted to $1 billion per month by 1966.

During the Johnson presidency Africa did not figure prominently in US geopolitical conduct because of the significant involvement with Vietnam. Events in Africa such as the leadership struggle in the Congo in 1965 received hardly any US foreign policy attention. Overall, US foreign policy in other Third World regions was overshadowed by the Vietnam conflict. Besides, due to their relative stability

149

compared to the Southeast Asian subregion they received little US geopolitical attention.

The Nixon and Ford eras represented a break with the past patterns of US foreign policy because of the proclamation of the Nixon Doctrine. [13] It became a rationale that largely structured US geopolitical behaviour in Third World regions. As a doctrine it eliminated the practice of committing US troops to aid countries fighting Communism. Emphasis was instead put on the supply of economic aid and military equipments to states willing and capable of fighting Soviet influence. The doctrine was a direct consequence of the Nixon Administration's reevaluation of US role in the Vietnam conflict. American economic and military aid would instead supplement the determination of recipient countries to fight their own wars of liberation.

In 1974 Congress gradually reduced aid to Vietnam as the beginning of a pull out process. In early 1975 there were hints that aid might be totally curtailed. President Ford's request in April 1975 for $72 million in military aid and $250 million in humanitarian and economic aid to Vietnam was denied by the Congress. This denial of aid to Vietnam marked a shift in regional geopolitical focus from Southeast Asia to the Middle East.

For the Nixon Administration in particular the major focus of foreign policy became the Middle East especially after the realization that Vietnam was lost. Besides, there was a need to shift focus because in the 1970's the USSR was militarily active in the region as an arms supplier and economic aid donor to several states including Egypt, Syria, and Iraq.

As in the past, the US again faced the formidable task of balancing its interests and relations among the Arab states on the one hand, and between the Arab states and Israel on the other. Egypt particularly became a target of US foreign policy influence. The Soviet Union at the same time was making strong efforts to exploit the hostile relationship between Egypt and Israel and other Arab states. This it did partly through the massive injection of advisers and technicians and the deployment of surface-to-air missiles in pro-Soviet countries. An aid race in military equipments gradually took shape in which the Superpowers became the major suppliers. The deployment by the USSR of numerous new sites for SA-2 and SA-3 ground-to-air missiles led the Nixon Administration to push for increased military aid to Israel, and moderate arms transfers to Lebanon and Jordan so that a military balance could be restored in the region.

Foreign aid was viewed in the Nixon/Ford era as playing a special role in furthering US objectives. Technology transfer in the form of military hardware together with significant levels of economic aid would enable, it was argued, regional powers like Iran to effectively contain hostile external threats without the direct military intervention of the US. To emphasize the corresponding focus on economic development the Nixon/Ford Administration underscored the importance of the private sector in extending development aid to Third World regions. At the same time as Soviet activities in the Middle East were taking root, its strategy in other parts of the Third World were undergoing change. The Soviet mode of operation was particularly changing in Africa where in addition to the transfer of large quantities of military aid and advisers, Cuban and other proxy forces were working to further USSR objectives.

Although facing formidable challenges in other regions, the US was determined to prevent any further Cubas in Latin America. The US therefore turned its attention to Chile and tried to thwart the electoral ambitions of pro-Marxist Salvador Altende and his supporters. Although aid was never cut off from Chile despite its subsequent Marxist regime, in September 1973 Altende was finally eliminated by an uprising of the military. In Asia the East Pakistan secession question led the US to move naval units to the Indian Ocean. Economic aid was cut off from India due to its invasion of East Pakistan and its cosy relationship with the USSR. The US shifted its support to Pakistan in order to restore some geopolitical and strategic balance in the Indian subregion. Overall the Nixon/Ford Administrations pursued limited objectives with the efficient use of limited economic and military resources. The idea of linkage became an integral part of US foreign policy thereby starting the tradition of tying US-Soviet issues to Soviet geopolitical conduct in the international arena.

The Carter Administration made a significant departure from a foreign policy structured by geopolitical concerns to one of international economic cooperation. After criticizing past administrations for their preoccupation with East-West issues and Soviet security threats, he proclaimed that his presidency would reject 'the inordinate fear of Communism which once led us to embrace any dictator who joined us in that fear.' [14] Issues of economic development, trade and investment, and human rights became the cornerstone of foreign policy. Closer political and economic cooperation between advanced industrial countries and the Third World was considered as the best way to solve the world's problems, and by extension the best way to further the US national interest.

However, by the second half of the 1970's, the previous superimposition of the US-Soviet struggle on the regions of Africa and Southeast Asia contributed to the intensification of the ever present US-Soviet rivalry. In the late 1970's the Soviet strategy of expansionism intensified in the regions of Southeast Asia and Southern Africa. This

151

development shattered President Carter's conviction that the East-West geopolitical struggles could be divorced from Third World issues.

Not long after his assumption of the presidency, Carter was confronted with a shifting of alignments in the Horn of Africa. By the Middle of 1977 the USSR had sided with Ethiopia in the Somali-Ethiopian conflict. This realignment was facilitated by the emergence of a pro-Marxist government in Ethiopia. Soviet presence in the Horn of Africa assumes grave proportions for US policy because of its proximity to the Persian Gulf. Besides, the presence of another pro-Soviet regime in South Yemen signalled a gradual and systematic Soviet advantage in the region.

The distinguishing feature of the Carter Administration was its deemphasis on foreign aid to contain Soviet intrusions. Since geopolitics was not a concern of the administration, aid transfer was not viewed as a significant foreign policy instrument. The administration withheld military aid to Somalia with the hope that the Soviet Union would agree to the withdrawal of all foreign forces and mediation of the Ethiopia-Somali conflict by other states in the region. Moreover, the Carter Administration often maintained a self-imposed restraint on military aid to friendly states as it did in the case of Somalia. Even in the Shaba incident in which Angolan-sponsored mercenaries were sent to destabilize the Zairean political system, the administration limited its military aid to the shipment of rifle ammunition. Within the subregion of Southern Africa the administration was bent on eliminating or sharply reducing the Soviet-Cuban military presence as well as the transfer of arms by both the US and USSR.

The normalization of relations with the PRC begun by the Nixon/Ford Administrations was completed by the Carter Administration. But it was not until the middle of 1978 that the PRC became the focus of US policy. In order to strengthen Sino-Soviet relations the administration assured the Chinese of US determination to contain Soviet expansionism and military buildup. The US also promised to reduce its military presence in Taiwan and work closely with the PRC in opposition to Soviet presence in key areas of the Third World such as the Horn of Africa, Southern Africa, and Southeast Asia.

The Soviet invasion of Afghanistan further motivated the US to forge closer ties with the PRC as a check to the expansionist tendencies of the USSR. After the invasion the sale of certain types of 'defensive' military weapons to the PRC was authorized by the administration. By 1980 relations had advanced to the level where the PRC was declared a friendly nation. More military equipment and air defense radar were added to the list of weapons authorized for sale to the PRC. This transfer and sale of arms marked a slight departure from Carter's policy of deemphasizing military aid and military concerns in the conduct of foreign policy.

In trying to dilute the Soviet-Cuban military cooperation, the Carter Administration made efforts to improve relations with Castro's Cuba in the hope of eventually undermining Soviet influence in that country. This strategy, if successful, would in turn eliminate the use of Cuban troops as surrogates for Soviet expansionist policies in Third World regions. Despite the establishment of some diplomatic contact with Cuba in early 1977, the use of Cuban proxy military forces by the USSR increased in Ethiopia and Southern Africa. In Asia, Afghanistan fell gradually into the Soviet camp. Radical leftist military elements were able to install in April 1978 a pro-Soviet regime in Afghanistan. Increased instability and opposition to pro-Soviet changes led the Soviet Union to eventually invade Afghanistan.

A series of events, all advantageous to the Soviets led the Carter Administration to reassess its foreign policy behavior. First there was the expansion of Soviet influence in Southern Africa, then the fall of the Shah, and the Soviet invasion of Afghanistan. The last event was even more ominous because it marked the first time the Soviets have invaded a country outside the Soviet bloc.

The Carter Doctrine proclaimed in early 1980 was a reaction to the apparent foreign policy failures. The Doctrine was particularly aimed at the Soviet moves in the Persian Gulf and read: 'Let our position be absolutely clear: An attempt by any outside force to gain control of the Persian Gulf region will be regarded as an assault on the vital interests of the United States of America, and such an assault will be repelled by any means necessary, including military force.' The Doctrine marked a departure from the earlier pattern of policy in the administration. It also underscored the geostrategic importance of the Gulf region to US and Western security. Thus in the end, the Carter Administration was forced by Soviet geopolitical gains to also adopt a geopolitical rationale as a pattern of foreign policy. Military capabilities and alliances were again invoked as instruments for containing the Soviets. This apparent change in the conduct of foreign policy was created more by events than by design. Both economic and military aid once more became a cornerstone of US geopolitical conduct. The creation of the Rapid Deployment Joint Task Force became the first manifestation of this foreign policy shift.

Taking over from the Carter Administration with its apparent setbacks in containing Soviet influence, the Reagan Administration became preoccupied and concerned about the decline in US power. President Reagan immediately decided to revert to the traditional view of the Soviet Union as the main geopolitical and strategic threat to US national security. Containing Soviet expansionism through the use of foreign policy capabilities once more became the focus of American foreign policy. All regions, it is argued, are linked to the security of the US, and therefore open to US intervention when considered appropriate.

In the early 1980's the US adopted a geopolitical and military strategy that involved two contrasting approaches: The 'peripheral strategy' and the 'continental strategy.' The former called for a substantial defense burden sharing by allies so that the US could concentrate more of its energies in containing the Soviets in other regions like the Persian Gulf. The latter strategy called for the presence of enough US military capabilities in Western Europe and Northeast Asia that would serve as a check on USSR objectives. A US-USSR linkage of geopolitical conduct as in the Nixon Administration, also became an aspect of the US determination to check Soviet expansionist goals.

In South America the Reagan Administration, more so than previous administrations, viewed the subregions of Central America and the Caribbean as geopolitically and militarily important to US security. Central America in particular constituted a territorial link between North and South America and would pose enormous obstacles to the US if controlled by the Soviets. The Central American question is made more complicated by the presence of Cuba as a Soviet client and the growing influence of the USSR in Nicaragua. Stemming the tide of Soviet influence in Nicaragua took the form of funding a growing anti-Sandanista force, now known as Contras, whose aim is to disrupt military installations. The determination to topple the pro-Marxist Sandanista regime is so strong that $100 million in aid was voted in 1985 for the Contras. In line with checking the spread of Soviet influence in the subregion, the Kissinger Commission recommended a massive increase in economic and military aid for the countries of El Salvador, Honduras, and Costa Rica.

The importance attached to the Caribbean is no less than that attached to Central America. In 1980, the Reagan Administration extended $90 million in bilateral aid to the new pro-capitalist Edward Seaga government. [15] The Seaga government also received support from the US for a $600 million loan from the International Monetary Fund (IMF) during the same year. Considered as a threat, the Soviet military buildup in Grenada became the immediate focus of the Reagan Administration in 1980. The close links with Castro's Cuba, the construction of a huge airport with Soviet and Cuban aid, and the political instability created by infighting among the leftist elite led the US to invade the island in 1983. The underlying and long term reason for invasion was the perception that completion of the airport

154

could serve as a base and landing area for Cuban forces in support of Soviet interests in the subregion and beyond.

The Reagan Administration, perhaps more than previous administrations, openly considers Israel as a strategic ally in the Middle East. In addition to the attempt to build a 'strategic consensus' embracing many Arab states in the area, it has also emphasized the importance of the Rapid Deployment Force created during the Carter Administration. Greater emphasis on US military power in the region is based on the conviction that, in the final analysis, there was no substitute for US power in any region. Interstate rivalry posed the most immediate security problem in the Middle East. Thus a massive extension of military aid or arms sale to Saudi Arabia affects Israeli perception of security even though Saudi Arabia is also a geostrategic pro-Western state in the region. The US offers protection to Saudi Arabia against radical forces and communist groups in the region because of their dislike for monarchical regimes.

Within Africa, in particular the Horn of Africa, the Reagan Administration was faced with the need to support Somalia against pro-Soviet Ethiopia regarding the dispute over the Ogaden. Foreign aid did not play a very significant role in Africa because of the selective use of aid by the Administration. In the whole region foreign economic aid is limited to just under $1 billion a year. The rest of the aid to the region comes from multilateral financial institutions like the IMF and the World Bank. In Southern Africa, the Reagan Administration shifted from Carter's strategy of confrontation to 'constructive engagement' with emphasis on quiet diplomacy. Constructive engagement, it is argued, would lead to improved relations and the eventual dismantling of Apartheid which is essential to US strategic interests because of South Africa's geostrategic location astride the vital sea lanes around the Cape of Good Hope between the Indian Ocean and the South Atlantic. This strategic importance is further reinforced by South Africa's vast deposits of some of the most important minerals that are critical to the defense and commercial industries of the West.

In the Asian region President Reagan pledged to maintain US forces in South Korea as a check on North Korean and Soviet aggression. This pledge was cemented by the announcement of a five-year military aid programme that included arms sales to South Korea totalling $4.7 billion. In the Afghanistan conflict the US extended arms and humanitarian aid to the anti-Soviet Mujaheddin through Pakistan. Egypt and Saudi Arabia also gave aid to the Mujaheddin through Pakistan. In the whole geopolitical balance in the region, Pakistan is very central to US objectives because it constitutes a barrier to southward Soviet expansion into South Asia. Thus in 1981 the US negotiated with Pakistan a $3.2 billion military and economic aid that included the transfer of F-16 aircraft, destroyers, and antiship missiles.

SUMMARY

In the evolution of US foreign aid, the shifts in distributional emphasis in terms of specific economic and military aid programmes (MAP, FMS, MASF, PL 480 and so on), priority recipient regions, and policy amendments have been structured by a combination of American reaction to international and/or regional systemic politics.   For example, the grant element in the military aid programme was dominant during the Cold War period, but with Bipolycentrism military aid programmes became more commercial in orientation as a result of the global recessions, the new-found wealth of oil-rich nations, and increased regional conflicts which produced an intensified demand-supply relationship.

Regions of potential and actual conflict are accorded top priority, especially in military resource allocations, such that most US foreign aid since the 1950s has been concentrated in the top two conflictual regions of Asia and the Middle East.   Geostrategic location, strategic minerals, in addition to crisis situations are key elements in superpower competition for influence underpinned largely by resource transfers.

Finally, the various stages in aid levels and orientation have been structured by a number of rationales such as: (1) traditional ties between the US and the Third World region or nation; (2) the degree of importance of the recipient state regarding trade and investment issues; (3) the geostrategic and economic commitments and interests of the US in a particular region; and (4) the perception of US administrations regarding the role of foreign aid in securing American goals overseas.   In line with the above rationales, US aid-giving behaviour has been mainly bilateral with the emphasis on the interrelationship of security and economic aid.   Security assistance in particular has become an integral part of foreign policy.   It obviates the necessity for a direct US intervention in regions of uncertainty and competition.   Consequently, bilateral security aid is directed at: (1) pro-American regimes that are threatened by domestic anti-America groups such as in El Salvador; (2) regimes that are unstable as a result of external factors such as Pakistan or Zaire; and (3) pro-American regimes threatened by both internal and external destabilizing factors such as South Korea.

NOTES

[1] See, for example, US, Department of State, Atlas of the US Foreign Relations Bureau of Public Affairs, June 1983.

[2] US, Department of Defense, Defense Security Assistance Agency. Foreign Military Sales and Military Facts, 1980.

[3] US Agency for International Development, The Foreign Assistance Programs: Annual Report to the Congress, Fiscal Year 1965, 1966.

[4] The Public Papers of the Presidents of the United States, April 16, 1954.

[5] US, Congress, Senate, Agricultural Trade Development and Assistance Act, April 1955.

[6] OECD, Twenty-Five Years of Development Cooperation: A Review, 1985 Report, p. 69.

[7] US, Agency for International Development, Proposed Mutual Defense and Development Programs, FY 1966, Summary Presentation to Congress, March, 1965.

[8] US, Department of State, Presentation Document, Foreign Assistance, FY 1968.

[9] US, Congress, Senate, International Development and Food Assistance Act, April, 1975.

[10] For details of President Eisenhower's focus on the Middle East, see, Charles C. Alexander, Holding the Line: The Eisenhower Era 1952-1961 (Bloomington, Indiana: Indiana University Press, 1975).

[11] See, for example, US, Department of State, The Foreign Relations of the United States, 1957, p. 57.

[12] The full text of President Kennedy's inaugural address is found in, The Public Papers of the Presidents of the United State, Department of State Publication, 1964.

[13] For further details about the Doctrine, see, Richard M. Nixon, The Memoirs of Richard Nixon (New York: Grosset and Dunlap, 1978).

[14] See, The Public Papers of the Presidents of the United States, 1978.

[15] See, for example, US News and World Report, 'Foreign Aid: Reaching Bottom of the Barrel,' December 13, 1982.

6 The Doctrinal Articulation: Presidential Doctrines and Foreign Aid

What makes American foreign policy and by extension its aid distribution policies unique is that its doctrinal basis gives structure, pattern, and justification to the pursuit of regional and global objectives. Doctrines articulate the goals of US foreign policy, the values that give life to those objectives, and the means through which those objectives are pursued and protected. They have been particularly useful in pinpointing continuity and change in US foreign policy such that distinct historical periods and developments and their impact on US foreign policy could be identified and analyzed.

By 1945 presidential doctrines had developed into a bedrock of American foreign policy since President James Monroe enunciated the now immortal Monroe Doctrine in 1823. Its specific objective was to forestall a possible European recolonization and expansion into the Western hemisphere. [1] In particular, it was a reaction to the intentions of a European reconquest of Latin American republics for Spain, as well as a warning to Czarist Russia against any Russian expansionist moves into the Americas. In contemporary times presidential doctrines are entirely a response to the hegemonic and expansionist tendencies of the Soviet Union. As a response to real or potential threats doctrines have since the nineteenth century been used to:

(1) preserve the status quo in volatile regions; (2) contain Soviet foreign policy objectives; (3) give coherence to US

foreign policy and justification for resource transfers; and (4) provide justification for defense of overall US national interest.

In this chapter the focus will be on a detailed exposition of presidential doctrines and their articulation into overall foreign policy and foreign aid distribution. The continuity and change inherent in successive doctrines have a direct bearing on the rhythm and flow of foreign aid dollars to specific regions. The questions that will be addressed are: (1) what role do presidential doctrines play in the aid distribution relationship? (2) how do they contribute to the effectiveness or ineffectiveness of foreign aid as an instrument of foreign policy? and (3) what will be the future role of doctrines in aid flows to regions? In order to facilitate the analysis, the impact of regional crises on doctrinal pronunciations will be emphasized, as well as the manner in which doctrines structure aid-giving assumptions and rationales. In sum, the relationship between crises, doctrines, and aid-giving will be underscored.

THE TRUMAN DOCTRINE

President Truman's address to a joint session of Congress in March, 1947 emphasized the concern of the US over the Greek and Turkish crises. Although the initial focus was on those two specific events the proclamation and its principles assumed the proportions of a doctrine which became known as the 'Truman Doctrine.' As the first post World War II pronouncement by an American president, it marked a watershed between the isolationist mood of the interwar years and the globalist mood of post World War II American foreign policy. Policies and programmes aimed at strengthening other nations from external communist interventions immediately became a cornerstone of US foreign policy.

The Soviet Union was the primary target of the goals inherent in the Truman Doctrine. At the request of Great Britain the US became very instrumental in guaranteeing Greek independence against what was believed in Western circles to be a Soviet-inspired crisis aimed at replacing the existing Greek regime with a Communist regime. [2] Greek complaints to the UN about Soviet intervention in its domestic affairs were used as a justification for the extension of foreign aid and the sending of a US technical aid mission to Greece. The implementation of the Truman Doctrine was further rationalized in terms of the announced British withdrawal from Greece. The threat posed by the USSR to Greece as well as the perception of overall Soviet intentions in the area led President Truman to ask Congress to appropriate $250 million of mostly economic aid to Greece. The request itself marked a significant step in the conduct of foreign policy. It was an indication that the US from that moment on would use foreign aid as an instrument as well as a cornerstone of foreign policy in the game of influence buying within regions.

The Truman Doctrine was also applied in the case of Soviet-Turkish relations. The Soviets were exerting undue pressure on Turkey because of their ambitions to gain unlimited access to the Mediterranean through the Turkish straits. [3] Pressure on the Iranian provinces of Kars and Ardahan which caused concern in Turkey was also followed by a Soviet propaganda pressure directed at the Turkish government. In order to strengthen Turkey from undue Soviet pressures a programme of foreign aid was considered necessary to guarantee its security. On March 1947, the Truman Doctrine found expression for a second time in the decision to provide $150 million of foreign aid to Turkey.

An immediate accomplishment and significant objective of the Truman Doctrine was the safeguarding of Greek and Turkish security from Soviet encroachments. The US focus on Greece and Turkey through the proclamation of a new doctrine backed by the distribution of foreign aid were effective in defusing the internal threat to the Greek government and the efforts by the Soviets to destabilize and eventually dominate Turkey. By the early 1950's Greek and Turkish political stability had been restored and Soviet expansionist moves slowed down. In particular an innovation in foreign policy characterized by the selective and penetrative use of foreign aid to contain the Soviet Union came into being. Selectivity in the conduct of foreign policy is in many instances structured by the tendency of policy makers to react to the real or imagined threats of Soviet Communism. Foreign aid extension is then used to gain entrance into a nation-state threatened by the USSR. The strategy of selective targeting underscores the reality of foreign aid being a costly way of conducting foreign policy and as a result the finite amount of aid available is distributed in significant amounts only at certain time periods if foreign aid is to be an effective and lasting instrument of policy.

The Truman Doctrine emphasized the economic developmental aspect of foreign aid and the recovery it could produce in recipient countries. The Greek-Turkish Aid Programme focused on economic aid and economic reconstruction instead of on military aid. The fact that economically and socially fragile societies are plagued by political instability, US foreign aid was designated to provide the social and economic strength that fragile countries need if they are to maintain their independence and territorial integrity.

The success of the Greek-Turkish Aid Programme created a new perception of foreign aid as a vehicle of foreign policy.

If aid-giving was a success in Greece and Turkey, it would be realistic to target other countries threatened by external pressures. This working assumption in fact set the pace for the global use of foreign aid in the conduct of foreign policy especially in Third World regions. Moreover, the effectiveness of foreign aid in the Greek and Turkish cases served as a diplomatic message to the Soviets that their expansionist moves would not always go unchecked.

The watershed effect of the Truman Doctrine on US foreign policy led many Third World countries to view the US as the source of economic and military assistance in their struggles against divisive domestic forces and external Communism. Aid to Greece and Turkey added a new dimension to US global power in helping nations preserve their independence. With foreign aid as a diplomatic weapon new avenues patterned and structured by the aid relationship were opened up in US foreign policy.

The Truman Doctrine also has implications with regard to US interventions in Third World regions. Instead of direct military interventions with US forces, foreign aid could be used for indirect intervention in the affairs of recipient countries. Such interventions could take the form of aiding the government in power or supporting a liberation movement. This dimension in aid-giving signified that foreign aid could be granted on a universal, regional, or country basis because the supply of capital is not limited by geographic factors like the sending of military troops. In other words, the type of intervention brought about by the emergence of foreign aid as a weapon of containment lacked any spatio-temporal limits. In sufficient amounts foreign aid could be distributed anytime and to any recipient that is willing to receive it.

In the Truman Doctrine foreign aid figured as the most prominent tool for the conduct of foreign policy. However, due to the finite amount of aid available certain criteria guided its extension to other countries. Specifically, the following criteria were referred to:
(1) US aid had to be requested by the governments seeking it, as had been the case with Greece and Turkey; (2) the threatened country must be making some effort to preserve its own security and independence; (3) American assistance was to be viewed as a 'last resort' by nations confronting a challenge to their independence; (4) in future cases the US would carefully study the 'conditions' prevailing in the countries making such requests; and (5) the US limited itself largely to extending financial aid, backed by a small scale programme of military aid and advice. [4]

In sum, the Truman Doctrine proclaimed during the Cold War rivalries period marked a watershed in the conduct of US foreign policy. Foreign aid was officially launched as a vehicle for the realization of goals and the containment of Communism. At this stage of the East-West rivalry it was assumed that only the US was in a position to provide the aid required by nations under attack. The success that followed the application of the doctrine helped in establishing the effectiveness of foreign aid in hotly contested regions of the Third World.

THE EISENHOWER DOCTRINE

In the same vein as President Truman's containment doctrine, his successor, President Eisenhower addressing a joint session of Congress on January 5, 1957 also proclaimed a new doctrine. The Eisenhower Doctrine as it came to be known was particularly directed at the volatile Middle East region. It set the stage for a perennial Soviet-American competition in the region. [5] The Eisenhower Doctrine specifically contained request for a new orientation to foreign aid policy that would put into motion more effective bilateral and multilateral aid distribution programmes geared towards strengthening the independence, territorial integrity, and overall self-preservation of states in the Middle East. As an indication of the emphasis on aid as a cornerstone of policy toward the region, military aid and military cooperation were introduced as new components of the aid relationship as well as a supplement to economic aid. In addition to the commitment to extend both economic and military aid, President Eisenhower asked for authority from Congress that would lead to the 'employment of the armed forces of the United States to secure and protect the territorial integrity and political independence of such nations, requesting such aid, against overt armed aggression from any nation controlled by International Communism.' [6]

The use of a three-pronged strategy: economic aid, military aid, and the possible use of US military forces, was adopted to bolster US power and prestige in the Middle East after the Suez crisis of 1956 in which the Soviet Union figured prominently in the scenario. The strategy was also an indirect warning to the Soviets indicating a US willingness to compete against real and imagined Soviet expansionist goals in the region. After the 1956 Suez crisis American foreign policy experts came to realize that the Middle East is one of the most volatile, potentially explosive, and crisis-prone regions in the Third World. The Eisenhower Doctrine was thus aimed at maintaining the status quo in a region of high conflicts during a Cold War rivalry period.

Two provisions of the Eisenhower Doctrine had a substantial bearing on the instrumentality of foreign aid in the conduct of foreign policy. First, the president was authorized to conclude agreements for the distribution of foreign aid to recipient nations demanding it. Second, the president was also empowered to distribute military aid to Middle Eastern countries requesting it. The military aid component was explicitly introduced into the doctrine because Egypt had set a precedent even prior to 1956 of acquiring Soviet arms. The military aid component would guarantee US arms to regional nations requesting them thereby diminishing Soviet arms influence in the region. Instead of just an economic aid-giving race, the dimension of a military aid race had been introduced into the region. The dual races were both patterned and structured by a high level of intra-regional conflicts in which the Superpowers had a stake.

The immediate motivation for the Eisenhower Doctrine stemmed from a perception of Soviet intentions and the methods used to achieve such goals in the Middle East region. The Soviet method of operation is to effect a status quo reversal and establish a Communist regime. The preferred methods of the Soviets are propaganda, economic and military aid programmes that would create dependence on them by the recipient state. More radical methods are campaigns, sponsoring of terrorism, destabilization and sabotage directed against the target government. In order to counter such revolutionary methods the doctrine reserved the option of direct military aid in the form of direct military intervention with US forces.

While the Truman Doctrine was basically a response to events in Greece and Turkey, the Eisenhower Doctrine on the other hand, was a reaction to perceived threat to US security in the Middle East region. The doctrine was enunciated to: (1) fill the vacuum created by British and French withdrawal from the region as a result of decolonization; (2) diminish the increasing growth of Soviet power and influence within the region; and (3) contain the destabilizing effects of the socialist leanings of Egypt's president, Gamal Abdel Nasser in the region. With independence, a new form of radical nationalism emerged especially in Egypt that led to the nationalization of the Suez Canal by Nasser in 1956. [7] The consequent attempt by Britain and France to reassert their authority over an international waterway led to a crisis situation which pitted the new nationalism against the former colonical masters.

Although Soviet influence was on the rise in the region, it became increasingly strong when the US refused to finance the proposed Aswan High Dam in 1955-56, thereby alienating Nasser. The alienation led to the decision by Nasser to nationalize the Canal. The later enunciation of the Eisenhower Doctrine was a realization by the Eisenhower Administration that the refusal to give aid particularly when requested could lead to the loss of a potential ally and result in a gain for the Soviet Union. While the radicalism of Nasser may not have been Communist-inspired, US policymakers interpreted his willingness to receive Soviet aid as an indication of his pro-Soviet orientation. In other words, the new nationalism was interpreted as communism. Nasser was perceived as even more threatening to US interests in the East-West competition because of the influence he wielded over the newly-emerging nations of Africa and the Middle East. The doctrine and its application would thus be instrumental in preventing other new nations from following the path of Egypt under Nasser.

The reaction of Turkey, Pakistan, Lebanon, and Iran towards the Eisenhower Doctrine was one of optimism. They saw it as a diplomatic innovation which would have positive and beneficial effects. Nonetheless the doctrine signalled US willingness to project its power in the Middle East and consequently get directly involved in various Middle Eastern crises, the major one being the traditional Arab-Israeli hostility. A vivid application of the doctrine in the region came in the Spring of 1957 during the internal instability in Jordan that prompted President Chamoun of Lebanon to request application of the doctrine fearing that the instability and possible overthrow of the monarchy in Jordan would threaten his own country. [8] The situation calmed down when the Sixth Fleet was ordered into the East Mediterranean. This military action by the Eisenhower Administration was followed by the extension of $10 million in US economic aid to Jordan as part of the doctrine's application aimed at containing the alleged communist-inspired forces that were attempting to topple the Monarchy. As instability unfolded between Syria and its neighbors the administration increased military aid to Syria's neighbors, especially to Turkey.

In sum, the Eisenhower Doctrine was more regionally specific than the Truman Doctrine. It was the first public and official expression of US interest in the region. The high level of intra-regional conflicts, aid racing, and increased superpower rivalry led to the expression of official US interest in the region as a check on Soviet expansionism. The geopolitical, military, and economic salience of the region is a primary factor for the high level of intra-regional superpower rivalry. The Eisenhower Doctrine is a justification to fill the vacuum left by British and French withdrawal from many parts of the region. As a doctrine it was comprehensive in scope, advocating economic aid, military aid, and direct military intervention in its application. The Middle East, as implied in the doctrine, was therefore the first Third World region to experience an economic aid and arms aid race between the US and USSR.

There are times when presidents accelerate the aid distribution process because of the perception of a potential crisis situation, and the need to impute a legal basis on aid-giving if it is perceived that it would encounter Congressional opposition. When aid distribution is justified in resolutions it usually involves a strong element of direct intervention under what became known as the 'imperical presidency.' [9] The first manifestation of the imperial presidency in aid distribution and intervention emerged during the Johnson Administration. Crisis situations in two regions -- South-East Asia and Latin America resulted in the proclamation of two doctrines: (1) the First Johnson Doctrine, and (2) the Second Johnson Doctrine. The Gulf of Tonkin Resolution was passed on 7 August 1964 by Congress as part of the First Johnson Doctrine focusing on South-East Asia. It was a response to two consecutive attacks on American destroyers in international waters, in the Gulf of Tonkin on 2 and 5 August by North Vietnamese PT boats. [10] The Gulf of Tonkin Resolution signed into law by President Johnson on 11 August was a statement of US determination to assist members of the SEATO either indirectly through foreign aid or directly through direct military intervention to resist communist aggression. Like the Eisenhower Doctrine for the Middle East the Johnson Doctrine for South-East Asia had provisions for both direct and indirect interventions.

In reference to the Tonkin Resolution, Secretary of State Dean Rusk described it in three ways: (1) a provision for defense of SEATO members who are allies of the US; (2) a means to aid regional allies requesting such aid; and (3) the resolution would be invoked and applied only to deter communist aggression. [11] The specific articulation of the Johnson Doctrine in the Tonkin Resolution signalled the beginning of a strong US commitment to the region of South-East Asia. On August 4, with the second attack on American naval units, President Johnson announced that the US was determined 'to take all necessary measures in support of freedom and in defense of peace in South-East Asia.' The president afterwards made reference to the now famous Munich Analogy in foreign policy that aggression should not be appeased but should be challenged and wiped out at all times. The Tonkin Resolution was specific about committing US forces in the region. This part of the Resolution was explicitly stated by the president himself: 'To any armed attack upon our forces, we shall reply. To any in South-East Asia who ask our help in defending our freedom, we shall give it.' [12] This pronouncement basically constitutes the major thrust of the Johnson Doctrine for the region. Like preceding doctrines it amounted to the articulation of a coherent and definitive US policy toward regional containment of the Soviet Union and communism in South-East Asia.

In the consequent escalation of events between North and South Vietnam, the US indicated its support of South Vietnam through a show of militarism. United States naval power was increased in the waters adjacent to Vietnam. This naval buildup was supplemented by the patrol of American destroyers in the Gulf of Tonkin. Well before the escalation of conflicts between North and South Vietnam, the Gulf of Tonkin Resolution was applied through military action. President Johnson ordered US aircrafts to carry out retaliatory raids against selected villages in North Vietnam for attacks on US ships. The rationale underlying the raids was that Hanoi would be deterred from further aggression through punishment.

Furthermore, in application of the Tonkin Resolution, President Johnson wanted to have a wide latitude to deter Communist expansion in South-East Asia. The Resolution thus contained certain elements that would guarantee this wide latitude: (1) retaliatory strikes against North Vietnam that would have the approval of Congress; (2) authorization of the president to take whatever steps necessary to combat aggression in the region; (3) the definition of 'aggression' would be left to the president to determine; and (4) the resolution would be operational until either the president or Congress found it unnecessary.

The Tonkin Resolution is perhaps the best case of a strong commitment by a president to his doctrine. President Johnson's level of commitment to the region and doctrine was so strong that as early as 1965 and 1966 he used $1.5 billion in contingency funds to finance military operations in the region. However, the First Johnson Doctrine was basically a failure. Communist aggression in South-East Asia was not eradicated and the failure of the doctrine's application resulted in the escalation of the conflict and a full scale war involving the United States.

While the First Johnson Doctrine targeted South-East Asia, the Second Johnson Doctrine focused on the region of Latin America and is summarized by President Johnson's statement to the American people on May 2, 1965: 'The American nations cannot, must not, and will not permit the establishment of another Communist government in the Western Hemisphere.' [13] The immediate motivation for the Johnson Doctrine was the Dominican Crisis, the justification being the need to forestall a Communist seizure of power in the country and thereby protect and safeguard the hemisphere from communist threat.

Similarly, the Second Johnson Doctrine was a reaction to a foreign threat in the form of political instability in Santo Domingo which quickly spread through the republic. In May 1961, the autocratic, repressive and exploitative rule of

166

Rafael Trujillo ended with his assassination. The new leader Juan Bosch was initially acceptable to the US. During his regime substantial amounts of foreign aid was extended to the Dominican Republic. The basic goal of the Kennedy Administration was to make the republic a model of democracy in the region. However, the Bosch regime gradually proved to be inefficient and became virtually influenced by people of Marxist leanings that proved very counterproductive of his regime and of US foreign policy objectives. On January 25, 1963 a military junta seized power thereby undermining the manifest goals of the Kennedy Administration in the region. The seizure of power was: (1) undemocratic and therefore would not make possible Kennedy's vision of making the republic a showcase of democracy, and (2) also counterproductive to Kennedy's new programme, the Alliance for Progress, whose major focus was the promotion of 'democracy' throughout the Western hemisphere. Despite these setbacks the Kennedy Administra-tion eventually recognized the new military regime. The recognition was reflected in the extension of some $4 million in economic aid to help solve the difficult economic and political situation in the country.

In April 1965 conditions deteriorated in the republic with the overthrow of the military regime by a group of pro-Bosch military officers. At this stage the republic was plunged into a crisis situation bordering on anarchy which threatened the lives of citizens and foreign nationals. After some serious escalation, a dominant faction emerged led by air force Colonel Pedro Benoit. The Benoit regime immediately requested American aid in the form of landing American marines to help contain the situation. About 1,200 marines were landed to help preserve order.

During the Dominican crisis as in the Cuban Missile crisis, the US role could be interpreted as a modern day reassertion of the Monroe Doctrine which emphasizes a special relationship between the US and Latin American republics. In keeping with that continuity in policy since 1823 when the Monroe Doctrine was proclaimed the US has intervened in Latin America on several occasions, one example being the overthrow of the Arbenz government in 1954 to prevent the creation of a communist regime in Guatemala.

In the case of the Dominican Republic in particular a special aid relationship cemented its relations with the US. Even before the Dominican crisis the Dominican Republic received military aid from the US largely in the form of the provision of military training for Dominican military officers in the US. Weapons transfers were also part of the US-Dominican Republic aid relationship. Finally, a parallel could be drawn between the Johnson Doctrine towards Latin America and the Truman Doctrine's focus on the Greek and

Turkish crises of 1947. In both instances the aim of US foreign policy was to contain Communism and establish democratic regimes in particular countries. Foreign aid became a key instrument in the whole process.

THE NIXON DOCTRINE

The Nixon Doctrine is better understood in the context of the US experience in the Vietnam War. Being its primary motivation the doctrine was aimed at a reduction of America's responsibilities and obligations overseas. Proclaimed during the period of detente it had an impact on the flow of foreign aid to Third World countries. By the late 1960's donor fatigue had become a reality, the Cold War had subsided and the mutual distrust and suspicion of the 1950s had decreased. Normalization of relations between the US and the PRC had also progressed substantially. The doctrine emerged as the new foreign policy road map of a nation about to end a long war that had challenged the entire basis of US foreign policy. As a new foreign policy guide it was aimed at: (1) reducing US political and military entanglements in the world; (2) restricting the use of American forces overseas and limiting the policy of interventions; and (3) shifting more responsibility to the threatened country in the process of containing hostile groups. [14]

The reexamination of US commitments, obligations, and interests correspondingly implied a reevaluation of alliances and foreign aid programmes. One indication of this characteristic of the Nixon Doctrine was the decision to significantly reduce the level of American military forces in South Korea. At the same time it was decided to significantly increase military aid to the country to make up for the reduction in manpower.

While the major themes of the doctrine point to a retrenchment in US commitments, the pledge to extend economic and military aid to threatened countries was also an indication of the desire to increase American responsibilities worldwide. The push to reduce US involvement was expressed in the condition that the endangered country provide the troops and show indications that it would in fact survive the threat backed by US assistance short of direct military intervention. The emphasis on reshaping post-Vietnam foreign policy had a broad geographic coverage. As the emphasis slightly shifted from South-East Asia it was directed at the Middle East in general, the Arab-Israeli dispute in particular, and African states. Developing a new and meaningful relationship was the major thrust of foreign policy in the Latin American region. US presence in South-East Asia was still maintained but on a limited level.

The Nixon Doctrine could be considered unique in the entire range of doctrines in American foreign policy. While other doctrines explicitly and unwaringly endorse direct interventions, it takes a critical look at foreign aid as an instrument of foreign policy. Foreign assistance may not even be extended unless the country under attack shows some signs of eventual survival. The significant number of American casualties of Vietnam and the estimated war cost of millions of dollars a month justified such a critical evaluation of global interests and responsibilities. When the transfer of resources runs into thousands of human casualties and billions of dollars then aid-giving becomes a very costly game of trying to maintain influence and power in only one country. The Nixon Doctrine implied that such a sacrifice was not worth it either in Vietnam or in other regions of the Third World that may not be as strategic as say the Persian Gulf region in the Middle East. To put it another way, the Nixon Doctrine was explicitly stating that US commitments would be rigidly prioritized with the utmost attention directed only to those states and sub-regions that are integral to the survival and security of the United States. In a foreign aid programme as extensive and profound as the assistance to Vietnam the consequences could be a tremendous cost in human lives as well as an enormous transfer of funds to one recipient.

The lesson of Vietnam also underscores another significant point, that foreign assistance in the form of economic and military aid, and direct military interventions are at times a necessary but not a sufficient condition for the realization of foreign policy objectives. Other far less costly means could also be employed, and the Nixon Administration was quick to seize upon the advantages of diplomatic contacts and rapprochement. Capitalizing on the rapprochement initiative, President Nixon in 1972 'normalized' relations between the US and the PRC. This diplomatic emphasis could be viewed as a case of the instrumentality of foreign aid being either supplemented by diplomacy or substituting it. The establishment of diplomatic relations with the PRC was one indication that the US was still prepared to maintain a presence in the region of South-East Asia, short of direct military involvement. Consequently, because of the Nixon initiative the US is today no less influential in the region particularly since Sino-American relations have been improving since 1972.

Perhaps the most important factor that motivated the Nixon Doctrine was the change in the configuration of power in the international system. The international system by the late 1960's had already evolved from a tight bipolar, loose bipolar, to a full-fledged bipolycentric system. Certain nations such as the PRC, India, Brazil and the like were emerging as major powers also seeking influence among smaller powers. Even the smaller nations were increasingly asserting their independence from the superpowers aided by major powers like the PRC. This reality in addition to US-Soviet competition made it difficult for the US to always achieve its goals. Thus there was a need to reassess US tactics and strategies in Third World regions in the light of: (1) Sino-Soviet-American competition; (2) competition from middle-level powers; and (3) increasing nationalism in Third World countries.

With the increased complexity of the international system the Cold War rivalry between the US and USSR was quickly overshadowed resulting in the consequent emergence of the era of detente. Decreasing US direct involvements abroad implied coming up with alternative means of protecting and realizing US goals. One alternative beside the rapprochement initiative was the introduction of the concept of 'linkage' to check Soviet actions. In other words, the continuation of peaceful relations between the US and USSR would be conditioned by the activities and behavior of the USSR in the regions of Africa, the Middle East, and South-East Asia.

A distinguishing factor in the Nixon Doctrine was its inclination toward a more realist approach to US foreign policy. The overall US national interest was emphasized by pronouncements that new US commitments would be conditioned by the national interests of the US That is if the overthrow of a particular nation would not endanger US national security then overt US support and intervention could be withheld from such a nation.

Donor fatigue was an aspect of the realist factor in the Nixon Doctrine. Donor fatigue or dissatisfaction with the effects of aid in Third World countries was also an aspect of detente. With the relaxation of tensions between the US and USSR foreign aid as an instrument of rivalry diminished in significance. By 1972 Congressional dissatisfaction with aid was reflected in decreasing support for foreign aid distribution among the American people. [15] Together with the declining support for aid flows emerged an increasing opposition to US foreign military interventions.

In sum, the Nixon Doctrine, despite its emphasis on retrenchment in overall US policy, still relied on resource transfers as a way of maintaining influence in Africa, Asia, Latin America, and the Middle East. However, the process of resource transfer became more structured by realpolitik, national interest, and national security concerns. The new emphasis on power politics and balance of power concerns was a reaction to the maturity of the new global power configurations of the 1970's as structured by characteristics of bipolycentrism. The reality of the international system

was an indication that an efficient way to implement the
Nixon Doctrine was through the selective targeting strategy.
Stated differently, US commitments were to be strictly
prioritized, selective, reduced, and carefully executed.

THE CARTER DOCTRINE

Until 1979 the Carter Administration's foreign policy was
predicated on the 'Vietnam War Syndrome.' Instead of an
interventionist, aggressive, and power oriented America,
there was an emphasis on the power of example, human rights,
and developing rapprochement with Third World and hostile
states. The subsequent proclamation of the doctrine was to
signal to the Soviets and the rest of the world that the
present foreign policy mood should not be construed as an
indication of weakness. At the same time the doctrine marked
a reawakening from the 'complacency' and lull after the
Vietnam quagmire. It was again the beginning of a globalist
and assertive foreign policy typical of the pre-Vietnam and
Vietnam era.
The immediate motivations for the proclamation of the
Carter Doctrine could be traced to three factors. By August
1979 the US became aware of the presence of some three
thousand Soviet forces in Cuba although they had already been
there for many years. Their discovery immediately raised two
questions about: (1) the efficiency of the nation's
intelligence community; and (2) the overall effectiveness of
the Carter Administration's foreign and national security
policy particularly since the US had to eventually accept
their presence as a fait accompli which was reflected in the
Soviet refusal to recall its forces. Far more important than
discovery of Soviet troops in Cuba were events in the Middle
East region that directly challenged US foreign policy.
These were the Iranian revolution and the Soviet invasion of
Afghanistan.
Early in 1979 the Shah was overthrown by radical religious
clergies, and in August the crisis was complicated by the
seizure of American diplomats as hostages. While the hostage
crisis lasted US diplomatic prestige suffered significantly.
Coupled with the US loss of influence in Iran was the March
1980 attack on Iran by Iraq. Because of their strategic
location within the Persian Gulf region the industrialized
nations experienced a reduction in their oil shipments from
the region for several months. The culminating event that
led to the proclamation of the Carter Doctrine was the 27
December 1979 Soviet military intervention in Afghanistan.
It was an indication that the Kremlin was finally successful
in imposing a Communist regime on that country after several
attempts in the past. [16]   The pro-Marxist Peoples

Democratic Party in a coup on 27 April 1978 seized power and subsequently relied heavily on the Soviet Union to maintain its rule. Because of the continuing resistance of the Afghans to Communist rule, Moscow decided to establish a more visible presence by direct military intervention.

While the three separate incidents eventually contributed to the proclamation of the Carter Doctrine, its immediate justification was the perception that Soviet domination of Afghanistan was a first step in a long term objective of blocking Western access to the oil fields of the Persian Gulf area. The doctrine denounced Soviet expansionism and continued military build up. The Soviet invasion was viewed as an incident which 'could pose the most serious threat to the peace since the Second World War.' President Carter then went on to summarize the entire Carter Doctrine by making direct reference to the Persian Gulf region and US willingness to defend it at all costs.

Doctrines once enunciated tend to be implemented, even if reluctantly. A strategy for its application should the occasion arise was guaranteed through the creation of a new Rapid Deployment Force (RDF). [17] The RDF became an indication of US military power projection and readiness to use it in both the Gulf region and other regions. Other measures integral to the Carter Doctrine that have a direct bearing on foreign aid distribution were: (1) a substantial increase in US military expenditure; (2) upgrading the defenses of the North Atlantic Treaty area; and (3) a renewed emphasis on US commitment to the security of Pakistan.

The Carter Doctrine like the Eisenhower and Johnson Doctrines in particular, again underscores the salience of the Middle East region in US foreign policy. Expressed differently, there is hardly a post World War II American presidential doctrine that does not make some reference to the Middle East region and US objectives to contain Soviet expansionist moves there. US presidential doctrines in general could be regarded as selective regional containment policies in which the Middle East figures more prominently because of its geopolitical importance as a major theatre of US-Soviet rivalry. The Carter Doctrine is also significant in another sense, it signalled America's willingness to reject the Vietnam War syndrome for a more aggressive stance on the Middle East. As a region it was too important to be plagued by the Vietnam syndrome, because it has become an integral part of US national security and for that matter the entire security of the Western powers. Moreover, the Carter Doctrine also underscores the strategic and critical importance of oil, the issue of which is quickly transformed into high politics. Critical raw materials fall into a special category of international politics that could easily elicit a military response by superpowers.

The period of detente which roughly falls between 1968 and 1978 practically ended with the proclamation of the Carter Doctrine. The doctrine signalled a reassertion of US power and with it increased commitments and obligations which translate into more resource transfers to the Third World. Direct military interventions also became fashionable as a means of rejuvenating the declining US influence around the world. Foreign aid would as from this point be viewed less as a costly game of buying influence and power. The idea of linkage in Soviet-American relations was also reactivated to buttress the Carter Doctrine. Perhaps more than anything the doctrine changed American foreign policy from one based largely on elements of idealism to an emphasis on realist behavior.

Although many of the Gulf states did not show much enthusiasm for the doctrine, Oman, Somalia and Kenya were willing to make their airfields and other military bases available in the event the need for implementing the doctrine arose. [18] Israel also offered base facilities for enforcement of the doctrine and strongly endorsed the new US reassertion of power in the region to contain the Soviets. Using the facilities of these countries had foreign aid implications. For instance, Somalia and Kenya offered their military bases as a quid pro quo for substantial increases in US military and economic aid. In the Mediterranean, Egypt expressed a willingness to provide limited use of Egyptian air bases for the security of the Gulf area. Egypt by this time was already heavily dependent on US foreign aid and would be expected to receive even more aid as a result of its support for the doctrine. After initial reluctance to join in implementing the Carter Doctrine, Pakistan eventually agreed in 1981 after serious negotiations to cooperate with the US in containing Soviet expansionism. The agreement was cemented by a military aid package totalling $500 million. The establishment of American military bases was not part of the agreement. The substantial increase in military aid was used to compete with an equally substantial Soviet military aid programme to India.

In sum, the Carter Doctrine was a response to a series of regional crises particularly in the Middle East. It was structured by two perceptions: (1) a Soviet attempt to change the global projection of power in their favor; and (2) a soviet challenge to vital US interests from the Sea of Japan to the Mediterranean. Thus, with the Carter Doctrine a Soviet-centric foreign policy view once more emerged as the primary focus of foreign policy behavior. Finally, other aspects of the Carter Doctrine involved suggestions for: (1) improving the effectiveness of the US intelligence community; (2) strengthening American forces in the Indian Ocean and Persian Gulf region; and (3) increasing overall

defense spending and by extension military assistance to
Third World regions. Trade and diplomatic ties with the PRC
were also employed to contain Soviet expansionism.

THE REAGAN DOCTRINE

While the Reagan Doctrine did not appear as firmly rooted
as preceding doctrines, nonetheless the foundations of what
resulted in such a doctrine had its beginnings in the Carter
Doctrine. The reversal of US foreign policy in the latter
part of the Carter Administration was accelerated by the
Reagan Administration. The conduct of foreign policy was
marked by the rhetoric and perceptions of the Cold War years.
The threat of Soviet expansionism was the underlying
rationale for a more assertive foreign policy in which
foreign aid was used more selectively to enhance US national
security.
The foreign aid policy of the Reagan Administration
reflected the emphasis of the Reagan Doctrine. The
selectivity of aid-giving, the unrestrained use of aid to
finance right-wing wars of liberation, and the militarism of
US foreign policy were three of its characteristics. [19]
In particular, that aspect of the Reagan Doctrine that had a
significant bearing on foreign aid distribution was stated
succinctly by Secretary of State, George Schultz. It
encompassed economic, politico-military, developmental, and
humanitarian considerations as rationales in the US
distribution of foreign aid. As outlined by Schultz foreign
aid-giving articulates into overall foreign policy to enhance
four US interests:

1. Our interest in a growing world economy which
   enhances the well-being of citizens in both the
   developing and industrialized world;
2. Our interests in security -- protecting our vital
   interests abroad, strengthening our friends,
   contributing to regional stability and back
   stopping our diplomatic efforts for peaceful
   solutions to regional problems;
3. Our interest in building democracy and promoting
   adherence to human rights and the rule of law; and
4. Our humanitarian interest in alleviating suffering
   and easing the immediate consequences of
   catastrophe on the very poor. [20]

As expressed in those four points, US aid policy
articulates into all aspects of US foreign policy including
national security. The second point is apparently the most
dominant and was reflected in selective targeting of friendly

states especially when geopolitically located and endowed with critical raw materials. The dominance of national security concerns led to foreign aid taking on a more military and political emphasis. Security aid was increased by 130 per cent since 1981, from less than half the total to over two-thirds. [21] With the renewed emphasis on utilitarian (economic, political, military) considerations in aid-giving, US aid-giving became explicitly tied to the behaviour of recipient states.

Congress accorded tacit approval to the Reagan Doctrine because of the change in US attitude towards funding the United Nations. There was a tendency to tie aid to UN performance. The expedient use of foreign aid for national security was clearly reflected in the final conclusions of the National Bipartisan Commission on Central America, headed by Henry Kissinger, and the Commission on Security and Economic Assistance headed by Frank Carlucci. Both reports concluded in agreement that:

1. economic and military assistance are equally servants of our national interest
2. rising standards in the Third World are vital to internal stability and external defense. Conversely, threats to stability impede development. [22]

The basic thrust of the Reagan Doctrine was three-fold: (1) the restoration of US power vis-a-vis the Soviet Union; (2) the support of right-wing 'Liberation' movements in any region of the world; and (3) the sparing and selective use of foreign aid to achieve foreign policy goals. The support of dictatorial regimes which has long been a factor in US foreign policy is a consequence of the attempt to prevent the emergence of radical regimes, while at the same time actively containing and trying to remove those that are already in existence.

The real application of the Reagan Doctrine was reflected in the US behaviour towards Nicaragua and Libya. [23] Through a foreign policy of compellence the US explicitly attempted to overthrow the Sandanista regime and eventually introduce a 'democratic' system in the country. Active containment of the regime took the form of opposition to a Nicaraguan military buildup through the acquisition of more advanced Soviet weapons. Within Central America itself active containment took the form of preventing aid to the El Salvador rebels by Nicaragua, Cuba, and the Soviet Union. The pressure against Nicaragua was four-fold: (1) overt and covert operations involving the Contras; (2) regional militarism in the form of military exercises in Honduras and off Nicaragua's shores; (3) denying and opposing both bilateral and multilateral loans to Nicaragua; and (4) serious efforts at diplomatically opposing the Sandanistas internationally. By the Spring of 1981 the US aid programme to Nicaragua was definitively cancelled. The US-supported attacks against the Sandanista regime were made possible by support of an aid bill of $100 million, renewal of which was prevented by the Boland Amendment.

Another instance of the Reagan Doctrine's application was in the case of Libya. Its application began with a dramatization of Libya's support for international terrorism which assumed the proportions of a belligerent policy toward Khaddafi different from the policy of the Carter Administration. The selective targeting of Libya then continued with a show of diplomatic toughness. Following the disclosures of attacks against Libyan students in the US in May 1981, Libyan diplomats were expelled as a retaliation. The expulsion was followed by warnings to American citizens to consider travel to Libya a risky venture.

The year 1981 saw the systematic application of the doctrine because after the diplomatic measures the Reagan Administration turned to militarism as the next policy of pressure against the radical government of Khaddafi. In August 1981 during routine naval exercises around the Gulf of Sidra, two Libyan aircraft were downed when they tried to intercept US aircraft over the Gulf. Militarism as manifested in occasional exercises around the Gulf of Sidra was followed by the application of comprehensive sanctions against Libya.

As in the case of Nicaragua, the Libyan case was one in which the strategies of military containment, diplomatic pressures, and economic sanctions were being simultaneously applied. With Libya in particular, the extension of military aid was also being increased to its threatened and hostile neighbors. These actions were based on the argument that strong hostile neighbors coupled with occasional US militarism and the pressures of economic sanctions would eventually soften the radical posture of Khaddafi. Thus resource power as an instrument of reward and punishment was couched in a dual strategy: (1) aid to threatened and hostile neighbors of Libya; and (2) diplomatic, economic, and military pressures on Libya.

Perhaps a more controversial aspect of the pressure on Libya concerned the resort by the administration to a foreign policy of deception, decoys, and disinformation. The questionable allegations were: (1) the announcement that Quaddafi had sent a hit squad to the US to assassinate President Reagan; (2) the assertion that Libya was behind the August 1985 bombing of the discotheque in Berlin which resulted in the death of an American; and (3) allegations of Libya's intent to bomb the Aswan Dam in Egypt. These allegations and a few others led to the decision by the Reagan Administration to apply an aspect of the Reagan Doctrine by ordering an air strike on Libya in April 1986.

In sum, the Reagan Doctrine had a strong similarity to the Truman Doctrine because of its emphasis on helping liberation movements everywhere. The Nicaraguan case was a vivid example of the doctrine in application. It was more realist in orientation and based on the balance of power approach to international politics. The insistence on overthrowing the Sandanistas is a case of trying to maintain a balance of power in favour of the US in Central America. The promise to support all right wing liberation movements regardless of who they were allied with was also another example of the realist focus of the doctrine. Thus, the support for UNITA led by Jonas Savimbi and also supported by the Apartheid regime of South Africa. The doctrine made a sharp distinction between friendly and hostile states. Thus selectivity in aid-giving became a dominant underlying pattern of the doctrine. Penetration of hostile regimes through liberation movements was a second dominant pattern of aid-giving in the doctrine's application. Overall, there was strong caution exercised in the use of economic aid, military aid, and direct military intervention in volatile regions.

SUMMARY

Foreign aid as a central element of US foreign policy still lacks an effective domestic constituency. What is there as a constituency has been growing weaker since the 1960s. [24] Based on surveys and polls about foreign assistance three conclusions have emerged: (1) there has been a consistent drop in the general level of popularity of foreign aid during the past three decades; (2) economic aid has always been less unpopular (more popular) than military aid; and (3) the general American electorate give a consistently lower approval than do the elites to both economic and military aid.

In connection with the above trend, doctrinal pronouncements have played a very useful role in the conduct of US foreign policy because they constitute: (1) a justification for the demand and supply of foreign aid; (2) a strategy for expanding presidential power in the conduct of foreign policy; and (3) a basis for the conduct of an effective foreign policy. Because of the legal and moral connotations inherent in doctrines, foreign aid-giving motivated by doctrinal pronouncements becomes invested with noble intentions because it is used in the solution of the geopolitical and economic problems identified by the doctrines.

In the conduct of American foreign policy the linkage between interests, commitments, responsibilities, and doctrines has generally been used to delineate regional spheres of influence, consolidate alliances, contain the Soviet Union, and maintain regional stability. This means that regions of high threat, volatility, geostrategic salience, and intense competition are the focus of the presidential doctrines-foreign aid nexus. Where client states are concerned, doctrines impute legitimacy on the demand-supply relationship such that they have almost become a legal and moral domestic constituency for the distribution of foreign aid.

US foreign policy is characterized by a proclivity to react to foreign threats through the proclamation of doctrines. This behavior has been particularly more pronounced in the post World War II era. While doctrines imply a certain amount of rigidity they also reflect a great deal of pragmatism. Doctrines now and in the future would present a credible threat against Soviet Communism. Except perhaps in the Persian Gulf region and Western Europe they would hardly be implemented to the point of a full scale war with the Soviet Union. The Vietnam syndrome and its deterrent effect on American interventionism would still have a significant impact on the regional conduct of US foreign policy.

The natural proclivity for doctrines could be interpreted as a case of superpower confidence that is manifested in the need to project domestic values to other parts of the world. Thus American presidential doctrines are basically value-laden. They are a reflection and expression of the ethos of American society yearning to be projected to the rest of the world. In other words, the doctrinal disposition is a cloak of idealism parading as realism in foreign policy. At the same time they are another form of containing Soviet Communism and therefore a manifestation of the age old balance of power in application.

Doctrines seek to guarantee peace and forestall war in volatile regions of the world including the Western hemisphere. The idea of peace is often implied and explicitly stated in the doctrinal pronouncements. As a superpower, the US perceives it has global interests but at the same time it has a global responsibility to ensure peace, and an obligation to protect friendly and peaceful states. The independence, sovereignty, territorial integrity, and self-preservation of nations is always the target of presidential doctrines particularly when the instituted government is struggling against communism.

While doctrines could forestall war and guarantee political stability, they could also be perceived as counterproductive and unprogressive. In their focus on stability they help maintain the status quo thereby undermining the objectives of national liberation movements that may not necessarily be communist inspired, but only trying to change oppressive and non-democratic systems. The increased feelings of anti-Americanism in Third World countries are party accounted for by this conservative tendency in US foreign policy doctrines. On the balance doctrines are at times antagonistic to the repressed, opposed to the goals of particular groups, and not necessarily peace and stability oriented. Furthermore, the pattern that emerges is that radical nationalism is equated with Communism. Thus doctrines in this regard tend to have an atmosphere of overreaction against the Soviet Union. With the Truman Doctrine, American foreign policy became vested with both geopolitical and ideological dimensions.

Of all the post World War II doctrines, the Nixon Doctrine stands in stark contrast to the others because of its explicit desire to reduce US global interests, responsibilities, and obligations. The Eisenhower, Johnson, and Carter Doctrines, in particular, explicitly promise the use of US resources and direct military intervention if necessary. Since doctrines are the pronouncements of presidents, they achieve significance because of the aura surrounding the presidency. That aura translates into a justification for applying the doctrine which then translates into resource transfers and at times direct military intervention.

The post World War II doctrines are all essentially in harmony with the first and most immortal American presidential doctrine, the Monroe Doctrine. The thrust of all of them is basically the global and regional containment of hostile forces. In post World War II terms, it is the regional containment of the Soviet Union. However, doctrines targeted at specific regions have contributed to regional enmities such as the Arab/Israeli, North Korea/South Korea, Ethiopia/Somalia, Egypt/Libya, and India/Pakistan polarizations. They tend to be emphasized and maintained by the promise to support the friendly side. On the other hand, a direct beneficial effect of doctrines is that they help deter war and Soviet expansionism. It would also be an exaggeration to say that they are the sole determinants of regional traditional enmities, although it would be reasonable to say that they also contribute in buttressing them.

The future effectiveness of American presidential doctrines will depend on two factors. First, conditions in Third World regions would play a dominant role. If doctrines are opposed to the goals of the growing number of dissatisfied people, then the choice would have to be more resource transfers for the elites to contain instability or it may require direct US intervention to save friendly but dictatorial regimes. The more opposed the US is to genuine nationalism the more anti-Americanism would surface in Third World regions. Second, the configuration of power in the international system would play a key role in aid flows. As bipolycentrism further develops into say tripolarity, a whole new aid race could emerge involving the US, USSR, and the PRC. The choice for US foreign policy would be whether to outgive two superpowers or to use other methods to achieve and maintain influence in the Third World. At present the PRC aid-giving focus is limited to parts of Africa and East Asia, but with more Chinese power and prosperity it would not be surprising to observe an increase in PRC global interests and commitments. Similarly, the more multipolar the configuration of power, the more adaptive US foreign policy would have to be. Multipolarity assumes increased assertiveness by middle level powers and a corresponding increase in their power, wealth, and prestige. The implication is that the US would be dealing with near co-equals in its conduct of foreign policy. Doctrines would then be more effective if they take into account the goals and objectives of the new actors and the new configurations of regional power.

While the foreign aid component of doctrines helps restore order in crisis situations, it has been viewed by its critics as instruments for propping up dictatorial regimes in Third World countries. Aid is mostly concessional transfer of funds but it is at the same time a vehicle that undermines democracy in many countries. United States aid-giving has a broad coverage in which funds are extended to democratic, socialist, and communist countries. The process which has been going on since 1947 has become such an integral part of US foreign policy that by 1983 over $200 billion in aid had been transferred. In the future presidential doctrines would still be the major medium through which US goals are articulated, justified, and implemented by the distribution of foreign aid as the vehicle to achieve the goals and objectives.

NOTES

[1]   Proclaimed on December 2, 1823, the Monroe Doctrine was presented to Congress by President James Monroe as a response to the perceived threats of Russian activities in the Northwest of the US, and as a reaction to the Holy Alliance formed in 1815 with the purpose of reimposing European colonialism in the Western hemisphere. For a discussion of the Doctrine, see, Monroe's Seventh Annual Message to Congress, in James

D. Richardson (ed.) A Compilation of the Messages and Papers of the Presidents, 1789-1897, II, pp. 207-20.

[2]   A detailed discussion of the Greek crisis following World War II is found in Hugh Seton-Watson, The East European Revolution (New York: Praeger, 1964).

[3]   For a complete account of the post World War II Turkish political situation and the Soviet role in it, see, Bruce R. Kuniholm, The Origins of the Cold War in the Near East: Great Power Conflicts and Diplomacy in Iran, Turkey, and Greece (Princeton, New Jersey: Princeton University Press, 1980).

[4]   These criteria are outlined in his Congressional message, the text of which may be found in Public Papers of the Presidents of the United States: Harry S. Truman (1947) (Washington, DC: Government Printing Office, 1963).

[5]   See, for instance, Department of State, United States Policy in the Middle East: September, 1956-June, 1957, Near and Middle East Series 25 (Washington, DC: Government Printing Office, 1957) pp. 15-23.

[6]   The thrust of President Eisenhower's Middle East strategy may be found in his statement on August 5, 1957, in Department of State, American Foreign Policy: Current Documents, 1957 (Washington, DC: Government Printing Office, 1961).

[7]   See, for example, US, Department of State, Senate Report no. 70, 85th Congress, American Foreign Policy: Current Documents, 1957.

[8]   A full account of the crisis in Jordan that led to the first application of the doctrine both directly through military intervention and indirectly through the extension of foreign aid may be found in Dwight D. Eisenhower, Waging Peace, 1956-1961 (Garden City, New York: Doubleday, 1965).

[9]   The idea of the Imperial Presidency refers to the ongoing tension between the Presidency and other branches of government as a result of the shift in the constitutional balance reflected in the appropriation by the Presidency of powers reserved by the constitution to Congress. This tendency was particularly manifested during the Indochina War and Watergate. The passage of the War Powers Act in 1973 limiting unilateral executive decisions regarding direct US military involvement is one example of the frustration of Congress over this development. For a detailed analysis of this phenomenon, see, Arthur M. Schlesinger, Jr. The Imperial Presidency (Boston: Houghton Mifflin Co., 1973).

[10] President Johnson's discussion of the crises in the Southeast Asian subregion are found in Public Papers of

the Presidents of the United States: Lyndon B. Johnson, 1963-1964, II, pp. 927-32.

[11] Additional references to the Resolution may be found in Secretary of State Dean Rusk's testimony in the US Congress, Senate, Committees on Foreign Relations and Armed Services, Hearings on Southeast Asia Resolution, 88th Congress, Second Session, 1964.

[12] See, for example, US, Senate, Hearings on Southeast Asia Resolution, 88th Congress 2nd. Session, 1964.

[13] The full text of the President's speech may be found in Public Papers of the Presidents of the United States: Lyndon B. Johnson, 1965 (Washington, DC: Government Printing Office, 1966), II, 461-74.

[14] For details of the Nixon Doctrine, see President Nixon's 'Second Annual Report to the Congress on United States Foreign Policy,' submitted on Feb. 25, 1971.

[15] Full accounts of the American public's attitude to domestic and foreign affairs are found in Barry B. Hughes, The Domestic Context of American Foreign Policy (San Francisco: W.H. Freeman, 1978); and Richard E. Dawson, Public Opinion and Contemporary Disarray (New York: Harper and Row, 1973).

[16] An interesting exposition of developments in Afghanistan since 1973 to the Soviet invasion may be found in James Phillips, 'Afghanistan: Islam Versus Marxism,' Journal of Social and Political Studies, IV (Winter, 1979) 305-21.

[17] In the initial plan it was decided that the RDF would comprise a military unit of 150,000 to 200,000 troops from the different branches of the armed services. It was estimated that about $25 billion would be spent between 1980-85 to bring the RDF into being. Units would be stationed in the Persian Gulf area, the Indian Ocean, the Pacific bases, the NATO area, and in the US. For more details on the formation of the RDF, see, 'Many Actions Taken, Studied in Response to Mideast Crisis,' Congressional Quarterly (Weekly Report), XXXVIII, January 26, 1980.

[18] The responses and demands of countries around the region are discussed in some detail in Cecil V. Crabb, The Doctrines of American Foreign Policy (Baton Rouge: Louisiana State University Press, 1982) pp. 355-360.

[19] In keeping with this emphasis on aiding liberation movements, the Reagan Administration has extended foreign aid to Jonas Savimbi and his UNITA movement even though he is also allied with the Apartheid regime of Pretoria in their attacks against Angola. Moreover, the ongoing Contra war against the Sandanista regime of Nicaragua is also another case in point of the practical applications of the Reagan Doctrine.

[20] For more details of the Reagan Administration's foreign aid policy, see Department of State Bulletin, May 1984, pp. 17-22.

[21] See, for example, The Economist 22 (Feb. 16) 1984, 'A bigger ban, a smaller boom, for the foreign aid buck.'

[22] Department of State Bulletin, May 1984, pp. 17-22.

[23] For a detailed discussion of these two cases and Afghanistan, Indochina, Southern Africa, and Iran, see Anthony Lake, 'Wrestling with Third World Radical Regimes: Theory and Practice,' in John W. Sewell, Richard Feinberg, and Valeriana Kallab (eds.) US Foreign Policy and the Third World (New Brunswick: Transaction Books, 1985) pp. 119-145.

[24] For futher information on American attitudes towards foreign aid, see, the following polls: Gallup Poll (January, 1957); Minnesota Poll (January, 1957); National Opinion Research Center Poll (January, 1957); and the Gallup Polls Sponsored by the Chicago Council on Foreign Relations (1974, 1978, and 1982).

7 Foreign Aid and American Military-Strategic Basing Access

Mutual deterrence in the context of the global military balance of power inevitably engages the geostrategic calculations of planners in the US as well as in the Soviet Union. In Third World regions, in particular, the superpowers have of late become deeply committed to the enhancement of their military-strategic advantages in critical locations like the Arabian Peninsular. The ongoing struggle to project power along the Third World littoral has served to deflect certain regions towards the gravitational pull of the perennial US-Soviet military competition. Moreover, the geographic location of many developing nations lying athwart the direct seaborne lines of communication and commerce to both the East and West has over the years thrust upon these regions the roles of a refueling station for ships bound for the East and West and a forward base for warring powers, among other roles. [1] The geostrategic relevance of the region of Africa, for example, extends as far back as the sixteenth century when the Portuguese led by Vasco Da Gama rounded the Cape route on their way to the East. In the modern era as in the past, perceptions of strategic imperatives are predicated on the rationale that sea lanes of communication could be threatened by the naval power of a hostile nation. The acquisition of military bases along and/or adjacent to sensitive choke points of a Third World nation has thus become a geopolitical imperative.

During the past fifteen years, the US has in fact

bequeathed a greater role to developing states in its quest for greater global power projection. The overall recent geopolitics of military-strategic basing access has been characterized not only by resource transfers on the part of the US and Soviet Union but also by competitive base denial strategies designed to prevent each other from either obtaining them or nudging each other out of theirs through the use of quid pro quos (economic and military aid), threats, propaganda, the formenting of domestic unrests, preemptive base acquisitions, among other strategies. [2] The key objective of these various strategies is to communicate to the new nation that by granting basing access it compromises its newly-won independence and sovereignty. The Soviets have directed propaganda at Oman and Bahrain which points to the possible future role of their US bases in support of Israel against other Arab states. Formentations of coups and revolutions have been blamed on outcomes in the Seychelles, Vietnam, Angola, among other locations.

Similarly, the US has variously used both subtle and overt means in its base denial competition against the Soviet Union. PL 480 food aid was used as a successful inducement to get Sekou Toure of Guinea to terminate Soviet Atlantic reconnaissance flights out of Conakry. Arms transfer relationships between Egypt and the US was instrumental in wresting Soviet control of Egyptian bases. Intentions by the Soviets to use Cuban bases as nuclear submarine bases have been prevented since 1962 by US threats.

In particular, both the US and Soviet Union use existing convergent interest with their client states to perpetrate their base denial strategies. In the recent geopolitics of basing the US and Saudi Arabia have worked extensively together to keep the Middle East free of Soviet bases. [3] The Saudis in conjunction with the US have freely used their money to keep Soviet bases out of North Yemen, the Sudan, and Egypt before the Camp David Accords. The Saudis may also be working on the radical South Yemen regime.

The above base denial strategies even when successful may not have a lasting impact because of the conditionality involved in the principle of rebus sic stantibus (terms of agreements remain valid only so long as the political conditions governing their signature remain), and regime changes which may undermine many of those strategies. The focus of this Chapter will be to analyze the evolving patterns of the more recent US overseas military-strategic basing in connection with the role of foreign aid in the renewed interest of the superpowers in the South Atlantic, Indian Ocean, and other critical regions. In particular, we will attempt to sketch the present and future implications for both the US and Third World nations of military basing, joint military exercises, and foreign aid as a quid pro quo.

SOVIET-AMERICAN MILITARY BASING ACTIVITIES

The US-Soviet competition to project influence no doubt started with the creation of networks of mostly military security alliances. [4] The US had an overwhelming advantage in this area during the Cold War, beginning with the 1949 NATO treaty which increased its membership in 1950 resulting in a military commitment of countries stretching from Europe to as far as Turkey in Asia. The Rio Pact committed the US to the entire defense of the western hemisphere. The ANZUS treaty took care of the Southwestern Pacific region. In East Asia the US had committed itself to the defense of Japan, South Korea, Taiwan, and the Phillipines in the early 1950s. With the establishment of SEATO in 1954 the US together with Britain, France, Australia, New Zealand, the Phillipines, Pakistan, and Thailand pledged itself to the maintenance of the status quo in that region of the world. The following year the Baghdad Pact (later known as CENTO) was sponsored largely by the US to link Britain, Turkey, Iraq, Iran, and Pakistan in a mutual effort against aggression and subversion.

The US continued in subsequent years to establish special security ties on a bilateral basis with more countries such that by the time of the Vietnam conflict it had created a vast network of alliances cemented by a massive transfer of economic and military aid, such that in 1970 observers noted that:

> The United States had more than 1,000,000 soldiers in 30 countries, was a member of four regional defense alliances and an active participant in a fifth, had mutual defense treaties with 42 nations, was a member of 53 international organizations and was furnishing military or economic aid to nearly 100 nations across the face of the globe. [5]

This enormous combination of alliances (some of which are presented in Table 7.1) and resource transfers was all part of a strategy to contain a Soviet Union equally determined to project its influence to a Third World groping in the dark for a development model that would enhance independence and eradicate lingering forms of 'neocolonialism.' Starting with 1953 the Soviets signed a trade agreement with India, in 1955-56 they and Czechoslovakia began an aid relationship with Egypt and even took over the funding of the Aswan Dam. Iraq, Afghanistan, Ghana, Mali, among others, became recipients of Soviet loans, a trend that culminated in the signing of a trade agreement with Cuba in 1960. By the early 1960s Soviet power projection and influence had stretched from its borders to a portion (Cuba) of the traditional

Table 7.1
US Alliances in the Early Post World War II Period

Treaty	Year	Other Signatories
1. Rio Treaty	1947	Mostly Latin American States
2. NATO	1949	West European Countries
3. Mutual Defense Treaty	1951	The Philippines
4. ANZUS Treaty	1951	Australia and New Zealand
5. Treaty of Mutual Coperation and Security	1952	Japan
6. Mutual Defense Treaty	1953	South Korea
7. The SEATO Treaty	1954	Australia, France, New Zealand, Pakistan, Phillipines, Thailand, U.K.
8. The Mutual Defense Treaty	1954	Taiwan

Source: US Senate, United States Security Agreements and
          Commitments Abroad, 91st Congress, Vol. 2, parts
          5-11, pp 1961-1962.

American sphere of influence.

Global power projection of the type described above is not only enhanced by, but also an integral part of military-strategic basing networks. In analyses of overseas bases, the terms 'base,' 'facility,' and 'access' have been used synonymously but strictly speaking the term 'access' is usually the umbrella term denoting all categories of bases and facilities both permanent and transitory which include overflight rights, port visit facilities, refueling rights, and the like. However, the recent global concern about military-strategic and economic access has prompted many analysts of diplomacy to use the term 'strategic access' to refer to bases and facilities as well as markets, raw materials sources, and investments. Strictly speaking bases refer to major military installations with a high degree of exclusive use by the external power, whereas a facility is dominated by technical installations, radio, TV, and other similar installations. [6]

In this analysis, 'base,' 'facility,' and 'access' will be used interchangeably and flexibly because our main focus is in underscoring their articulation into patterns of economic and military aid distribution. Whenever necessary, a contrast can always be made between nations with major US military bases versus those with US facilities.

The probability of exclusive use, retention, and control over a base is higher if basing is intertwined with alliance formation (for example NATO) or purposely done in defense of the host country as in South Korea. If on the other hand they have not been expressly established as part of an alliance system or to perform a trip-wire function they tend to be more subject to the whims and caprices of Third World leaders as in Libya after 1969 and Ethiopia in 1978.

The US has in the past and in its recent power projection behaviour used areas of Egypt and other North African states for bombing practice and for aerial dog-fight training because of the availability of large air and ground spaces coupled with the appropriate terrain and facilities that are limited in Western Europe due to congested space. To reduce the degree of vulnerability to political pressure in connection with the continued use of the facilities and also create an image of military commitment to the host country, US military forces conduct periodic exercises with the armed forces of the host country. In the 1980s, air, naval, and ground facilities have been very instrumental in the new geopolitics of military-strategic access characterized in part by occasional joint exercises of US and host nation forces.

The use of port facilities and overflight privileges have become increasingly important in a world plagued by ideological divides exacerbated by the US-Soviet competition and the foundering behavior of Third World nations over political ideology. The consequences of these two interrelated factors is a rather acute division of many regions into rival ideological camps which produce local and regional conflicts. The issue of ideology and foreign aid will be treated in some detail in the next chapter, and in it we will touch upon the various ideological camps in Third World regions. Meanwhile, the granting of port facilities and overflight privileges to the superpowers is increasingly contributing to regional tensions caused by many Third World nations putting pressure on neighboring states to deny overflights from superpowers to their neighboring rivals.

Use of port facilities can be viewed as a form of subtle power projection either in relation to a military alliance or to signal military commitment to a Third World state. [7] Port visits or fleet movements are used to deter a neighboring antagonist or to support a client state by threatening a rival neighbor. Kenya and North Yemen have been similarly supported by the US when threatened by neighbors, while the Soviets have done the same in relation to Mozambique and Angola against South Africa in the Southern African subregion.

Factors and developments in military-strategic thinking such as intelligence ships, ground ships, aircrafts and satellites, and surveillance of radars and communications emanating from a rival region are integral to basing access. In many cases these instruments and activities may require port facilities or airport facilities for repairs, replacement, refueling, and manpower rotation. Port facilities and overflight rights in particular have become a central element of antisubmarine warfare practices by the US and USSR. Countries such as Oman, Kenya, Thailand, among others are stations for the numerous computerized US S-3A and P-3C aircrafts used in pinpointing submarines. [8] This is all part of the ongoing superpower competition aimed at finding new ways to detect, locate and destroy their opponents nuclear ballistic missile and attack submarines.

In the interwar years and the era of colonialism, Western powers and corporations owned or controlled numerous port facilities and overflight privileges were less restricted. However, the competition for basing access became more intense starting with the decolonization process which ushered in numerous independent nations seriously jealous of their newly-won sovereignty. [9] The existence of sometimes politically opposed or antagonistic neighboring countries has resulted in regional interstate and domestic conflicts in which the major powers find themselves either directly or indirectly involved. Provision of basing access by a nation embroiled in a regional conflict often translates into extension of military assistance by the major powers. The arms transferred or the military advice provided is ultimately used in the war effort, such as Soviet military assistance to Ethiopia in its war with Somalia, or US military assistance to Morocco in relation to the Western Sahara conflict.

Prior to the end of the Second World War, there were no US forces or bases in Africa and the Middle East. In Asia there was a 'station fleet' at Shanghai primarily intended before World War II, for the protection of US nationals and business ventures against the regional Chinese civilian conflicts. Furthermore, the various post World War II developments - the seemingly monolithic Sino-Soviet Communist bloc, coupled with their massive land armies added logistical advantage to the rival Eastern bloc. Faced with such a seeming strategic disadvantage the maintenance of naval and air superiority became an obvious preoccupation of the West. Moreover, the introduction of new military technology (in particular nuclear weapons) produced a new and modified need for overseas bases for deterrence and reconnaissance purposes. Collecting intelligence on the Soviet Union became a strategic imperative especially because of the 'closed' nature of Soviet Society.

The transfer of economic and military aid to underpin basing access, a feature of foreign policy absent during the interwar years, became a key element of world politics following the end of the war. The acquisition and retention of facilities by the West was made possible by either the existing colonial domination over overseas territories or the still lingering remnants of past colonial rule. In time, the network of bases was extended by common membership in alliances and converging regional interests resulting from Third World domestic and interstate conflicts.

By the mid 1960s the outlines of a US-Soviet basing competition were already being shaped by a more assertive Third World, and by new forces and developments in a period that has been referred to as the 'intermediate postwar period.' The key elements of this period can be summarized as:

1. The shift in the international system from a tense competitive environment to a weakening of East-West tensions as reflected n the Sino-Soviet split, a stronger reassertion of French sovereignty from NATO, and the emergence of a North-South split underpinned by economic issues.

2. The continued reassertion of radical nationalism among a number of Third World nations following the decolonization process. Non-alignment, neutralism, and socialism emerged as ideas with which the US had to contend. The establishment of diplomatic

relations between these countries and the USSR
signalled the end of American diplomatic monopoly.

3.   The slow but steady projection of Soviet military
      and diplomatic power in the new nations of Africa,
      Asia, and the Middle East gave a new momentum to
      the military-strategic competition for global power
      projection.

4.   There was a reduced need for forward bases in the
      area of strategic nuclear deterrence.

5.   The lessened need for forward bases was replaced by
      the proliferation of new military technology for
      intelligence gathering, surveillance, telemetry,
      antisubmarine warfare, among others.

Basing networks have been at the center of US-Soviet
confrontations since the immediate postwar years. The
tremendous advantage of the US in this matter led the Soviets
in a meeting of the Big Four foreign ministers regarding
tensions in Europe to identify bases as part of 'the
principal cause of the tense stuation in Europe.' [10] This
complaint was prompted by the US actions following the end of
World War II to effectively consolidate its hold on basing
facilities under its control. As the new leader of the West,
the US gained permission to reopen the strategic Wheelus Air
Force Base in Libya, and partial use of an air facility at
Dhahran in Saudi Arabia. [11] The expansion of the US
basing network was facilitated in large part by British
retention of an extensive network of bases in Egypt, Cyprus,
Libya, Jordan, Iraq, among other locations in the 1950s.
The Korean War of 1950-1953 further served as a catalyst in
the expansion of the US basing network, in addition to the
perceived growing Soviet threat. Priority in base
acquisition was given to air bases as part of the Eisenhower
massive retaliation nuclear strategy doctrine. In 1951 the
US which already possessed 232 Air Force Bases envisaged
increasing that number by more than 33 per cent to arrive at
a total of 309 facilities at home and abroad. That same year
$2.2 billion was appropriated for overseas construction of
installations with the Air Force receiving over 70 per cent
($1,487,000), the army $478 million, and the navy $242
million. [12]
Up till 1960 the access advantage was on the side of the US
with some of its bases in close proximity to the USSR which
lacked similar basing facilities. The interconnectedness of
overseas bases and nuclear deterrence meant that between 1950
and 1960 the former was perceived to play a critical role in
strategies of nuclear balance, mutual deterrence strategies
against surprise first strike vulnerability. The maintenance
of credible offensive and defensive systems was considered to
hinge largely on access to foreign bases for crucial

intelligence monitoring activities and other communication activities.

United States overseas facilities also played a crucial role in the surveillance and detection of Soviet missile developments and buildup. The latter part of the 1950s saw the second in a series of 'gaposis' now commonly known as the 'missile gap.' [13] In 1955 the Soviets began testing IRBMs with a range of 1,000 miles. The following year the Soviets were working on ICBMs and the 1957 launching of the first satellite to orbit the earth (Sputnik) added fresh fears to the American concern over a Soviet military technological breakthrough that could place the US far behind in the military-strategic competition. Overseas facilities enhanced the US competitive edge because they served as take-off points for U-2 surveillance planes, facilitated satellite reconnaissance activities and other forms of intelligence gathering activities. In the recovery of satellite photos ground facilities both in the US and overseas were particularly crucial. Since the mid 1950s the Seychelles Islands, Ethiopia, among others served as ground stations to recover satellite photos. The need for foreign ground, sea, and air facilities increased with the proliferation of technical intelligence capabilities even though during the same period the need for forward overseas nuclear bases was diminished by the advent of ICBMs.

The massive Soviet nuclear and conventional buildup between 1950 and 1961, coupled with the closed nature of Soviet society which made human intelligence gathering extremely difficult, made overseas bases increasingly relevant to the overall US military containment strategy. [14] The use of aircraft for electro-magnetic reconnaissance and intelligence (ELINT) and the use of numerous ground-based intercept stations for communication intelligence (COMINT) were all being directed at the Soviet Union from foreign bases in Turkey, South Korea, Iran, and other places.

United States basing access was dependent on British maintenance of prewar basing structure during the Cold War. The Americans had filled in the vacuums in some areas where British overseas access was either diminished or eliminated. The US was able to gain a foothold in Greece (Salonika) following British withdrawal and enunciation of the Truman Doctrine. In Somalia, British withdrawal in 1950 made it possible for the Soviets years later to gain basing access in the Horn. Between 1945 and 1956 Britain lost all of its bases to the new Egyptian nationalism spearheaded by Gamal Abdel Nasser. In sub-Saharan Africa, however, Britain maintained most of its prewar base acquisitions throughout the 1950s. Kenya became an important basing access for British military activities in the surrounding regions. In the mid 1950s, the British troops deployed variously to

Malaya, Aden, and the Persian Gulf were dispatched from Kenya. [15] However, by the early 1960s the reality of decolonization with its attendant nationalism provided in various degrees American and Soviet access to the former elaborate system of British bases in Asia, Africa, and the Middle East.

Similarly, the end of the various other Western colonial empires resulted for the Soviets access to a number of bases and for the West in the loss of a number of basing assets. Soviet influence was later to become dominant in Algeria, Mali, Guinea, Guinea-Bissau, Angola, and Mozambique. The competition for influence over these ex-French, Portuguese, and Spanish colonies was to have wider ramifications in terms of the direct or indirect US and Soviet material support of client states in their regional conflicts.

During this immediate post World War II period, US basing access and forward alliance system were focused primarily in the Far East and in Western Europe and the Mediterranean. American basing needs were fulfilled by the British basing network stretching from Cyprus to Singapore, touching on Iraq, the Persian Gulf, Kenya, the Seychelles, and Mauritius. Later in the 1960s the gradual withdrawal of the British presence in those countries would result in a US takeover of facilities in Bahrain, Mashirah, and Diego Garcia, while the Soviets would fill the vacuum in other vacant areas.

It was only after the mid 1960s that the US basing network extended to Southeast Asia and the Eastern coast of Africa. The exceptions were Pakistan, Iran, and Turkey which provided the US with intelligence listening posts and a staging ground for its U-2 flights over the USSR. The Dharan base in Saudi Arabia and the Kagenw station in Ethiopia were respectively staging points as well as refueling points and communication facilities for the United States.

The developments of US basing access in Latin America and the Caribbean, and in sub-Saharan Africa lagged far behind that of other territories during the highwater mark of the Cold War period. Most of these regions were either still uncontested US spheres of influence or in the case of Africa still largely under the aegis of the former colonial powers. Except for the US use of Roberts Field in Liberia for staging purposes, and the use of the South African intelligence and communication centre at Silvermine, US military installations were absent from sub-Saharan Africa.

From 1947-1957 the Soviets were almost totally lacking in overseas facilities. Towards the second half of the 1950s, they entered the arms transfer business of the Third World. [16] This development paved the way for basing access and provided the Soviets with the opportunity to gradually get out from under 'capitalist encirclement.' In 1955 arms agreements were signed with Egypt and Syria. Later years saw

193

Table 7.2
US Third World Bases in the Late Cold War Period

Country	Medium of Access
South Korea	Alliance-Agreement
Taiwan	Alliance Agreement
Laos	Agreement
Vietnam	Alliance-Agreement/Military Aid
Phillipines	Alliance-Agreement/Military Aid
Thailand	Alliance-Agreement (SEATO)
Singapore	Agreement
Pakistan	Agreement (CENTO, SEATO)
Iran	Bilateral Agreement, CENTO
Saudi Arabia	Agreement, Arms Sales
Ethiopia	Security Agreement/Military Aid
Kenya	Agreement/Foreign Aid
Liberia	Agreement/Foreign Aid
Madagascar	Agreement
Liberia	Agreement until 1969
Morocco	Agreement
Panama	US Control/Agreement

Source: US Senate, United States Security Agreements and Commitments Abroad, 91st Congress, Vol. 2, Parts 5-11, pp 1961-1962.

the initiation of arms relationships with North Yemen (1957), Indonesia (1958), Guinea (1959), and India (1961).   Arms transfers were selectively targeted in large doses at a few client states.   The transfer of arms, though it did not immediately guarantee base acquisitions, nonetheless paved the way for achieving this foreign policy objective.   The Cuban revolution, radical nationalism, or left-leaning non-alignment on the part of some Third World states would later translate into more arms transfers as a quid pro quo for basing access. In subsequent years the evolving American and Soviet network of bases and alliances would be increasingly consolidated by massive military and economic aid packages to host countries, and by an equally ever increasing convergence of military-security interests between superpower and host country.

After 1965 following the lessening of tensions inherent in the Cold War period the military-strategic map of global competition for political influence and basing access had changed.   They came to depend increasingly on political compatibility and resource transfers.   The geopolitical underpinnings of military basing access had altered from the traditional Mackinderian heartland/rimland basis of access to one based on a bipolycentric, diffused, and globally dispersed spatial configuration of competition.

During this modern era US military basing access is subject to Third World regime stability and change. In roughly the past two decades the US basing access has been totally lost or nearly so in Libya, Iran, Ethiopia, Laos, South Vietnam, the Seychelles, among other locations.   Withdrawals of its allies--Britain and Portugal in particular--from countries such as Malta, Angola, Mozambique, Cape Verde, and the Maldives, resulted in the loss of easy military access. Another reason for the loss of easy access may stem from the lessened cohesion of the Western alliance which has eroded the Cold War convergence of military-security commitments between the US and its allies, and the commonly perceived Communist threat of the 1950s.

In the evolving geopolitics of superpower military basing, the Soviet Union penetrated Latin America and the Caribbean once an exclusive US geostrategic preserve.   Soviet centers of influence were equally found in Africa, the Middle East, South Asia, Southeast Asia, among others.   The rapid Soviet gains were attributed to the global decolonization process which produced a host of new Third World regimes espousing radical nationalism and/or anti-Western political orientations, or left-leaning 'non-alignment.' The political foundation laid in the 1950s based on the establishment of arms transfer relationship with Egypt, Syria, Somalia, Tanzania, India, and Indonesia, among others was a major factor in the acquisition of Soviet bases in these new nations. In more recent years Soviet basing objectives have been extended to Third World nations considered largely pro-Western. [17] Columbia, Ecuador, Kenya, Mexico, Pakistan, Tunisia, and Uruguay, among others, have all extended access to the Soviets in the area of diplomatic port visits.

The North African, East African, Persian Gulf, and Indian Ocean areas are the major focus of recent Soviet and American geopolitical basing competition. There were reports of Soviet attempts to secure full use of Libyan onshore naval facilities, in addition to developing the Libyan port of Bardia as a future naval facility and the construction of air bases in Southern Libya as future staging areas for operations in neighboring regions. More recently South Yemen has replaced Somalia as the major site of Soviet basing activities in the Persian Gulf region.

A key element of Soviet global strategy that facilitates its base acquisitions is provision of military assistance during wars of independence or national liberation. In such an instance material support precedes basing access. Following the Mozambiquan independence victory in 1975, due largely to Soviet arms supply, Soviet vessels were allowed to make calls at the ports of Lourenco Marques (Now Maputo), Nacala and Beira. Indications of further security commitments were signalled by the Soviets after a South African raid into Mozambique. The Frelimo government has apparently been resisting a major Soviet basing access, unless South Africa engages Mozambique in a major conflict with South Africa.

Beginning with the mid 1960s to the late 1970s, Soviet basing network was primarily concentrated in the Mediterranean and Indian Ocean areas. Developments in the 1980s point towards Soviet expansion in the Pacific and in Africa. The shift in focus is due to the change in alignments in Asia particularly following the erosion of US presence in Southeast Asia. In Africa, Guinea-Bissau, Cape Verde, Benin, Congo, Nigeria, and Equatorial Guinea have developed arms transfer relationships with the Soviets and some have apparently allowed Soviet staging operations en route to Angola. [18] In Mali which participated in the Angola staging operation, there were reports of Soviets building a large air base earmarked for future staging operations to Southern Africa.

Finally, this global air and naval access network of the Soviets has been readily used to assist pro-Soviet states in conflict such as Algeria, India, South Yemen, Ethiopia, Angola, Mozambique, among others. The use of these networks of facilities to assist client states also helps strengthen the credibility of Soviet commitments in the perception of Third World nations. In the final analysis, Soviet basing success like the American basing access network will also be underpinned by convergent regional military-security interests and its fortunes affected by vicissitudes of regime instability and change. Egypt and Somalia have not too long ago been removed from the client network system due to shifts in alignments. The complex nature of many regional conflicts is bound to bring about more changes in the future.

THE BASE-AID-JOINT TRAINING NEXUS

In order to capture the most recent trends in US basing objectives, it will be worthwhile to examine the base-aid-training nexus around Africa and the Middle East. The subregion of North Africa - Morocco, Algeria, Tunisian, Libya, and Egypt - has always figured prominently in the geopolitics of US military basing because of its physical location, it borders on the Mediterranean and is therefore relevant to the strategic calculations of the NATO defense system. The significance of the North African states is largely based on their geographic proximity to Europe and to NATOs bases in Spain, Italy, Greece and Turkey. In the geopolitical writings of Mackinder and Spykman, North Africa is portrayed as an integral part of the rimland in explanations of the heartland theory. [19] The rimland, in fact, starts from the southern shores of the Middle East and South Asia and eventually reaching Japan. For Mackinder and Spykman, control over the heartland (Germany and/or Russia) could hardly be accomplished without control of sensitive choke points along the rimland, over coastlines, and the hinterland.

The importance of Africa and the Middle East in these geopolitical calculations regarding the rimland has been strongly expressed in this manner:

> From this rimland, nuclear B-36 bombers could strike at Soviet military concentrations if required; war supplies could be prestocked with assurance they would not fall into adversary hands; Soviet maritime and naval activities could be kept under surveillance; facilities in North Africa and Middle Africa could be used to transport...equipment into the Middle East; communications and other intelligence activities could be carried out in comparative security; antisubmarine patrols in the Atlantic, the Red Sea, and the Indian Ocean could be facilitated. [20]

The trend of US military basing has closely followed the central thrust of the heartland theory. In the early 1950s the cold war competition compelled the US to construct four air bases in Morocco. It lost Wheelus Field, a major strategic Libyan base, following the Libyan revolution of 1969.

Egypt was one of the first African countries to provide military facilities for the US Rapid Deployment Force in 1980. The Cairo-West air base has been used for training exercises for American forces. The agreement to use the base was signed between President Carter and President Sadat with the understanding that it would not constitute a permanent American military presence. Further agreements were that military exercises were to be held jointly between American and Egyptian forces, with all installations to include Egyptian officers. Moreover, Egypt's importance in the recent geopolitics of US military basing is reflected in its inclusion in the encirclement strategy set in motion by the Carter administration following the 1978 realignment of forces in the Horn. [21] The strategy involved influencing Ethiopia's neighbors - Egypt, Kenya, Somalia, and Oman - with military, security, and economic aid as a quid pro quo for the establishment of military facilities and use of their territories as staging grounds for the RDF's military operations in the Middle East in particular. Furthermore, Egypt, especially, is critical as an East-West axis because of its strategic link between Western Europe, the Balkans, and the Black Sea.

Also included in President Carter's encirclement strategy in the geopolitics of African and Middle Eastern basing were Somalia and Kenya who agreed to provide bases for the staging operations of the RDF in the Persian Gulf, roughly a thousand miles away. Somalia allowed the use of two of its facilities: the port at Mogadishu and the facilities at Berbera on the Gulf of Aden. The latter comprised of a port and air base with two air strips of roughly 15,000 and 18,000 feet respectively which were built and used by the Soviets between 1974 and 1977. [22] In general, the importance of the East African littoral to the geopolitics of US military basing increased from the minor to major level in the 1980s as a result of US-Soviet competition in the Indian Ocean. The Indian Ocean, in addition to the commerce that is transported through its waters is also a prowling environment of American and Soviet submarines. Access to the Ocean would enhance the launching capacity of nuclear delivery systems of the major powers. The two superpowers are particularly active in the Indian Ocean, each trying to search out the other's missile-bearing submarines and antisubmarine forces.

Unlike North Africa, East Africa, and parts of the Middle East, Southern Africa is yet of low intensity in terms of the competition for superpower military basing, with both superpowers presently content with maintaining the military-strategic status quo. The subregion's military significance to the US largely revolves around South Africa because of the following reasons: (1) its key location around the sea lanes of communication - the Cape of Good Hope, the Madagascar Channel, and the Mascarene Passage, among others - between the South Atlantic and the Indian Ocean; (2) the country is endowed with excellent port facilities for military as well as commercial vessels; and (3) the countries in the subregion and South Africa in particular, contain minerals critical to the military and space industries.

The unprecedented domestic upheavals in the mid 1970s in Southern Africa, coupled with Soviet and Cuban external interventions compelled the US to abandon its complacency towards the subregion. The present US support of low-intensity warfare against the Marxist-Leninist regimes in the subregion is viewed by critics as an alliance between the US and the Apartheid regime of Pretoria. However, the US, as part of the Reagan Doctrine, abandoned its long standing complacency for two main reasons: the existence of radical regimes espousing Marxist-Leninist ideology following the collapse of the Portuguese African empire; and Moscow's proclivity to move in and fill up the political vacuums created by civil wars and general instability.

An inevitable and interlocking relationship has developed between the use of military facilities and the transfer of resources as a quid pro quo. While US military bases and other facilities are intended to enhance American global power projection, at the same time it is in the regional interest of the US as well as the client state to use economic and military assistance to strengthen the latter's self-defense capabilities. [23] The interconnectedness of bases, aid, and the client state's domestic and external defense is revealed in superpower relations with countries like Ethiopia, Somalia, Kenya, and Egypt, among others. For FY 1982 Egypt, Sudan, Liberia, and Somalis were among the top 15 recipients of the US Economic Support Fund. The ESF as we have already discussed in Chapter One, is used for countries with short-run economic, political, and development needs. Table 7.3 shows the major recipients among countries in and around Africa of the ESF and 'Development Assistance' (DA) for FY 1982. These are basically countries with US military facilities and overlooking sensitive choke points. In addition to receiving ESF and DA, special military sales agreements are concluded with such forward defense countries. Table 7.4 also shows the major arms agreements between the US and host countries in the early 1980s. During the initial stages of the application of the encirclement strategy, the US-Somali alliance was strengthened by the sale of $42 million worth of defensive military hardware to Somalia. The US Navy also proposed to spend $24 million in Somalia in 1982

199

Table 7.3
Africa: 1982 Recipients of US Economic
Support Fund (ESF) and Development Assistance (DA)

Country	ESF	DA
Botswana	11.0	4.9
Chad	2.8	3.4
Egypt	771.0	239.9
Kenya	10.7	48.6
Liberia	35.0	30.5
Mauritius	2.0	1.7
Oman	15.0	0.5
Seychelles	2.0	0.4
Somalia	20.0	35.8
Sudan	.100.0	51.8
Zambia	20.0	7.1

Source: US Department of State. Agency for International Development Foreign Assistance Program, 1982.

for the upgrading of military facilities in the country. In the same year $20 million in development aid and $25 million in PL 480 food aid was proposed for Somalia. The 1983 US security assistance proposal even called for an increase of $10 million. [34]

The US fiscal year 1983 budget promised close to half a billion dollars in economic and military aid to Djibouti, Kenya, Somalia, and Sudan for making their military facilities available to the RDF. Egypt, under President Sadat was all too willing to enter into a military relationship with the United States. The Egyptian naval facilities at Ras Babas on the Red Sea, its air base at Cairo West were put at the disposal of the US. In 1980 three months of joint military exercises and training were held between US and Egyptian Air Force Squadrons. The acquisition of Egyptian facilities which was also part of the Camp David Accords between Israel and Egypt pledged a US arms transfer of $4.5 billion in arms and other military aid over a three-year period to the two countries. [25] Egypt received approximately $1.5 billion in arms as part of the process of cementing the political settlement between the two countries.

The inevitable linkage between access to military facilities and resource transfers is part of a reverse leverage on the US applied by the host country. In the case of the US in particular, acquiescing to such leverage is based on the need to deny the Soviets sensitive choke points along the Third World littoral for the following reasons: (1) the geographic location of many countries in relation to Europe, the Middle East, and South America; (2) their endowment with many of the minerals critical to the military and space industries; and (3) the need for the US to maintain and protect its already acquired communication and military facilities. While acquisition of strategic points may constitute the most effective way of denying an enemy use of a base for offensive purposes, at times it is also the most expensive because of the element of increased demands for higher levels of economic and military aid involved in the reverse leverage applied by the host country. Moreover, the superpowers are at times dragged into the ongoing regional conflicts, or they may be perceived as taking sides in the sometimes complex and multifaceted local disputes.

SUMMARY

The evolving geopolitics of US and Soviet military basing in the Third World is bound to be a checkered one due to the endemic instability and frequent regime changes characteristic of Third World nations. In 1969, following the Libyan revolution, the US lost its major strategic base,

Table 7.4
The Third World and the US: Major Identified
Arms Agreements, JUNE 1980 - JUNE 1981

Recipient	Date of Agreement	Cost	Expected Delivery
		(millions of dollars)	
Egypt	7/80	104	1981-82
Morocco	3/81	182	NA
	6/81	100	1982
Oman	10/80	17	1981
	3/81	1.3	1981
Sudan	8/80	14.5	1981
		9.5	1981
Tunisia	7/80	24.6	1981
	8/80	23.8	NA
	3/81	15.0	1981
Kenya	10/80	14.0	1981
Somalia	2/81	NA	1981
Saudi Arabia	2/81	117	1981-82
Pakistan	6/81	NA	1982
Thailand	8/80	58	1981

Source: The International Institute for Strategic Studies,
The Military Balance 1981-1982, pp 115-117.

Wheelus Field. Again, in 1978, as a result of the realignment of forces in the Horn of Africa, the US lost all use of Ethiopian military facilities but gained access to the Somalia facilities.

The increasing intensity of US-Soviet geopolitical power projection in the Third World will continue to push the relevance of military base acquisition into center stage. In other words, military relationships and mutual security arrangements will remain a permanent feature of the strategic calculations between superpower and their regional clients. The recent intensity of US basing efforts is still on the rise as reflected in the recent US military activities in Zaire. In April 1987, US-Zairean military manoeuvres coincided with the upgrading of two 7,000 foot-long runways at the Belgian-built Kamina airfield in Zaire's Shaba province. In all, US army engineers made $50,000 worth of repairs at Kamina in addition to establishing five new bases at Kitona, Kincuso, Kimpese, Kahemba, and Dilolo near the Angolan border.

Despite the remarkable developments in electronic and communications intelligence, in side-angle and overhead photography, and sophisticated satellites, overseas military facilities are still germane to US military-strategic calculations. Furthermore, the future usefulness of overseas military facilities in the Third World is presently reflected in their role in theatre nuclear weapons in Europe. These weapons in most cases need foreign bases. The relevance of West European bases in terms of GLCMs and Pershing IIs, among other medium range weapons has already been demonstrated. In the long run many Third World nations could also end up playing the role of staging ground for these weapons.

In addition, the Third World's geopolitical and military importance to the US will continue to increase because control of overseas foreign bases is also essential in satellite tracking, an activity that has a dual purpose for the US: the tracking of the USSR's space systems and the control and tracking of US' own system. The evolving geopolitics of space technology and nuclear defensive weapons seems to strongly point towards more satellite tracking either of rival SDIs or ASATs. At present, several strategic US overseas bases are used to control satellites with the objective of data collection, photographs, and redirection of the satellites.

Finally, while the renewed superpower basing interests in the Third World are likely to continue far into the future, one can only speculate about their continuity and stability. For instance, how will the political instability and deteriorating economic conditions in the Third World affect the evolving pattern of military basing? Or, to what extent will a resurgence of Islamic fundamentalism in predominantly

203

Islamic countries like Egypt, Oman, Morocco, or Somalia disrupt US basing objectives in Africa and the Middle East? In the final analysis, the inevitable linkage between military bases, economic and military aid, and joint military exercises and training will continue to be a key element of US military policy in the Third World. The last two elements - resource transfers and joint military training - will enhance the US' ability to acquire, retain, and increase control over military bases.

NOTES

[1] Third World regions have played various roles in great-power global power projection. For example, a detailed discussion of Africa's many roles in great-power world politics is found in W.J. Foltz, 'Africa in Great-Power Strategy,' in W.J. Foltz and H.S. Bienen (eds.), (New Haven: Yale University Press, 1985).

[2] Further discussions of these strategies are found in Alvin Cottrell, 'Soviet Views of US Overseas Bases,' Orbis 7 1 (Spring, 1963) pp. 77-95.

[3] See, for example, Adeed Dawish, 'Saudi Arabia's Search for Security' (London: International Institute for Strategic Studies, 1980), Adelphi Paper No. 158.

[4] For more details on the nature and extent of these alliances, see, Roland Paul, American Military Commitments Abroad (New Brunswick, NJ: Rutgers University Press, 1973).

[5] R. Steele, Pax Americana (New York: Viking Press, 1977) p. 134; and Paul Kennedy, The Rise and Fall of the Great Powers (New York: Random House, 1987) pp. 389-390.

[6] For further discussions of these terms, see, Robert Harkavy, Great Power Competition for Overseas Bases (New York: Pergamon Press, 1982) pp. 14-18.

[7] An elaboration on such strategies is found in Charles C. Petersen, 'Showing the Flag' in B. Dismukes and J. McConnell (eds.), Soviet Naval Diplomacy (New York: Pergamon Press, 1977) pp 37-87; and Barry Blechman and Stephen Kaplan, Force Without War (Washington, DC: Brookings Institution, 1978).

[8] This issue is treated in more detail by Lt. David T. Easter, 'ASW Strategy: Issues for the 1980s' US Naval Institute Proceedings, (March 1980) pp 35-41; and R. Garwin, 'Anti-Submarine Warfare and National Security,' in Arms Control: Readings from Scientific American (San Francisco: W.H. Freeman, 1975).

[9]   See, for example, P.M. Dadant, 'Shrinking International Airspace as a Problem for Future Air Movements - A Briefing Report,' Report R-2178-AF, Rand Corporation (Santa Monica: Rand Corporation, 1978).

[10] Buel W. Patch, 'Overseas Bases,' Editorial Research Report, Vol. II, No. 2, July 14, 1951, pp. 441-2.

[11] James L. Gormley, 'Keeping the Door Open in Saudi Arabia: The United States and the Dhahran Airfield, 1945-46,' Diplomatic History 4, 2 (Spring 1980) pp. 189-205.

[12] See, Buel W. Patch, 'Overseas Bases,' p. 437.

[13] Post World War II US military development have been characterized by eight gaps: Bomber Gap (1950s), Missile gap and ABM gap (1960s), Hard-Target-Kill gap (1970s), Spending gap, Laser gap, Tank-Armor gap, and Chemical Warfare gap (1980s). For a discussion of these, see, Ruth Sivard, World Military and Social Expenditures 1987/88 (Washington, DC: World Priorities, 1987) p. 9.

[14] See, for example, Phillip Klass, Secret Sentries in Space (New York: Random House, 1971).

[15] For an analysis of Western overseas basing structure in the immediate postwar years, see, Robert Harkavy, Great-Power Competition for Overseas Bases pp. 112-127.

[16] Amelia Leiss, Changing Patterns of Arms Transfers (Cambridge, Mass: MIT Center for International Studies, 1970).

[17] See, for example, Charles C. Petersen, 'Trends in Soviet Naval Operations,' in B. Dismukes and J. McConnell (eds.), Soviet Naval Diplomacy.

[18] A. Shulsky, 'Coercive Diplomacy' in B. Dismukes and J. McConnell (eds.) Soviet Naval Diplomacy.

[19] Halford Mackinder, 'The Geographical Pivot of History,' in Halford Mackinder, Democratic Ideals and Reality (New York: W.W. Norton, 1962) pp. 241-264; and Nicholas Spykman, 'Heartland and Rimland,' in his The Geography of the Peace (New York: Harcourt, Brace, 1944), pp. 38-41.

[20] W.H. Lewis, 'How a Defense Planner Looks at Africa,' in H. Kitchen (eds.) Africa: From Mystery to Maze (Lexington, Mass: Lexington Books, 1976).

[21] See, for example, E.J. Kelley, 'United States Foreign Policy on the Horn of Africa: Policymaking with Blinders On,' in G.J. Bender, J.S. Coleman and R.L. Sklar (eds.), African Crises Areas and US Foreign Policy (Berkely: University of California Press, 1985).

[22] A.J. Pierre, The Global Politics of Arms Sales (Princeton: NJ, 1982) pp. 259-261.

[23] M.T. Klare and C. Arnson, Supplying Repression, US

Support for Authoritarian Regimes Abroad (Washington, DC: Institute for Policy Studies, 1981).

[24] See, H. Wolpe, The Horn of Africa and the United States (Washington, DC: Congressional Research Service, 1982).

[25] US Department of State, US Overseas Loans and Grants, 1982 (Washington, DC: Government Printing Office, 1982).

8 Third World Ideological Preferences and Resource Allocation

A key component of the new strategic environment, also a sequel of the Second World War, was the seemingly overriding impact of ideology. Ideology undoubtedly played a major role in nineteenth-century European diplomacy as reflected in the actions of European statesmen like Metternich, Nicholas I, and Bismarck, among others. In the interwar years ideology seemed to have increased as a factor in world politics with the Russian revolution and the ultimate creation of the Soviet state recognized by the United States only in 1933. Nonetheless, the multifaceted nature of multipolar international politics characterized by alliances that transcended ideological lines, coupled with the isolationist tradition of the US, relegated ideology as a factor in world politics to a secondary role. In the US, even Churchill's celebrated 'Iron Curtain' speech of March 1946 did not help greatly in molding an American world view based on an ideological divide of Communism versus Capitalism.

It took almost three years after World War II before the heightened role of ideology in world politics became a critical element of the Cold War between the East and West. The 'Truman Doctrine' speech exactly a year after the Churchill 'Iron Curtain' speech finally acknowledged a new world politics based largely on ideological differences:

> One way of life is based upon the will of the majority, and is distinguished by free institutions, representative

government, free elections, guarantees of individual liberty, freedom of speech and religion and freedom from oppression. The second way of life is based upon the will of the minority forcibly imposed on the majority. It relies upon terror and oppression, a controlled press, framed elections and the suppression of personal freedom. [1]

Evidence of the ideological divide in the new international system was reflected in the reluctance of the Soviets to conduct free and fair elections in areas under their control, in the struggles between Communist and non-Communist groups in Greece, China, and in some parts of Eastern and Central Europe. One major reason for American global projection of power would be 'to help free people to maintain their institutions and their integrity against aggressive movements that seek to impose upon them totalitarian regimes.' [2]
This chapter will have as its focus the ideological element in world politics in terms of US material support of Third World nations. In other words, we will explore the linkage between the ideological preferences of Third World states and the nature of US-Soviet global competition as revealed in the transfer of arms, and the extension of economic and military assistance. Is there a strong correlation between the ideological preference of a Third World nation and United States regime support? How have ideological affinities shaped American global power projection? Does American aid distribution transcend ideological preference? The above questions will be the concern of this chapter on ideology and the distribution of American foreign aid.
Much like the concepts of imperialism, geopolitics, or liberalism, ideology constitutes a thorny theoretical issue often underpinned by conceptual confusion and therefore difficult to pin down. In Third World politics, in particular, ideology is heavily influenced by factors that produce ideological mutation. In other words, the manifestations of ideological differences between the US and Third World nations vary greatly from one situation to another. We shall classify regimes primarily in terms of their avowed official policy that either Socialism, Marxism-Leninism, or Capitalism is their state ideology. We shall also broaden our conceptualization of ideology based on empirical evidence of US relations with nations that are anti-American due to, say, religious differences. The above approach leads us to identify four strands of regime orientations that have ideological implications for US foreign policy as follows:

1. Marxist-Leninist states such as Ethiopia, Cuba, South Yemen, Laos, among others.

2. 'Socialist' states. These are states that bandy about with the concept of socialism and tend to show an ideological preference for socialist policies. In the 1960s, Kwame Nkrumah's Ghana, Modibo Keita's Mali, and Sekou Toure's Guinea in Africa fell into this category. At present, Tanzania, Libya, and Algeria would fall into the same category. [3]

3. Capitalist states. These are states that have wholly adopted or are seriously following the capitalist model of development. Nigeria, Brazil, Thailand, the Phillipines, among others, fall into this group.

4. 'Anti-Americanism.' This is a situation where individual elite-groups feel resentment, anger, ill will, or even hatred toward the US government and/or American people because of religious orientations like Islamic Fundamentalism in Iran, Egypt, and other countries. This is basically a question of attitudes towards the US irrespective of political and economic differences. [4]

SOVIET-AMERICAN IDEOLOGICAL STRUGGLES

The major geopolitical ramification of the Cold War was its steady extension from Europe to other regions of the world such that by the early 1960s, the US and Soviets were already engaged in ideological struggles over Congo (Zaire), Egypt, Ghana, Cuba, and other locations. While the US was determined to maintain the status quo in former West European spheres of influence, the Soviets were equally interested in future developments in the Middle East and the Far East. As early as 1945, it was already evident from the scramble for vacuums created by the war that American containment of the Soviets would eventually have a wider geographic focus, particularly since the outlines of the competition were being shaped by two rigidly opposed ideologies: Communism and Capitalism.

The geographic transfer of the US-Soviet conflict was precipitated among other factors by the loss of China (1948), the Korean War (1950), the existence of Communist insurgents in Indonesia, the resistance against the British in Malaya, and the French in Indochina. By the early 1950s, the US was already relying increasingly on geostrategic guarantees to contain the Communist threat. In 1951, US air and naval rights to the Phillipines and to the defense of those islands was signed. [5] The same year the ANZUS treaty was also signed. Massive economic and military support was extended to Taiwan and the US increased its military and economic support of Japan.

The Third World instability that produces regimes ideologically incompatible to the US has proved worrisome to US policymakers, especially when such regimes are pro-Soviet in orientation. This concern has resulted, as we stated in chapter two, in the polarization of US foreign policy between globalists and regionalists. The points at issue are what priority should be accorded to containment of the Soviets and what are the sources of radicalism and professions of socialism. The globalists prefer a Cold War, Soviet-centric foreign policy and blame Third World radicalism on the Soviets, whereas the regionalists view conflicts and expressions of radicalism as primarily shaped by domestic factors.

The foundering behavior of Third World leaders over ideology and policy has often been responsible for much of the conflict in Third World nations stretching as far back as the Korean War (1950-53), the Congo Crisis (1960-64), the Angolan Civil War (1974-76), and the Ethiopian conflict (1977-78), among others. The intervention of the superpowers often created situations of increased conflicts and confusions as groups became more rigid in their stance. Moreover, the superpowers are more than prone to view Third World regions only in the context of cold war competition with strong ideological overtones. This tendency which started in the 1950s has been blatantly manifested in many prolonged and internecine conflicts with the Afghan and Nicaraguan ones being the most recent. By the early 1960s the United States became concerned mostly from a psychological point of view, instead of concrete strategic factors, about any Communist penetration of newly independent states. This concern was precipitated by the loss of Cuba to Communism and the growing Communist incursions in Asia. American policymakers then came to believe that any Communist successes in other parts of the Third World would give the ideology added momentum. [6] The containment strategy in many parts of the Third World then became predicated first and foremost on the role of new nations in the battle against the Communist ideology, rather than on the basis of their economic assets or domestic needs.

Moreover, the political vacuums that emerged after independence presented in large part a sudden opportunity for the US to gain new spheres of economic and political influence by maintaining the status quo in former European colonies. It also became the political and economic duty of the US as the new dominant capitalist power to ensure continued Western economic and political access in areas that were formerly British, Belgian, or French preserves. Similarly, the independence of India (1947), Sudan (1956), Ghana (1957), among others, signalled an opportunity for the

Soviet Union to establish a foothold in those countries by advertising its Marxist-Leninist values to political elites groping in the dark in search of an ideological roadmap to modernization.

United States ideological interests intersect with Third World interests on three main levels: in the quest for regime stability, in US-Soviet global power competition, and in the internationalization of Third World conflicts. Many real and potential Third World conflicts have a strong undercurrent of ideological differences among elites, which in turn invite superpower entanglements. In many conflicts the US finds itself increasingly allied with the 'conservative' and/or 'moderate' states against the Soviet Union and the 'progressive' and/or 'radical' states. The conflict over the Western Sahara pitting Morocco against Algeria and the Polisario is one such example. Another is the potential for conflict between Zaire and its neighbors, Angola and Congo-Brazzaville. [7] In the Middle East it is between Saudi Arabia and Iran, in Central America between Honduras and Nicaragua, and in South-East Asia between Thailand and Vietnam.

By the mid-1960s the bedrock of US Third World policy had become anti-Communism. Economic and military aid were purposely used to contain Communism because as the argument goes, Communism exploits the frustrations produced by poor conditions. Economic aid, in particular, could mitigate such conditions. More important, the US put into operation a global strategy based on a ring of alliances designed to frustrate international Communism. Many developing countries would link up with the NATO countries. They then became the recipients of generous economic and military aid while even hard loans were sometimes denied to radical states. One such example was the US refusal to give a loan to Kwame Nkrumah of Ghana but was given to his moderate successor Joseph Ankrah immediately after he toppled Nkrumah from power.

For the United States as well as the Soviets, interrelationships with Third World nations revolve primarily around military linkages (alliances, arms transfer agreements, and basing access). The commitment of massive support in the form of disbursing enormous funds is often triggered by conflict situations with ideological overtones. Between 1979 and 1983 Soviet and other Eastern bloc aid to Nicaragua exceeded $1176 million all geared towards maintaining the Sandanista regime in power. [8] Similarly, military cooperation between Honduras and the US in support of the Contras strengthened considerably.

Closely tied to, and shaped by, ideology, is the pursuit of US military-strategic basing access which we have already discussed in the preceding chapter. The countries that have granted the US special rights for naval and other military

211

activities in their territories are, to say the least, headed by regimes ideologically acceptable to the United States. Egypt, Kenya, Somalia, and Oman, among others, have provided access to the RDF for most of its foreign operations. The military agreements between the US and these countries constitute a seeming convergence of interests between moderate and/or conflict-ridden Third World countries and the United States. Providing military facilities to the US has resulted in the conclusion of generous and very substantial military sales agreement with these countries. [9] Egypt, Kenya, Morocco, and Oman in particular are inclued in the encirclement strategy. While Somalia, Kenya, and Mauritius provide the US easy access to the Indian Ocean, Ethiopia, Mozambique, and South Yemen are transit points for the substantial number of ships (32 ships during September, 1980) maintained by the Soviets in the Indian Ocean. The largest aircraft carriers and dozens of other ships belonging to the two superpowers prowl the Indian Ocean exposing the surrounding nations to the risks involved in potential or actual conflict resulting from such naval power projection competition.

United States and Soviet attempts to gain influence in Third World nations have not been without their problems. After an initial period of seeming success in Guinea, Ghana, Mali, and the Congo in the early 1960s, Soviet efforts faded in intensity due to regime changes and the indecisiveness of the new nations regarding the adoption of Communism as a model of development. In the early 1970s, the Marxist regime of Salvador Allende was overthrown, thereby eliminating a Communist foothold in Chile. In 1983, the US invasion of Grenada also eradicated what seemed like the beginnings of a Soviet-Cuban influence in that country. Similarly, US ideological gains in Third World countries have been affected by the shaky foundations of the ideological commitments of many regimes. Startling reversals are frequent possiblities, such as the sudden declarations for Marxism-Leninism of the military regimes of Benin and Madagascar. Realignment of forces such as the one in the Horn of Africa in 1978, and the indecisiveness of new leaders are other factors that challenge US ideological objectives in developing nations. Perhaps the most recent and far-reaching ideological challenge for the US was the 'loss' of Mozambique, Angola, and other former Portuguese colonies to Marxism-Leninism.

IDEOLOGY AND ALIGNMENTS

The underlying fluidity of Third World ideological alignments means that no condition - at least up to the present - is ever permanent. Some nations in the recent past seemed to be the exclusive preserve of the US, such as Iran under the Shah, or Egypt under President Sadat. Countries such as Iraq and Algeria seem to sit on a fence separating the two superpowers, maintaining relationships with, and receiving resources from both, without being aligned to anyone.

In parts of the Middle East such as the Arabian Peninsular, the US has long remained an ally of Saudi Arabia, most of the Gulf emirates, Kuwait, and Oman. It was only in 1985 that the United Arab Emirates, Kuwait, and Oman established diplomatic relations with Moscow. South Yemen remains a Soviet preserve with a Soviet military base. Nonetheless, all the Gulf Cooperation Council (GCC) members - Saudi Arabia, Kuwait, Oman, Qatar, Bahrain, and the United Arab Emirates - could be classified as pro-Western or 'conservative,' while the states of Iran, South Yemen, and to a certain extent Iraq, could be regarded as hostile or potentially so. [10]

In Southeast Asia, the ASEAN countries (the Phillipines, Indonesia, Singapore, Thailand, Malaysia, and Brunei) are all capitalist and anti-Communist although quasi-authoritarian. All leftist political orientations are regarded with suspicion largely because of security reasons. In both South Korea and the Phillipines there are situations of precarious stability characterized by cycles of unrest and violence. Communist-led guerrillas persist in their objectives as they seem to be increasingly growing in strength. In both countries there are recurring crises of legitimacy.

In the Middle East, another development that has had ramifications for US global power projection has been the ideology of Islamic Fundamentalism or militant Islam. Although it emphasizes 'non-alignment' towards the two superpowers, it has nonetheless been more hostile to the United States. Iran, for example, under Ayatollah Khomeini has ignored all resource relationships with the US, and has often referred to the US as a satanic power.

In the ideological battle against Communism, what has been called the Reagan Doctrine has added new momentum to US government support for right-wing insurgencies struggling to overthrow Marxist-Leninist and/or repressive regimes in Nicaragua, Afghanistan, and Angola. In its focus it had more of a global orientation compared to many past doctrines of American foreign policy. At present, arms sales, economic and military aid, alliances, among other things, constitute the key elements in the equation of ideological containment. In 1984 the selective distribution of foreign aid to Third World nations was based on perceptions of ideological affinity and convergence of interests in the US. In Africa, for example, the key recipients of aid were Somalia, Liberia, Chad, Sudan, and Kenya. [11] These nations were either part of the encirclement strategy, or were fighting against a Communist-supported faction. The rejects in the aid disbursement process were Tanzania, Mali, Sierra Leone, Togo, and Burkina Fasso, countries with regimes considered less ideologically compatible with the United States.

The ideological underpinning of superpower Third World policy has often been shaped by a continuous interplay of realignments with domestic and regional groups. In the 1960-64 Congolese crisis the Soviets were aligned with the Lumumba/Gizenga faction along with the then radical regimes of Sekou Toure (Guinea), Gamal Abdel Nasser (Egypt), and Kwame Nkrumah (Ghana). [12] In Gizenga's opposition to Mobutu and Kassavubu, Sekou Toure and Nasser had even extended diplomatic recognition to the Gizenga regime in Stanleyville. The US, on the other hand, threw its support behind the moderates, Mobutu and Kassavubu, along with Belgium and other American allies. By October 1962, Mobutu was already receiving bilateral aid in the form of vehicles, communication equipment and US military advisors. United States European allies also initiated a plan (the Greene Plan) whose objective was to speed up Mobutu's rise to power. Although it was later abandoned, the West European powers were totally in support of the US role in the country. The alignment with Mobutu resulted in $6.1 million in US aid by mid-1964, almost two years following the outbreak of the crisis.

The alignment of forces in the Congo (now Zaire) has since the first crisis followed a strict pattern of 'conservatives' versus 'radicals.' During the Shaba invasions of 1977 and 1978, Morocco joined forces with the US, Belgium, and France to repulse an invasion of former Katanga (now Shaba) launched from Angola. Following the 1978 invasion in particular, Mobutu was supported by 2,500 troops from moderate African countries in this order: 1,500 soldiers from Morocco, 600 from Senegal, 180 from Togo, and 80 from the Ivory Coast. [13] This Force interafricaine, as it is known, is composed of soldiers from predominantly conservative African countries.

The continent of Africa is especially replete with examples of conflicts underpinned by ideological differences and alliances between moderate and radical regimes, with indirect involvement by the US and the Soviet Union. The ideological accentuation of the Angolan conflict was started during the Nixon Administration and later underscored by Henry Kissinger, who defined the Angolan struggle for independence and the subsequent civil war as a manifestation of Soviet expansionism. The decision was therefore made to support the FNLA and UNITA because of Soviet support of the MPLA. By January 1975, a CIA proposal for $300,000 in covert US support to the FNLA was already under consideration by the 40

Committee of the National Security Council. The proposal
received the overwhelming approval of Secretary of State,
Kissinger. [14] Again, by June 1975, the NSC was
considering more ambitious options in connection with support
for the FNLA and UNITA. One of the recommendations included
financial support of $40 million as well as covert action to
enhance the fighting capacity of the two pro-Western groups
over the MPLA. Pro-Western and moderate Zaire served as a
forward defense for the transfer of the material support for
the US allies in Angola. The FNLA used Zairean territory as
a launching pad for its attacks on the MPLA, reflecting in
large part Mobutu's concern about the possibility of a
Marxist-Leninist MPLA regime as his neighbor. For both
ideological and strategic reasons he allowed Zaire to be used
as a forward base in US intervention in Angola.

The ideological alignments in the Angolan civil war had
already solidified by the Spring of 1975 into a US-Zairean
alliance versus a Soviet-Congo Brazzarille alliance. Congo,
a socialist state, allowed its territory to be used as a base
for the supply of huge quantities of Soviet arms - rockets,
AK-47 rifles, machine guns and bazookas - which were
transported directly at points along the Angolan border. By
the Summer of 1975, the Angolan civil war became multifaceted
with local, regional, and external actors involved. On the
Western moderate wing were the FNLA, UNITA, South Africa,
Zaire, Great Britain, West Germany, Belgium, and the United
States; and on the socialist pro-Soviet wing were the MPLA,
Congo-Brazzaville, Cuba, and the Soviet Union. In the 1980s
the Angolan conflict is winding down but is still underpinned
by ideological divisions.

In Third World-Superpower relations ideological affinities
play a significant role in decisions to extend material
support, intervene, or enter into an alliance. At the same
time the impact of ideology is decreased by other
determinants of Third World-superpower interrelationships.
Overriding geopolitical factors or raison d'etat
considerations on both sides tend to transcend simple
political ideological considerations.

Socialist regimes of diverse hues have cooperated willingly
with US multinationals, programmes and projects. American
oil companies operate successfully in Libya and Angola. In
1961 the regime of Kwame Nkrumah in Ghana cooperated
successfully with Kaiser in the Volta Dam project. Sekou
Toure's Guinea tolerated without conflicts Olin Mathiesen and
Harvey Aluminum. Currently, Gulf Oil still works amicably
with Marxist-Leninist Angola, although still unrecognized by
the US government. The so-called Marxist-Leninist and
Socialist states of the Third World have mixed policies and
do not adhere to any rigid Soviet model of development. In
speaking of the ideological factor in the Third World,

reference is being made to the political and military influence of the Soviet Union, Cuba, and China in these countries.

In the realm of international relations, most Third World nations desire to establish diplomatic relations with both superpowers, as an indication of nonalignment and a mark of sovereignty. Moreover, the nature of regional conflicts and the perception of threats to the survival of the regime play a crucial role in the priority given to ideological affinity. Saudi Arabia is presently receiving substantial military assistance from China because of the overriding objective to strengthen its missile defense system. Similarly, in the 1960s, Somalia began building a military-security relationship with the Soviet Union under a market-economy regime, when the US refused to provide it with military assistance because of its irredentist goals directed against Ethiopia and Kenya. When the Soviets chose to change sides and align with Ethiopia in 1977, the Somalis, although Marxist-Leninist, ruptured their Soviet ties and allied with the United States.

Finally, we would expect large-scale US aid to be transferred to countries that are ideologically compatible to, and have an ongoing convergence of interest with, the United States. Table 8.1 presents a random selection of US economic and military aid recipients in rank order from 1946-1981. We see that resource allocations reflect to a large extent the factors of ideological affinity, convergent regional interests, and historical ties. Pakistan, Morocco, and Zaire rank high in economic as well as military aid. But at the same time during this time period, 1946-1981, foreign aid has been used to maintain diplomatic relationships with states that have very few interests with the United States. Syria, Libya, Iraq, Angola, and Congo, states that for most of their existence have been either Marxist-Leninist, Socialist, or pro-Soviet received aid from the United States. The above patterns are discernable because in the twentieth century foreign aid is an instrument for conducting diplomacy. US economic aid programmes are made to sustain, at least, some semblance of aid relationships with many countries.

SUMMARY

The US anti-communist reaction, which is explicitly ideological, has not been the sole motivation of foreign policy toward the Third World, but its expressions have been abundantly clear in connection with its interrelationships with economic interests. This ideological basis of foreign policy has always aimed at the support and maintenance of

Table 8.1
A Random Selection of US Economic and
Military Aid to Third World Nations 1946-1981

US Economic Aid (1946-1981. $ millions)		US Military Aid (1946-1980. $ millions)	
Pakistan	5,047.7	Thailand	1,719.5
Morocco	1,061.3	Pakistan	713.7
Zaire	668.3	Indonesia	468.0
Syria	587.9	Morocco	350.7
Afghanistan	536.9	Tunisia	192.1
Kenya	333.8	Zaire	162.9
Tanzania	308.8	Malaysia	159.1
Somalia	256.6	India	146.3
Libya	212.5	Kenya	116.3
Algeria	203.3	Sudan	65.3
Malaysia	89.8	Iraq	50.0
Mozambique	70.6	Somalia	40.4
Iraq	45.5	Libya	17.6
Angola	12.7	Guinea	1.0
Congo	12.7	Syria	0.1

Source: The New Book of World Rankings (New York: Facts on File, 1984).

moderate pro-Western leadership in developing countries. The competition between the US and the Soviets to enlist a regime's ideological commitment to either capitalism or socialism commenced in the late 1940s and has since been reflected in the pattern of their interventions in the material support of Third World crises and conflicts. The developing countries became targets of increased resource transfers punctuated by regime changes brought about by coups, revolutions, and civil wars that found the two superpowers either losing or gaining clients and getting involved in regional conflicts.

In the 1980s, US involvement in conflicts has been more indirect, one example being the Western Saharan conflict. Morocco has served many times as the custodian of Western interests in the region, providing a staging ground for the RDF since 1982. The convergence of interests between the US and Morocco led the former to provide massive amounts of military aid to the latter. The weapons were obviously used in the Western Sahara conflict against the Polisario. Although the Carter Administration tried to distance itself from the conflict, the Reagan Administration did not hesitate to supply Morocco with weapons.

However, while ideological affinities may play a big role in interrelationships, at times cooperation is predicated on geopolitical factors. Soviet access to the Somali airbase complex at Berbera in the early 1970s was made possible more by the Somali-Ethiopian conflict than by the degree of ideological affinity (Marxist-Leninism) between the two countries. This observation is supported by the subsequent realignment of forces in the region in which Ethiopia - for long a US ally - became a Soviet ally, and Somalia an avowed Marxist-Leninist state entered into an alliance with the US in 1980.

Finally, although ideology is a key motivating factor in US global power projection, the dominoes have not fallen in many Third World countries as theorized in the 1950s. In South-East Asia, the ASEAN nations are still intact and largely successful in their capitalist orientation. In other words, the loss of South Vietnam did not mean the fall of other pro-capitalist nations in the region. In Africa and the Middle East there is reluctance among self-ascribed Marxist-Leninist or Socialist states to adhere to a rigid Soviet model of development. The existence of these states (Angola, Mozambique, Algeria, South Yemen, and others) has not affected the pro-capitalist choice of other states. More recent trends seem to strongly point to a weakened ideological appeal of Communism as a model of development. The reforms of China (experimentation with the market system), followed by the ongoing economic and political restructuring (Perestroika) of Soviet society, may weaken

218

even further the political and economic appeal of Communism and reduce the Communist underpinning of American foreign policy.

NOTES

[1]   See, M. Balfour, The Adversaries: America, Russia, and the Open World, 1941-1962 (London: Routledge and Kegan Paul, 1981). p. 71.

[2]   Quoted in Paul Kennedy, The Rise and Fall of the Great Powers (New York: Random House, 1987), p. 372.

[3]   Crawford Young categorized African states into three ideological orientations: Afro-Marxist, Populist Socialism, and Capitalist. For details on these categories see, Crawford Young, Ideology and Development in Africa (New Haven: Yale University Press, 1982), pp. 9-12.

[4]   A detailed study of anti-Americanism is found in Alvin Z. Rubinstein and Donald E. Smith, Anti-Americanism in the Third World (New York: Praeger, 1985).

[5]   For a chronology of the lateral escalation of the Cold War from Europe to the Third World, see, Paul Kennedy, The Rise and Fall of the Great Powers, Chapter 7.

[6]   In the case of Africa in particular, US concerns about Communism were largely psychological because of the continent's low priority in US military-strategic calculations, especially in the 1960s. For a fuller account of this aspect of American foreign policy, see Henry F. Jackson, From the Congo to Soweto: US Foreign Policy Toward Africa Since 1960 (New York: William Morrow and Co., 1982).

[7]   A comprehensive discussion of actual and potential conflicts in Afree is found in Gerald Bender et al., African Crises Areas and US Foreign Policy (Berkeley: Univ. of California Press, 1985).

[8]   Jorge I. Dominguez, 'US, Soviet, and Cuban Policies toward Latin America,' in Marshall D. Shulman (ed.), (New York: W.W. Norton, 1986), p. 66.

[9]   See, for example, The Military Balance, 1981-82 (London: International Institute for Strategic Studies).

[10]   The GCC members met in Abu Dhabi in May 1981 and signed the Charter of the GCC establishing the first Persian Gulf collective security system. For the text of the GCC Charter, see The Gulf Cooperation Council (Riyadh: GCC Secretariat, 1982).

[11]   Crawford Young, Ideology and Development in Africa, Chapter 5.

[12] See, for example, Catherine Hoskyns, _The Congo Since Independence_ (London: Oxford Univ. Press, 1965).

[13] For more details on the Shaba invasions, see Henry F. Jackson, _From the Congo to Soweto_, Chapter 1.

[14] See, Gerald Bender, 'Kissinger in Angola: Anatomy of Failure,' in Rene Lemarchand (ed.) _American Policy in Southern Africa: The Stakes and the Stance_ (Washington DC: Univ. Press of America, 1981).

[15] See Henry F. Jackson, _From the Congo to Soweto_, Chapter 2; and Nathaniel Davis, 'The Angolan Decision of 1975: A Personal Memoir,' _Foreign Affairs_, Fall, 1978.

9 Mutual Power-Dependence: an Alternative Interpretation of the Foreign Aid Relationship

In the preceding chapters, I set out to explore the linkage between US foreign policy and the distributional trends of its foreign aid programmes with a particular focus on the impact of geopolitical, strategic, and socioeconomic characteristics of regions and recipient countries on such a linkage. I also discussed regional, programme, and policy shifts in the distribution of economic and military aid as well as the impact of presidential doctrines on their geographic allocation. In the process we have arrived at some conclusions regarding the connection between foreign aid flows and US geopolitical behaviour that focused on international systemic changes, the level of intraregional conflicts, the donor-recipient aid supply-demand relationship, and the foreign policy output strategies of selectivity and penetration. At this point, it is appropriate to reflect on the entire aid distribution process, and on that basis to offer an alternative interpretation -- as a way of concluding -- of the foreign aid relationship between donor and recipient.

Such an interpretation need not apply to every donor-recipient aid relationship; rather it should provide a set of alternative clues and insights that will be helpful in understanding present and future trends in aid-giving behaviour and the multiple factors involved in the process and in terms of regional politics.

To begin this interpretation, let us recall that in chapter

three we defined the national interest as the sum total of geopolitical, military, and socioeconomic objectives sought by the state in its conduct of foreign policy. Earlier on in chapter one we also mentioned the four fundamental US national interests: preventing the expansion of Soviet power and influence in the Third World; upholding the commitment to the independence and security of friendly states; enhancing global political and economic cooperation to promote US security; and maintaining freedom of access to critical raw materials and passages. With the national interests of both donor and recipient in mind we can now develop an alternative interpretation of the aid relationship -- one that underscores the interlocking security concerns and interdependence of donors and recipients rather than just the dependence of the recipient country on the donor. No doubt, such an interpretation will largely reflect my conceptualization of certain donor-recipient aid patterns; however, my perspectives will substantially be buttressed by empirical evidence unearthed in the course of this study.

EXPLAINING MUTUAL POWER-DEPENDENCE

Most discussions of the foreign aid process have focused on the leverage exercised by the donor state on the recipient state. However, in certain aid relationships it is reasonable to view the interactions involved in terms of bargaining or negotiations between donor and recipient structured by symmetrical power relations. [1] In other words, the geopolitics and economics of foreign aid distribution has been evolving in the direction of mutual power-dependence between Superpowers and recipient countries in actual or potential high-threat, high-conflict, and geostrategic regions. Four factors establish a relationship of mutual power-dependence. First, the superpower donor is not in a dominant position because it cannot terminate its aid without great loss or cost to its national interest. Second, the mutual possession of valued things ('utilities') by both donor and recipient place them in advantageous bargaining positions, which may enable them to dictate a number of conditions to each other on the basis of which concessions are made. Third, the type of aid and utilities involved allow both donor and recipient to intervene and exercise leverage in each other's internal affairs. Fourth, repayment of debts incurred from aid and renewal of utilities like military bases often require that both donor and recipient reschedule debts and renegotiate terms which again place both of them in advantageous bargaining positions.
What are most likely to accelerate mutual dependence between a Superpower donor and a recipient country are:

(1) the intensity of local conflict within the recipient country and between it and rival regional neighbors; (2) the extent of foreign (superpower) competition in the region; and (3) the scope of foreign commercial transactions as well as the economic salience of the region. Regions of high conflict, in particular, regard the supply of foreign aid as a necessity because of many reasons, among which are: (1) their involvement in actual or potential conflict with an equally strong regional nation; (2) the fact that they may be engaged in a protracted confrontation with guerrilla forces; and (3) the regime in power may simply want to enhance the prestige of the armed forces, or engage in conspicuous industrialization through modernization of its military.

In mutual power-dependence, the influence of a Superpower over a Third World recipient nation is determined by the dependence of the latter on the former for foreign aid and its corresponding valued outcomes. In the case of the US the level of military, project, and programme aid, as well as the size of the US market for the recipient's raw materials are all influence factors. Influence is best understood by the importance attached by the recipient to the strategic and economic value of the aid as well as the outcomes at stake in the overall donor-recipient relationship; and the capability of obtaining similar aid from a rival donor.

Similarly, the influence of a recipient country over a Superpower donor is based on the dependence of the latter on the former for the pursuit of its foreign policy goals in a particular region. Valued things like military bases, landing rights, resupply lines, strategic raw materials and other factors are central to the influence relationship. Thus, the special geostrategic significance of either donor or recipient is a function of the extent of the other's dependence on the valued capabilities provided by the other. When dependence on valued capabilities on both sides equally counterbalance each other, a situation of mutual power-dependence is the outcome.

THE EMPIRICAL EVIDENCE

The mutual power-dependence argument is predicated on the assumption that the flow of outcomes in the aid relationship are structured by reciprocity. Outcomes can either be positive or negative depending on the nature of the relationship as it is affected by systemic factors. The provision of air and naval facilities for the US by a geostrategic country like the Philippines would increase the power of the US in the region to the degree that overseas military facilities are of great significance to the US and not actually possessed by other nations in the region.

Similarly, the military presence of the US in Philippino soil would increase the external defense of the Philippines and strengthen the regime against domestic insurgents. Revenues earned from use of military bases also contribute to a healthy economy, particularly if similar revenues are not readily extended by alternative donors.

At the end of World War II, the Philippines grew strong due to US aid and support in the process of rebuilding the country. During the Vietnam crisis, Philippino influence vis-a-vis the US grew enormously as the military and economic ties between the two countries strengthened. In connection with the two military bases, there was a general agreement between the two countries that they should maintain security ties after Philippine independence in 1946, and that the US should retain military bases there. The military base agreement was signed in 1947 and was to last for 99 years providing rent free use of the bases. Since 1947 the base agreement has been amended forty-two times. In 1966 the fixed term of the bases was reduced from the 80 years remaining on the original 99-year term to 25 years (ending in 1991) with the agreement to continue indefinitely thereafter subject to termination by either side with one year's notice. [2]

The influence of the Philippines over the US becomes critical in relation to the bases. If the present Philippine government decides to terminate the agreement in 1991, new base sites must be considered. Other sites, such as Japan or Guam, could be used, but the US could never get two major bases so close together as they are in the Philippines, and no other location has better strategic value. It would also take a considerable amount of time and money (approximately 2.5 billion) to build new bases. Thus, in US-Philippine relationship the issue of the bases seems to confer a power advantage on the Philippines over the US. In other words, although both the US and the Philippines are cooperating to ensure a particular regional outcome, the termination of such cooperation may result in the US suffering more costs or loss than the Philippines. This influence relationship regarding the bases was manifested in 1986 when Congress proposed a FY 1986 aid package which linked economic and military aid to reforms in the Philippine government as well as a provision for one-fourth of food aid to be disbursed by non-governmental institutions. The proposal which in essence was 'blackmail' of the Marcos regime was immediately countered by Marcos with a threat to immediately terminate the base agreements. [3] As a result, the final resolution was modified, at the urging of the Reagan Administration, to exclude those provisions. The influence relationship between the two has produced a situation of interlocked national interests such that the US is concerned about safeguarding

224

the security of the Philippines, and more important
to Clark and Subic, which are the symbols of US
interests in the area.

South Korea stands as another example of inter
converging national security interests of a donor
and a recipient country. Since the Korean War in
1950s South Korea has been dependent on
assistance. The commitment to South Korea
geostrategic implications based on rivalry with the Soviets.
From Syngman Rhee, South Korea's first leader, to Park Chung
Hee, and until recently Chun Doo Hwan, the country has
experienced increasingly repressive regimes. For their part,
the leaders have always justified autocratic rule in the name
of keeping South Korea secure. Despite the pattern of human
rights violations, and successive authoritarian regimes the
US is permanently locked in commitment to the country. In
1977 the US agreed to modernize the Korean military by
extending $2 billion in equipment to it. [4] The extent of
US commitment to the country, itself serves as a kind of
leverage over US foreign policy in the region. For instance,
when President Carter decided to pull out American forces in
the country, he chose as a replacement for the withdrawal to
extend military sales credits to the country over a five year
period for the purchase of aircraft, surface-to-air missiles,
antitank missiles and other sophisticated weapons. He also
promised that US weapons and equipment used by American
forces in Korea would be given to the Korean military. The
US commitment to South Korea is not only geopolitical, it is
also economic. The loss of Korean markets and investment
outlets will adversely affect US exports and level of
employment, in addition to contributing to the inflation
rate. In sum, the relationship between the US and South
Korea could be characterized as one where commitment by a
donor has reached a point of no return such that the
commitment itself acts as a leverage over the donor to the
advantage of the recipient.

A third example of interlocked national interests that
produce mutual dependence are the ties between the US and
Israel. Israel occupies a special place in US geostrategic
objectives in the Middle East. It shares the same values and
democratic traditions as the US but at the same time it is
surrounded by hostile Arab states most of whom do not share
common values and ideals with the US. The US recognizes the
importance of Israel as a reliable ally in the Middle East
and at the same time Israel's strength is to a large extent
due to US economic and military support. In addition to
giving Israel enormous amounts of aid, it has also modernized
the military facilities of Israel. The power relationship
between the two countries could be described as one of mutual
leverage. When the US protested against Israel's annexation

the Golan Heights in 1981, the former Prime Minister of Israel, Menachem Begin, vividly portrayed the relationship when he said:

> What kind of talk is this, 'punishing Israel?' Are we a Vassal state of yours? Are we a banana republic? Are we 14-year-olds, who, if we misbehave, we get our wrists slapped? ... He who threatens us will find us deaf to his threats. [5]

The Israeli leverage on the US stems from its unique place in the Middle East as the only reliable US ally, and the US domestic support for Israel that comes from the American Jewish community, a community that exercises considerable leverage over prominent politicians. Moreover, the US commitment to Israel is further enhanced by the latter's increasing technological capability in the arms industry. Israeli manufactured arms include the Shafrir air-to-air missile, the Gabriel sea-launched missile, the Chariot tank and the impressive Kfir fighter which is an imitation of the French Mirage III. [6] While Israel may be dependent on US aid, at the same time, it has enough leverage over the US because of its own capabilities and status in the region. These factors have been largely responsible for the limited leverage the US has over Israeli policies in the Middle East. Such is the outcome when national security policies converge and interlock in a region of high conflict and rivalry.

Evolving patterns of interlocking interests

In discussions of the evolving patterns of foreign aid relationships it is important to distinguish between a High level of Mutual Power- Dependence and a Low Level of Mutual Power-Dependence. The former refers to a situation in which the scope and intensity of mutual interests have become so interlocked that the relationship could not be broken without great cost or loss to the national interests of both countries. The examples discussed above of the Philippines, Israel, and South Korea fit this situation. In the bilateral relations involved the two nations are a central part of each other's security interests and they work hard to strengthen the alliance between them. Conversely, the latter situation refers to shifting alliances with rivals in which ties may be broken without great loss or cost because of the existence of, and willingness to switch to alternative rivals. It describes a relationship of uncertainty with a low level of commitment because areas of policy convergence are few and in many issues non-existent. The on and off ephemeral relationships between the US and Egypt, Ethiopia, and Somalia, or that between the USSR and Egypt, Ethiopia, and

Somalia fit this description.

A substantial portion of US foreign policy is focused on strengthening and protecting regional powers with whom the US shares critical security interests. The Nixon Doctrine articulated this aspect of foreign policy when it underscored the role of economic and military aid and de-emphasized direct US military intervention. In a pattern of interlocking interests, the US steadily becomes entrapped in its commitment and finds itself protecting their stability at great cost. Oftentimes it is a commitment to unstable regional friends with regional enemies.

In both high and low levels of mutual power-dependence, the US inevitably becomes a part of the regional rivalries that may be territorial, ethnic, or religious in origin. The US experience in the Horn of Africa is a case in point as the President of Somalia (Siad Barre) tried to involve the US in his goal of annexing the Ogaden region which legally belongs to Ethiopia but which is ethnically Somali. The attraction of the abandoned Soviet base at Berbera acted as a leverage over the US in its negotiation with Somalia. In 1980 the US had to overcome its reluctance to get involved in the dispute and extended military aid to Somalia while at the same time telling Somalia to withdraw its troops from the Ogaden. This action by the US completed the rupture in US-Ethiopian relations, made the US an ally of Somalia, and the USSR an ally of Ethiopia.

Military aid is a key element in a mutual power-dependence relationship because with arms the pattern of Superpower competition through 'allies' is enhanced. The US-Soviet competition is reflected in the demand of regional friends for aid, and their increase in defense spending. The commitment of the Superpowers has changed the evolutionary character of military assistance. [7] It was the pattern before the 1970s to confine military aid to unsophisticated and sometimes outdated weaponry, but with increased systemic changes, wealth, and more intraregional conflicts, commitment has grown tighter and so has the nature of the demand-supply relationship. For example, the sophisticated F-15 has been sold to Israel and Saudi Arabia; similarly the Soviet Mig-23 has been made available to many Middle Eastern nations. In 1973 the TOW anti-tank missile, was first released to the outside world only during the Yom Kippur War. The decision of the Superpowers to modify their military aid patterns is one indication that the ties between them and their allies has grown stronger over the years triggering a transfer of more valuable military technology.

In a situation of low level mutual dependence, aid can be given on preventive grounds: to forestall the penetrative moves of a rival donor. For a long time the US was reluctant to satisfy Jordan's request for military aid to strengthen its defenses. But when Jordan began to turn to the Soviets for help the US reacted to King Hussein's move in 1975 and provided the country with 500 Hawk surface-to-air missiles.

In both high and low levels of mutual dependence foreign aid could be used as an instrument of leverage through promises and threats. In 1975 the US promised Israel the transfer of the F-15 and other military assistance in exchange for effecting the Sinai disengagement agreement. Similarly, in 1978 the US persuaded President Sadat to keep Egypt in the Middle East Peace negotiations by making available to Egypt F-5E fighters. Threats are also a part of the influence relationship. Despite widespread human rights violations in the Philippines during the Marcos regime, Marcos demanded substantial economic and military aid in return for the American use of the Clark and Subic military bases by threatening to refuse renewal, and even the cancellation of the agreements regarding the bases.

Moreover, in a relationship of high level mutual dependence, it is common for the recipient nation to ignore the policy wishes of the donor because it is aware of its strategic importance. Similarly, it is common for the donor to refrain from directing sanctions against the recipient country because of the latter's critical importance to the national security of the former. In the area of human rights, the US through the Kennedy Amendment barred all military aid to Chile because of human rights violations after the overthrow of Salvador Allende. However, provisions like the Kennedy Amendment do not affect countries with critical interlocking objectives with the US. Iran during the Shah's reign, South Korea, and the Philippines were not affected by the Amendment because of their geostrategic salience to US national security which acts as a leverage over foreign policy decisions. At the same time, aid to Argentina, Uruguay, and Ethiopia was reduced because of human rights violations and because their ties to the US did not involve critical geostrategic and economic interests.

SUPERPOWER COMPETITION AND RIVAL REGIONAL INFLUENTIALS

The national interest since the 1970s has become increasingly multidimensional in nature for every nation state. The major themes discussed in this book are essentially elements making up such a multidimensionality. For instance, a country's profile, especially its possession of critical resources constitutes one component of its power base which impacts on the national interest of other countries. In addition the networks of aid, trade and investment of which countries are a part, increase the mutual interests between them which in turn enhances the mutual leverage they are capable of exercising over one another.

The US support of Israel during the 1973 Yom Kippur War triggered an oil embargo by the Arab states against the US, Western Europe, and Japan. Since they accounted for about 17 per cent, 55 per cent, and 90 per cent respectively of most Arab oil imports, the embargo was in part responsible for modifying their foreign policies towards the Arab-Israeli conflict. [8] Moreover, being the primary consumers of the world's energy resources, their dependence and vulnerability provided a bargaining edge for the Arab states and especially for Saudi Arabia.

Partly as a result of the 1973-74 experience and largely because of Soviet behavior, President Carter in his 1980 State of the Union address, proclaimed the Carter Doctrine to emphasize the importance of the Persian Gulf, the narrow Straits of Hormuz, and the importance of moderate states like Saudi Arabia and Kuwait to the national security of the US and the West in general. Since the Arab oil embargo, the US has been forging closer ties with Saudi Arabia a regional influential among moderate Arab states and also the state with one of the most highly concentrated oil deposits.

The concentration of other strategic minerals has also been steadily conferring leverage on the endowed countries over the importing countries. Minerals such as cobalt, chromium, manganese, and platinum group metals, among others, are critical to the military and civilian industries of the West. [9] Their strategic element confers on their few owners influence over multinational corporations and their parent states. In Africa, for instance, South Africa is the leading location of these minerals. Although it could not be considered a major recipient of US foreign assistance, as a leading producer of strategic minerals, it has been able to exert influence over the US in connection with the issue of Apartheid. The realization that South Africa is a key producer of critical minerals outside the Communist bloc is largely responsible for the Reagan Administration's refusal to adopt tougher measures against the Apartheid system. The cosmetic reforms made by the regime since 1985 and the reluctance of the US to press for profound changes are an indication of the mutual influence between the two countries, structured by the commercial relations in the area of critical raw materials and geostrategic location.

In the global ranking (status) of nation states regional influentials come after superpowers and major powers. They constitute a group of state actors that exercise, in certain regions, and at certain times, considerable influence over both superpower and major powers. Regional influentials are characterized by a substantial power base: a strong military, a large population, a large geographic size, critical raw materials, and a strategic location, among other things. They sometimes aspire to regional hegemony and become directly involved in the foreign policy goals of the Superpowers as allies cooperating in political, military, and intelligence activities. Nations such as Israel, Syria, India, Pakistan, Egypt, Brazil, Nigeria, among others generally possess many or all of the geostrategic and economic characteristics of regional influentials.

As a result of their importance, regional influentials have been able to develop a special relationship with the Superpowers that in varying degrees, and depending on which regional influential, is one of mutual leverage. They can influence a Superpower's foreign policy goals by threatening a particular line of action; Superpowers in turn can enlist the support of the influential by promising action (for example, increase foreign aid) that would enhance the latter's regional prestige.

The existence of rival regional influentials and Superpower competition means that the former would have continuing leverage over, and commitment to, the foreign policy goals of whichever Superpower they happen to be allied to at any point in time. They lose their leverage only if: (1) the two Superpowers move to the point of full convergence in terms of their national interests and foreign policy goals; and (2) one Superpower completely withdraws from competition in a particular region leaving the other to exercise complete hegemony and establish a sphere of influence.

Furthermore, there are regional influentials whose importance has profound economic implications. The debt crisis usually revolves around them with substantial implications for the viability of the Western economic system. Brazil, Mexico, and Argentina, among others, are very central to the smooth running of the Western economy. They have been the recipients of significant amounts of both private and official foreign aid such that they owe billions of dollars to US private banks and to the US government. Four countries: Argentina, Mexico, Brazil, and South Korea together accounted for about 84 per cent of floating-interest debt in 1982. In 1982, over 50 per cent of the $350 billion private bank debt was owed by borrowers in only seven recipient countries: Mexico (about $40 billion), Brazil ($85 billion), South Korea ($20 billion), Argentina ($40 billion), Venezuela ($30 billion) Chile ($15 billion), and Poland ($25 billion). [10] Since the debt crisis is tied up with international trade and direct foreign investments the US government has to intervene occasionally to help both the banks and the debtor nations. Their central role in the Western economic system means the debtor nations have interlocking economic interests with the US qualifying them for continuous balance of payments support in the form of increased foreign aid to enable them to service their debts and play their role in the international economic system.

The phenomenon of the regional influentials coupled with the Bipolycentrism of the 1980's, and the continuing US-Soviet competition means that interlocking national interests and strong commitments would continue to develop in world politics. This trend as already discussed is structured by restraint in the use of power. An increase in the cost of foreign aid or its curtailment may encourage a recipient state to turn to a rival donor. Similarly, a reduction in the use of foreign utilities or shortening the lease period may encourage a Superpower to find alternative facilities.

In a situation of converging and interlocking interests, advantages in bargaining could be complicated. The direction of the influence relationship is usually determined by a number of factors. In a foreign aid relationship we would expect a donor's leverage over a recipient country to be greater if the latter: (1) is unable to find alternate donors; (2) is unable to meet the conditions accompanying the aid; (3) is not geostrategically located; (4) perceived it may not survive a threat or conflict without the Superpower's help; and (5) has strong political (ideological) ties with the Superpower and is not prepared to find alternate donors. On the other hand, we would expect a recipient country's leverage to be greater if: (1) it maintains aid relationships with several donors; (2) it occupies a geostrategic location; (3) it does not perceive any potential or real threat to its security; (4) it is endowed with critical minerals with no substitutes; and (5) it has no ideological qualms about switching donors.

In the ebb and flow of regional politics there will continue to be occasional realignment of forces because of the complicated nature of the influence relationship in a process of interlocking national interests. Recipient countries that are geostrategic, have very critical raw materials, and are prepared to switch Superpowers regardless of ideology will continue to present dilemmas for US foreign policy. For instance, US ties with Somalia may strain relations with Kenya because of the border and ethnic disputes between the two countries. A similar dilemma exists in US foreign policy in connection with India and Pakistan in South Asia, Brazil and Argentina in South America, and Angola and Zaire in Africa.

Finally, it will not be proper to end this analysis without examining the falling levels of foreign aid in recent years in relation to the new trend in US regional commitments and alliances. The programme cuts embedded in the Gramm-Rudman-Hollings Act will require reductions in many government programmes including foreign aid. Already the act has had a direct impact on foreign aid appropriations by

Congress. Between 1981 and 1985 foreign aid experienced a huge increase of 65 per cent. [11] Since 1986 it has been decreased significantly as part of the efforts to satisfy the Gramm-Rudman-Hollings guidelines to reduce the US deficit. In FY 1986, the first year of the act, foreign aid fell by 13 per cent below the 1985 level. For FY 1987 Congress appropriated 2 per cent less than the previous year's aid level. Although many efforts were made to save foreign aid programmes from cuts, the 1988 aid level fell by still another 2 per cent from the 1987 level. In other words, foreign aid levels will continue to fall if Gramm-Rudman-Hollings guidelines remain in effect.

These cuts in foreign aid programmes which have recently been protested by President Reagan, and Secretary of State George Shultz, among others, has ramifications for US global power projection, and in particular for the existing US commitments and alliances in Third World regions. The decreasing amounts appropriated by Congress since 1986 have been inadequate to fulfill American commitments, responsibilities and obligation. If foreign aid continues to shrink, the very basis for US global power projection and leadership in the world will be in jeopardy. That may also mean that the foreign aid available will be more selectively targeted at only the most valued Third World nations thereby running the risk of alienating or losing many client nations.

Recent trends seem to suggest that security aid will be the wave of the future in US foreign policy. The Reagan administration's emphasis on promoting military and security objectives abroad was cemented largely by security aid. In 1981 security-focused aid represented 50 per cent of total US aid, five years later in 1987 it represented more than 62 per cent. Since 1980 ESF and FMS credit programmes actually doubled and MAP increased by 600 per cent. At the same time, between 1980 to 1987 economic and humanitarian assistance fell by $100 million. [12] In addition, FMS has been transformed steadily from market-rate loans to concessional loans, with some of the loans even being forgiven. Eventually all military aid programmes may be converted to grant programmes.

The converging US-Third World interests in addition to the mutual power-dependence mean that despite the falling levels of aid, the programmes for many of the largest aid recipients - Egypt, Israel, Pakistan - have not been affected by the cuts. Besides, the programmes for base access countries rose by roughly 60 per cent between 1981 and 1987 to over $1.5 billion. [13] Furthermore, the recipients of US foreign aid have increased in number since 1981. Thirty-two countries receive ESF in 1988 an increase of 11 from 21 in 1981.

Although the relevance of foreign aid seems to have decreased, recent years have seen the United States create a global network of security arrangements and commitments largely within the Third World. The agreements with Kenya, Oman, and Somalia in connection with the use of military facilities is largely a result of the desire to protect the Saudi Monarchy and its enormous oil supply which is so vital to the West. The Reagan administration concluded a $3.2 billion military aid package with Pakistan because of its willingness to support the Mujahadeen struggle against Soviet occupation in Afghanistan. [14] These, in addition to the commitments with Morocco, Thailand, Honduras, and the support of various right-wing guerrilla movements are included in the equation of rising US commitments in an era of declining levels of American foreign aid.

The Middle East represents the area with the most significant extension of US security commitments. The process reached one of its highest points in 1978 with the Camp David peace accords which called for far-reaching American financial and military guarantees to Egypt and Israel. The arms transfer relationship between the US and Egypt has reached about $20 billion since 1979. In other parts of the Middle East, the Carter administration enlisted US support of moderate Arab states: Saudi Arabia, North Yemen, among others. South Yemen's attack on North Yemen in March 1979 prompted a US military aid package of $390 million to North Yemen. The Carter administration, following the US foreign policy reverses of 1979 and 1980, asked selected states bordering the Indian Ocean to provide their facilities for US peace time military operations in return for a long-term security partnership with the United States. The mutual security commitment would involve a US foreign aid package to expand and improve their facilities, the maintenance of a continuing economic and military aid relationship, and assurances of protection against external aggression.

The widening trend in US security commitments took-off during the Carter Presidency, they accelerated, strengthened, and expanded during the Reagan years. The Reagan administration continued to use far greater amounts of foreign aid to secure the military cooperation of nations in geostrategic locations. In particular, it relied on security assistance to maintain these new commitments and alliances. Between 1980 and 1986, nominal US economic aid declined 8 per cent while security aid increased 130 per cent to $10.3 billion. [15] Morocco, Oman, Somalia, South Korea, and Sudan received increases in military aid from 50 per cent to 100 per cent. Egypt, El Salvador, Honduras, Pakistan, Thailand, and Tunisia received significant increases from 100 per cent to 200 per cent.

A final facet of this mutual-power dependence and convergence of regional interests has taken the form of rejuvenating the existing alliances to serve as major instruments for US power projection. The ASEAN and GCC especially the targets of US support during the Reagan administration. United States arms transfers to the ASEAN states dramatically increased from $916 million between 1972 and 1978 to $3.37 billion between 1979 and 1985. [16] In terms of the GCC, President Reagan extended the Carter Doctrine to include domestic threats to Persian Gulf regimes. Between 1981-1986, US arms sales to GCC countries reached approximately $15 billion, in addition to a substantial amount of military assistance to some nations in the region. This new convergence of interests between the US and Third World nations involves no formal treaties, is diffuse and often improvised as a reaction to Soviet behavior, and respectful of the political sensitivities of regional states. The longevity of a particular alliance or commitment will largely be dependent on continued common security interests. Despite the falling levels of foreign aid appropriations it will remain a key element of American foreign policy.

NOTES

[1]   For further exposure to the literature on bargaining and negotiations within the context of power, see, S.B. Bacharach, and E.J. Lawler, 'The Perception of Power,' Social Forces 55(1976):   123-134; O.R. Young, (ed.) Bargaining: Formal Theories of Negotiation (Chicago: University of Illinois Press, 1975).

[2]   Details on the politics and economics surrounding the issue of the military bases could be found in San Juan, E.   Crises in the Philippines: The Making of a Revolution (South Hadley, Mass.:   Bergin and Garney, 1986).

[3]   See, Nayan Chanda, 'The 'All Powerful' US With Its Hands Tied,' Far Eastern Economic Review Nov. 21, 1986.

[4]   For further details on the US-South Korean military assistance relationship, see, Andrew J. Pierre, The Global Politics of Arms Sales (New Jersey: Princeton University Press 1982) pp. 210-213.

[5]   New York Times, 'Transcript of Prime Minister Begin's Statement to the US Envoy to Israel,' December 21, 1981.

[6]   See, for example, Andrew J. Pierre, The Global Politics of Arms Sales, pp. 156-164.

[7]   It should be noted that commitment is multidimensional in relation to the donor-recipient relationship. First, commitment and mutual dependence can be produced through various political and economic means, among

which are aid, trade and investment. Second, economic and military aid are instrumental in establishing commitment, but they do not guarantee commitment itself and mutual dependence. That is recipients can undermine commitment and mutual dependence by switching donors, refusing a permanent aid relationship or playing off one donor against another. Third, even in the case of a successfully completed commitment and mutual dependence relationship, both donor and recipient may not derive any benefits. Or it may be the case that the benefits derived are based on asymmetrical aid ties, thereby reducing the relationship to one of simple dependence by either the donor or recipient. For theoretical discussions of commitment, see, Roby, T.B., 'Commitment.' Behavioral Science 5:1960, pp. 253-264; Schelling, T.C. The Strategy of Conflict (New York: Oxford University Press, 1963); and Weinstein, F.P. 'The Concept of Commitment in International Relations.' Journal of Conflict Resolution 13 (March, 1969) pp 39-56.

[8]   For facts on the West's dependence on oil imports, see Central Intelligence Agency, International Energy Statistical Review (Washington, DC: Directorate of Intelligence, October 26, 1982).

[9]   See, for example, Herbert E. Meyer, 'How We're Fixed for Strategic Minerals,' Fortune, February 9, 1981.

[10]   For further facts and figures on the debt problem, see, IMF Survey, 'World Recovery Failing to Reverse Restrictions on Trade and Payments,' July 16, 1984; World Bank, Annual Report 1983 and World Bank, World Debt Tables, 1982-83; and OECD, External Debt of Developing Countries: 1982 Survey (Paris 1982).

[11]   See, Larry Nowels, Congressional Research Service (January 1988).

[12]   David R. Obey and Carol Lancaster, 'Funding Foreign Aid,' Foreign Policy No. 71, (Summer 1988) pp. 141-155.

[13]   Ibid., p. 152.

[14]   See, Terry L. Deibel, 'Hidden Commitments,' Foreign Policy, No. 67, (Summer 1987), p. 46.

[15]   Larry Nowels, Congressional Research Service (January 1988).

[16]   Terry L. Deibel, 'Hidden Commitments,' p. 56.

Amin, Samir, Giovanni Arrighi, Andre Gunder Frank, and
    Immanuel Wallerstein. Dynamics of Global Crisis (New York:
    Monthly Review Press, 1982).
Arkes, Hadley. Bureaucracy, the Marshall Plan, and the
    National Interest (Princeton: Princeton University Press,
    1972).
Askari, Hossein and Michael Glover. Military Expenditures
    and the Level of Economic Development (Austin: University
    of Texas, Bureau of Business Research, 1977).
Avery, William P. 'Domestic Influences on Latin American
    Importation of US Armaments,' International Studies
    Quarterly, 22, (March, 1978): 121-42.
Baldwin, David A. Economic Development and American
    Foreign Policy 1943-1962 (Chicago: University of Chicago
    Press, 1965).
Balfour, M. The Adversaries: America, Russia, and
    the Open World, 1941-1962 (London: Routledge and Kegan
    Paul, 1981).
Bauer, Peter T. and Basil S. Yamey. 'Foreign Aid: What is
    At Stake?' in W. Scott Thompson (ed.), The Third World:
    Premises of US Policy (San Francisco: Institute for
    Contemporary Studies, 1983).
Bell, David E. 'The Impact of Foreign Aid on the American
    Economy,' Department of State Bulletin, XLIX, no. 1274
    (November 25, 1963): 830-31.
Bender, G.J., J.S. Coleman, and R.L. Sklar (eds.). African
    Crises Areas and US Foreign Policy (Berkeley: University
    of California Press, 1985).
Blechman, Barry and Stephen Kaplan. Force Without War
    (Washington, DC: Brookings Institution, 1978).
Block, Fred L. The Origins of International Economic
    Disorder: A Study of US International Monetary Policy
    from World War II to the Present (Berkeley: University of
    California Press, 1977).
Cardoso, Fernando Henrique and Enzo Faletto. Dependency
    and Development in Latin America (Berkeley: University of
    California Press, 1980).
Chase-Dunn, Christopher and Richard Rubinson. 'Toward a
    Structural Perspective on the World System,' Politics and
    Society, 7, 4(1977): 453-476.
Chilcote, Ronald H. and Dale L. Johnson (eds.). Theories of
    Development: Mode of Production or Dependency (Beverly
    Hills: Sage Publications, 1983).
Chubin, Shahram. 'The United States and the Third World:
    Motives, Objectives, Policies,' in Third World Conflict
    and International Security Part II Adelphi Paper No. 167
    (London: IISS).

Cohen, Saul. Geography and Politics in a World Divided (New York: Random House, 1963).

Cottrell, Alvin. 'Soviet Views of US Overseas Bases,' Orbis 7, 1(Spring, 1963).

Crabb, Cecil V. Jr. The Doctrines of American Foreign Policy (Baton Rouge: Louisiana State University Press, 1982).

Cressey, George. The Basis of Soviet Strength (New York: McGraw-Hill, 1945).

Dacy, Douglas C. Foreign Aid, War, and Economic Development, South Vietnam, 1955-1975 (Cambridge: Cambridge University Press, 1986).

Dawish, Adeed. 'Saudi Arabia's Search for Security.' (London: IISS, 1980) Adelphi Paper No. 158.

Deibel, Terry L. 'Hidden Commitments,' Foreign Policy (Summer, 1987).

Dougherty, James E. and Robert L. Pfaltgraff, Jr. American Foreign Policy: FDR to Reagan (New York: Harper and Row, 1986).

Extension of Public Law 480, Hearings before the House Committee on Agriculture, 86th Congress, 1st Session (Washington, DC: Government Printing Office, 1959): 199-208.

Ferris, Elizabeth G. (ed.) Refugees and World Politics (New York: Praeger, 1985).

Fitch, John Samuel. 'The Political Impact of US Military Aid in Latin America,' Armed Forces and Society, V (Spring, 1979) 360-86.

Foltz, W.J. 'Africa in Great-Power Strategy,' in W.J. Foltz and H.S. bienen, Arms and the African: Military Influences on Africa's International Relations (New Haven: Yale University Press, 1985).

Gimble, John. The Origins of the Marshall Plan (Stanford: Stanford University Press, 1976).

Gray, Colin S. The Geopolitics of the Nuclear Era (New York: Crane, Russak, 1977).

Green, Stephen. International Disaster Relief Toward a Responsive System (New York: McGraw-Hill, 1977).

Gunder-Frank, Andre. 'Global Crisis and Transformation,' Development and Change, 14, 3(July, 1983).

Hall, Thomas D. 'World System Theory,' Annual Review of Sociology 8(1982): 81-106.

Hanan, Alfred T. The Problem of Asia and Its Effects Upon International Policies (Boston: Little, Brown, 1980).

Harkavy, Robert E. Great Power Competition for Overseas Bases: The Geopolitics of Access Diplomacy (New York: Pergamon, 1982).

Helleiner, G.K. (ed.). A World Divided: The Less Developed Countries in the International Economy (Cambridge: Cambridge University Press, 1976).

Hoogvelt, Ankie M.M. The Third World in Global Development

(London: MacMillan, 1982).

International Monterary Fund. Survey (March 7, 1983).

Jackson, Henry F. From the Congo to Sovieto: US Foreign Policy Toward Africa Since 1960 (New York: William Morrow and Co., 1982).

Johansen, Robert C. The National Interest and the Human Interest (New Jersey: Princeton University Press, 1980).

Jones, Stephen. 'Global Strategic Views,' The Geographical Review, 45, 4 (July 1955) 492-508.

Kaldor, Mary. 'The Military in Third World Development,' in Richard Jolly (ed.) Disarmament and World Development (Oxford: Pergamon Press, 1978).

Kamarck, Andrew. Economies of African Development (New York: Praeger, 1967).

Kaplan, B.H. (ed.). Social Changes in the Capitalist World Economy (Beverly Hills: Sage, 1978).

Kemp, Geoffrey. 'The New Strategic Map,' Survival 19, 2(March/April 1977).

Kende, Istvan. Guerres Locales en Asie, en Afrique et en Amerique Latine (Budapest: Centre pour la Recherche de l'Afro-Asie de l'Academie des Sciences de Hongrie, 1973).

Kennedy, Paul. The Rise and Fall of the Great Powers (New York: Random House, 1987).

Klare, Michael. Resurgent Militarism (Washington: Institute for Policy Studies, 1981).

_____ and C. Arnson, Supplying Repression, US Support for Authorization Regimes Abroad (Washington, DC: Institute for Policy Studies, 1981).

Klass, Phillip. Secret Sentries in Space (New York: Random House, 1971).

Kolko, Gabriel. The Politics of War: The World and US Foreign Policy 1943-1945 (New York: Random House, 1968).

Kurian, George Thomas. The Book of World Rankings (New York: Facts on File, 1979).

Leiss, Amelia. Changing Patterns of Arms Transfers (Cambridge, Mass.: MIT Center for International Studies, 1970).

Lewis, W.H. 'How a Defense Planner Looks at Africa,' in H. Kitchen (ed.), Africa: From Mystery to Maze (Lexington, Mass.: Lexington Books, 1976).

Limqueco, P. and B. McFarlane (eds.). Neo-Marxist Theories of Underdevelopment (London: Croom Helm, 1983).

Lumsden, Malvern. 'Militarism: Cultural Dimensions of Militarization,' in Asbjorn Eide and Marek Thee (eds.), Problems of Contemporary Militarism (London: Croom Helm, 1980).

Mackinder, Halford. 'The Geographical Pivot of History,' in Halford Mackinder, Democratic Ideals and Reality (New York: W.W. Norton, 1962).

Mahan, Alfred T. The Influence of Seapower Upon History 1669-1783 (Boston: Little, Brown, 1980).
Makin, John H. The Global Debt Crisis: America's Growing Involvement (New York: Basic Books, 1984).
Mallalieu, William C. British Reconstruction of American Policy (New York: Scarcecrow Press, 1956).
McKinlay, R.D. and R. Little, 'A Foreign Policy Model of US Bilateral Aid Allocation,' World Politics, 30, 1 (Oct. 1977): 58-86.
Mende, Tibor. From Aid to Recolonization (New York: Pantheon, 1973).
Moll, Randall D. 'Arms Race and Military Expenditure Models,' Journal of Conflict Resolution 24 (March): 153-85.
Mosley, Hugh G. Economic and Social Consequences of the Arms Race (Lexington, M.A.: D.C. Heath and Co. 1982).
Neuman, Stephanie G. Military Assistance in Recent Wars: The Dominance of the Superpowers (New York: Praeger, 1986).
Nowels, Larry. Congressional Research Service (January, 1988).
Obey, David R. and Carol Lancaster, 'Funding Foreign Aid,' Foreign Policy, no. 71, (Summer, 1988).
Organization for Economic Cooperation and Development, Development Cooperation: Efforts and Policies of the Members of the Development Assistance Committee (Paris, 1984).
_____ Geographical Distribution of Financial Flows to Less Developed Countries 1966-1967 (Paris, 1969).
Pastor, Robert A. Congress and the Politics of US Foreign Economic Policy 1929-1976 (Berkeley: University of California Press, 1980).
Patch, Buel W. 'Overseas Bases,' Editorial Research Report, vol. II, no. 2, July 14, 1951.
Paul, Roland. American Military Commitment Abroad (New Brunswick, NJ: Rutgers University Press, 1973).
Pierre, Andrew J. (ed.). Arms Transfers and American Foreign Policy (New York University Press, 1979)
_____. The Global Politics of Arms Sales (Princeton: Princeton University Press, 1982).
President's Committee to Study the United States Military Assistance Program, Composite Report (Washington, DC: August, 1959) 146-56.
Price, Harry B. The Marshall Plan and Its Meaning (Ithaca: Cornell University Press, 1955).
Public Papers of the Presidents of the United Stated: Harry S. Truman (Washington, DC: Government Printing Office, 1964).
Ravenhill, John. 'Comparing Regime Performance in Africa: The Limitations of Cross-National Aggregate Analysis,' Journal of Modern African Studies, XVII: 1 (March): 99-126.

Rockefeller, Nelson A. 'Widening Boundaries of National
Interest,' Foreign Affairs, 29, 4 (July 1951): 527.
Rostow, W.W. Eisenhower, Kennedy, and Foreign Aid (Austin:
University of Texas Press, 1985).
Rubin, Jacob A. Your Hundred Billion Dollars: The
Complete Story of American Foreign Aid (Philadelphia:
Chilton, 1964).
Rubinstein, Alvin Z. and Donald E. Smith, Anti-Americanism
in the Third World (New York: Praeger, 1985).
Seversky, Alexander P. de. Air Power: Key to Survival (New
York: Simon and Schuster, 1950).
Sewell, John W. et al. The United States and World
Development Agenda 1977 (New York: ODC, Praeger, 1977).
_____. US Foreign Policy and the Third World: Agenda
1985-86 (New Brunswick: Transaction Books, 1985).
Shulsky, A. 'Coercive Diplomacy' in B. Dismukes and J.
McConnel (eds.) Soviet Naval Diplomacy (New York:
Pergamon, 1979).
Slessor, John. The Great Deterrent (New York: Praeger,
1957).
Smith, R.P. 'Military Expenditure and Capitalism,'
Cambridge Journal of Economics (I): 61-76.
Sprout, Harold and Margaret. 'Geography and International
Politics in an Era of Revolutionary Change,' in W.A.
Douglas Jackson (ed.) Politics and Geographic
Relationships: Readings on the Nature of Political
Geography (Englewood Cliffs, N.J.: Prentice-Hall, 1964).
Spykman, Nicholas. America's Strategy in World Politics
(New York: Harcourt, Brace, 1942).
_____. 'Heartland and Rimland,' in Nicholas Spykman, The
Geography of Peace (New York: Harcourt, Brace, 1944).
Steele, R. Pax Americana (New York: Viking Press, 1977).
Stephens, Lynn H. and Stephen J. Green (eds.). Disaster
Assistance Appraisal, Reform and New Approaches (New York:
New York University Press, 1979).
The committee to Strengthen the Security of the Free World,
The Scope and Distribution of United States Military and
Economic Assistance Programs (Washington, DC: March,
1963).
Thornton, Thomas Perry. The Challenge to US Policy in the
Third World (Boulder: Westview Press, 1986).
United Nations Secretary-General. Economic and Social
Consequences of the Arms Race and of Military Expenditures.
Revised Report of the Secretary-General. (New York: United
Nations, 1978).
United States Agency for International Development,
Proposed Mutual Defense and Development Programs FY 1966,
Summary Presentation to Congress (Washington, DC:
Government Printing Office, March 1965).

United States Agency for International Development. Overseas Loans and Grants and Assistance from International Organizations: Obligations and Loan Authorizations, July 1945-June 1970 (Washington, DC: Government Printing Office).

United States Arms Control and Disarmament Agency. Undated. World Military Expenditures and Arms Trade, 1963-1973 (Washington, DC: Government Printing Office).

United States Department of State and Department of Defense. The Mutual Security Program, Fiscal year 1958 (Washington, DC: International Cooperation Administration, 1957).

Walters, Robert E. The Nuclear Trap (Baltimore: Penguin Books, 1974).

Wiggins, James and Helmut Schoeck (eds.). Foreign Aid Re-examined (Washington, DC: Public Affairs Press, 1958).

Wilhelm J. and Gerry Feinstein (eds.). US Foreign Assistance Investment or Folly? (New York: Praeger, 1984).

Wolf, Charles Jr. Foreign Aid: Theory and Practice in Southeast Asia (Princeton: Princeton University Press, 1960).

Wolpe, H. The Horn of Africa and the United States (Washington, DC: Congressional Research Service, 1982).

Wolpin, Miles D. Military Aid and Counterrevolution in the Third World (Lexington, MA: D.C. Heath, 1973).

Wood, Robert E. From Marshall Plan to Debt Crisis (Berkley: University of California Press, 1986).

Wulf, Herbert. 'Dependent Militarism in the Periphery and Possible Alternative Concepts,' in Stephanie G. Newman and Robert Harkaby (eds.) Arms Transfers in the Modern World (New York, Praeger, 1979).

Young, Crawford. Ideology and Development in Africa (New Haven: Yale Unviersity Press, 1982).

Index